URBAN EUROPE
1500–1700

ALEXANDER COWAN

Senior Lecturer in History, University of Northumbria

A member of the Hodder Headline Group
LONDON • NEW YORK • SYDNEY • AUCKLAND

In memory of Lionel Cowan (1905–95),
printer and man of peace

First published in Great Britain 1998 by
Arnold, a division of Hodder Headline PLC,
338 Euston Road, London NW1 3BH
http://www.arnoldpublishers.com

Co-published in the United States of America by
Oxford University Press Inc.,
198 Madison Avenue, New York, NY 10016

British Library Cataloguing in Publication Data
A catalogue entry for this book is available from the British Library

Library of Congress Cataloging-in-Publication Data
A catalog record for this book is available from the Library of Congress

ISBN 0 340 71981 8 (pb)
ISBN 0 340 66324 3 (hb)

1 2 3 4 5   95 96 97 98 99

Production Editor: James Rabson
Production Controller: Helen Whitehorn
Cover designer: Terry Griffiths

Typeset in 10/12 pt Sabon by Prepress Projects, Perth, Scotland
Printed and bound in the United Kingdom by MPG Books, Bodmin, Cornwall

Contents

Acknowledgements

The idea for this book first grew out of a final-year course at the University of Northumbria. I am greatly indebted to several generations of students at the university, whose questions and contributions to seminars helped me to form some initial ideas about how the subject could be approached, and to the university itself for the leave to complete the writing process.

Peter Coss, Henry Cohn and Mia Rodriguez-Salgado offered encouragement and useful ideas when the book was in its early stages. Brian Pullan and Richard Mackenney read draft chapters, which have greatly benefited from their comments. Parts of this book were first rehearsed as papers at the Anglo-American Historians' Conference, the Centre for Urban History at the University of Leicester and the Third International Urban History Conference in Budapest. As the book's editor, Christopher Wheeler has been courteously supportive throughout, at a time when a less patient man might have given up.

Michèle, Charlotte and Benjamin saw much of modern urban Europe in my company and have been very tolerant about the intrusion of its historical roots into their lives.

Newcastle
November 1997

Introduction

The urban dimension is not the first image that springs to mind when considering the history of Europe in the sixteenth and seventeenth centuries. The world in which most contemporaries lived and worked, loved and fought, prayed and feared, was predominantly rural. The ownership of land was the chief source of power and large-scale income. Agriculture in its various forms provided direct employment or sustenance for most of the population. Networks of authority, both ecclesiastical and secular, were organised on a rural model, even if the nodal points of these networks were located in urban centres for convenience. Such comments are as valid for the beginning of the eighteenth century as they are for the end of the fifteenth.

Why, then, should one write of an 'urban Europe' between 1500 and 1700 when it was patently obvious to contemporaries that the predominant feature of the continent was its rural character? This book has been written on the premise that there was a shared urban dimension to the history of early modern Europe, a dimension whose influence far outweighed the relatively small numbers of people who lived in urban centres. One of the most important characteristics of every urban centre was its dynamism – the way in which it was at the centre of forces of attraction and repulsion, which reached out far beyond the boundaries of urban settlement, influencing patterns of consumption, modes of thought and facilitating change on a broad front.

This urban dimension can be illustrated by what could be seen by an observer standing by the side of a road anywhere in western Europe. The road is a broad one, wide enough to take an ox-cart, a group of horsemen or pedestrians or a herd of sheep. It is not metalled, but it does show all the signs of more than local use. It is dusty and muddy in turns according to the seasons. The countryside through which it runs could be mountainous or flat, meadowland or cultivated with a variety of crops. The road users, on the other hand, are affected by more than rural concerns. Most of them are country people, but their business takes them to and between urban centres: peasants on their way to or from a market, journeymen on the 'tramp', pedlars, pilgrims, mendicant clergy, soldiers, subsistence migrants. By taking to the road, they have each implicitly recognised the influence of the town on their lives. The town may be their ultimate destination or a staging post on a longer journey. Whichever it is, it offers something that runs through the rural Europe of the majority like a gleaming ribbon, attractive, insubstantial, yet inescapable.

In order to appreciate the economic, political, social and cultural impact of urban centres on the broader history of early modern Europe, it is necessary to focus on the urban centres themselves, the chief characteristics of urban life, the social and economic organisation that contrasted with the rural environment and to examine the impact of forces for change, which, although also experienced outside the towns, were amplified in the urban context. How did urban economic and social organisation respond to the demographic changes of the sixteenth and seventeenth centuries? What was the impact of external political change on urban centres that had hitherto experienced considerable political autonomy? Were the Reformation and Counter-Reformation expressions of individual religious belief or willing tools for the extension of secular authority? Was the increasing social distance between members of urban élites and other townspeople responsible for more or less social stability in the course of the period? The consideration of these questions is a more modest objective than a detailed discussion of the role of urbanisation and, while certain pointers do emerge through the chapters of this book, its major emphasis remains the organisation and complexity of urban life in western Europe during the sixteenth and seventeenth centuries.

Such an approach inevitably irons out many of the differences between individual towns and between the various regions of western Europe. In a general study of this kind, it is not necessary to excuse oneself for not doing enough detailed justice to the histories of individual urban centres. This is only a minor contrast with the approach taken by contemporaries. Although the celebratory chroniclers of the sixteenth and seventeenth centuries, who reconstructed the ancient roots, great deeds, famous men and notable buildings of their native towns, only referred to other urban centres by name in order to rank their own towns in the pantheon of the famous, there were already others who formulated more general questions. Giovanni Botero's late sixteenth-century *Treatise Concerning the Causes of the Magnificency and Greatness of Cities* attempted to identify the factors that enabled large European urban centres to prosper. The growing literature on the ideal city, on the other hand, largely written by architects and military theorists, concentrated on the unsatisfactory aspects of existing urban centres and the ways in which the organisation of urban life could be improved by creating an effective model from scratch.

The question of size is a much more difficult issue. In order to cover the field comprehensively, any urban history of Europe should take into account the experience of townspeople living in centres ranging from minor settlements numbering no more than a few hundred inhabitants to the great metropolitan centres of London, Paris and Venice, whose populations numbered hundreds of thousands. On the other hand, the range of available published evidence for the smallest centres, while growing, remains relatively inaccessible. The work of the small towns history projects in England and France directed by Peter Clark and Jean-Pierre Poussou, respectively, is beginning to bear some very interesting fruit and will continue to do so as time passes. However, with the exception of the valuable collection of essays on small towns in early modern Europe recently edited by Peter Clark, little comparative work has been published for other regions of Europe, and this is reflected in this study.

It would be tempting to limit an urban history of Europe to the largest towns at the other end of the urban scale, the cities or capitals and great commercial centres, and many have done so in the past, particularly in the area of architectural history. While the number of detailed studies of such large agglomerations is reflected in this book, the range of centres under consideration is much broader, resulting, it is to be hoped, in a relative assessment of the extent to which the changes particularly associated with the largest urban centres were also experienced elsewhere. The range of centres considered for this study is based on the criteria used by Professor de Vries when constructing the immensely valuable urban database for his study of European urbanisation between 1500 and 1800. De Vries chose a lower limit of 10 000 inhabitants when collecting his data but built in enough flexibility to enable him to include all urban centres that reached this threshold at any time during his chosen period. The database consequently includes both Dresden, which only had a population of 5000 in 1500 because it reached 12 000 by 1600, York with 8000 at the beginning of the period and Montpellier with 6000. While the corollary of such a choice still means that more emphasis is placed on that minority of urban centres that played more than a local role than on smaller settlements like Wetzlar in Hesse, Ostend in Flanders, Rovereto in the Veronese or Northallerton in the North Riding of Yorkshire, this study does attempt to address those features that created an urban continuum between urban centres at every point on the demographic scale.

The chronological limits for this book have been set at 1500 and 1700. Other definitions of 'early modern' would extend this period at least 50 years in each direction, and a case can be made for doing so. The decision to consider this particular block of 200 years was partly based on the convention that the period was an important one in the context of the development of modern Europe, often studied on undergraduate courses, which had a certain inner coherence that longer periods lacked. Closer study of the different regions of Europe suggests that such a view needs to be modified. None of the periods usually associated with the 'early modern' label are entirely congruent with the timing of similar developments in different parts of Europe. Sophisticated town planning and poor relief policies developed much earlier in the towns of northern and central Italy than in England or France, for example, while the experience of rapid demographic and economic growth in mid-sixteenth-century Seville was not matched by Amsterdam for at least 50 years. The new organisation of the urban fabric symbolised by late seventeenth-century Turin only came to be imitated elsewhere during the eighteenth century. Nor were the roots of all the developments experienced by the majority of larger west European towns within the 200 years 1500–1700. Many, like the European urban network itself, went back much further. The choice of 1500–1700, then, should be seen as a historical tool, a segment, which cuts across much longer-term developments in order to throw them into greater relief, but one whose comparatively short length enables more attention to be paid to religious change and the development of the centralised state.

The book has been organised into two distinctive sections. Part I is concerned with the urban framework. Chapters on the urban economy, government, élites, social horizons and religion set out the formal and informal structures within which townspeople lived and worked. Part II shifts the emphasis from organisation to rapid change and the tensions that arose from it – changes to the urban fabric, poverty and poor relief and the difficult balance between order and disorder. It is followed by a concluding chapter, which attempts to draw together some of the changes and continuities of the urban history of western Europe in the early modern period.

The opening chapter focuses on five themes: economies, hierarchies and networks; demographic trends; changes in economic organisation; economic relationships between town and countryside; and expanding and contracting urban economies. This is followed by a discussion of the changes in the distribution of authority inside and outside the town, which affected the ways in which urban government operated when faced with problems and pressures. It explores the ways in which the slow and difficult process of state-building created conditions in which the relationship between urban governments and central administrations developed more as a wary partnership than as a relationship of urban dependence on external authority.

As political authority was increasingly concentrated in the hands of a political élite and the participation of other burghers in decision-making consequently declined, it seems logical to follow a framework chapter on urban government with one that discusses urban élites. This discussion, however, extends the definition of the élite beyond the small group of men holding political office at any one time to a consideration of the 'social élite', a cohesive social group whose male members held leading positions in a broad range of activities: politics, wealth, culture, ideas and the practice of highly regarded professional occupations, such as the law, education or administration, and whose female members played an important part in ensuring the cohesiveness and continuity of the group. The role of these social élites in shaping and responding to urban change remains one of the constant themes of this book.

The consideration of social relationships, social cohesion and social stratification is amplified in the chapter on 'Social horizons', which examines the nature of urban society less from the outside in than from the inside out. By using the concept of social horizons, it addresses the extent to which urban societies cohered together as single communities, while examining the range of overlapping groups to which most individuals belonged and which, to a certain extent, helped to create their own public identity.

The chapter on religion and society that completes Part I is intended to function as a kind of bridge between the framework chapters and those in the second part of the book. It examines how, although the Reformation and the Counter-Reformation appeared to give members of both sexes more opportunities to express their religious beliefs in private and in public, this took place increasingly within a framework of strict orthodoxy in which more popular or individualistic forms of expression were placed under strict controls. In order to explore this, the chapter is divided into three linked sections: the nature and impact of the urban Reformation and Counter-Reformation; the expansion of urban lay piety throughout western Europe; and the complex impact on urban life of the widespread presence of religious minority groups.

Part II opens with a consideration of the interplay between economic, social and political change and the urban material environment. In the context of the economic stagnation and the retention of the existing urban fabric experienced by most of the urban centres considered in the sixteenth and seventeenth centuries, the changes in town planning and in the overall appearance of streets, buildings and open spaces that affected a relatively small number of towns are discussed less in terms of their immediate importance than for their roles as models for other towns during the eighteenth century.

The increase in urban poverty and in subsistence migration to towns by the rural poor during the sixteenth and seventeenth centuries posed considerable problems for the urban authorities and for the stable core of urban society. The chapter on 'Poverty and poor relief' juxtaposes a discussion of the causes of urban poverty with a consideration of the practical and ideological formal and informal responses of townspeople, religious institutions and the urban authorities.

The final substantive chapter is concerned with the relationship between the fear of disorder in towns, the extent to which such fears were justified and the measures that were taken by the urban authorities to forestall or control outbreaks of disorder.

PART

I

FRAMEWORKS

1

The urban economy

When through the Lindgasse you've been led,
You'll see the market place ahead,
Where wool is sold and textiles rare,
Velvet and silk, and camel's hair.
Dealers in herbs and apothecaries
Here have their shops; and peas and cherries
And cheese and cabbage are for sale,
And pubs dispense fine white wine and ale.

(Strauss, 1976, 65)

Johann Haselberg's lively rhyming description of Nuremberg in 1531 is an evocative depiction of the urban centre as an economic organism. It is a place for buying and selling, for making and meeting, for contacts between the urban and the rural and the local and the distant. Urban centres and their economic functions were inseparable. The location, size and prosperity of great towns in early modern Europe were largely dependent on the nature and scale of the economic activities that took place within their boundaries. Much of the character of the European urban experience in the sixteenth and seventeenth centuries was informed by, if not entirely dictated by, economic circumstances. This chapter is an attempt to discuss the nature of the urban economy in western Europe, the scale and range of activities that took place within it and the extent to which it changed in the course of two centuries.

The history of the urban economy was, of course, far more than the sum of the experiences of urban centres in different parts of Europe and at different times. Each town had its place in much larger networks of economic activity. These networks had several different dimensions, all of them defined by the exchange of goods. At a European level, long-distance trade by sea, navigable waterway and road created links between ports and major inland entrepôts.

These urban centres, which were distinguished by their size and the complexity of their functions, both economic and non-economic, in turn disseminated goods down through dependent regional hierarchies and acted as the gateway for the wider diffusion of goods and services produced by other members of the hierarchy. From another point of view, although many urban centres were cut off from their rural surroundings by high walls, their survival was inextricably linked to the fields and forests around them. Not only did they serve as centres of production and consumption for their rural hinterlands, they depended on the latter for food, labour and contact with other urban centres overland or by water.

The economic history of the sixteenth and seventeenth centuries was marked by sharp contrasts: demographic growth, economic expansion and inflation in the sixteenth century; recession, falling prices and a slowing down of the money supply in the 'long seventeenth century'. These changes were mirrored in the urban economy in general and in the economies of those regions, such as England and the Netherlands, which bucked the trend, in particular. What was striking about the urban economy, however, was its capacity to amplify the changes taking place at a macroeconomic level and the diversity of its responses, leading to temporary expansion for most centres in the sixteenth century and widespread stagnation or decline in the seventeenth.

In order to explore the reasons for this diversity and to establish more clearly how urban economies operated, this chapter has been divided into five sections: economies, hierarchies and networks; demographic trends; changes in economic organisation; town and countryside; and expanding and contracting economies.

Economies, hierarchies and networks

What are the minimum criteria for identifying a town? Most obvious forms of measurement are not entirely satisfactory. While it is generally agreed that towns had a greater concentration of population than villages or isolated settlements, the point at which such a concentration signalled the presence of a town rather than a village varied from one part of Europe to another. In the sixteenth century, urban settlements of fewer than 500 inhabitants were to be found in Scandinavia, Germany, Flanders and parts of France and Italy. The threshold for English market towns during the same period appears to have been slightly larger. But size was a deceptive indicator of what separated town from village. Some towns with a population of 500 or fewer were fully fledged. Some, particularly in France and Germany, even had their own defences. Others were only micro-towns, villages whose semi-urban functions had the potential to develop into fully fledged towns but often did not do so. Rather than looking at size alone, it is necessary to place these tiny urban settlements in context. There were only 10 towns in early sixteenth-century Norway. Seven of them had populations of 500 or fewer. In an area such as Norway where there was no fully developed urban network, even very small towns fulfilled urban functions. The fragmented nature of political authority in medieval Germany, which permitted very large urban centres to develop, also encouraged local rulers to foster small towns in the area under their jurisdiction to take advantage of the profits to be made from controlling trade and production. The contrast with a more centralised England where market towns were much larger is striking.

Ultimately, it was neither size nor legal status, nor the presence of fortifications, but 'urban' functions that distinguished even the smallest centres from villages. Some villages could be relatively large. Some had their own walls. On the other hand, many towns were unfortified and lacked a charter. In terms of its economic functions, Stratford-upon-Avon, which did not receive a charter from the English crown until 1553, was what we would recognise as a fully fledged town.

Early modern towns were multifunctional. Whether they were large or small, this was what they shared, and this in turn is what distinguished them most from rural settlements. Not all of these functions were economic, but the economic functions were the foundations upon which all others were constructed. Only newly established military towns, such as Palmanova in north-eastern Italy or Neufbrisach on the Franco-Imperial border, and the occasional ecclesiastical centre were an exception to this pattern. Without the money and demographic momentum generated by economic activity, towns were not selected as the location for administrative centres, law courts, capital cities, colleges and universities, cathedrals or the sites for religious orders. They might be transformed in the process, as were Madrid, when it was chosen definitively by Philip II in 1561 as the capital of Spain, and Weilburg in Hesse, which was reconstructed for a similar purpose in the late seventeenth century by Count Johann Wolfgang of Nassau, but the preconditions for growth were already there.

Five economic functions distinguished towns from the countryside: their location as centres for exchange; the presence of artisans; occupational diversity; regular links with other centres of exchange; and influence over a hinterland. These distinguishing characteristics were then reinforced by the presence of social and cultural indicators, such as more complex forms of government, the presence of a stratified society with an identifiable élite, the presence of professionals, such as lawyers or schoolteachers, and of religious orders and educational establishments. As time passed, new cultural indicators were added, such as discussion groups, mutual societies and charitable groups.

By using these urban characteristics and indicators, it is possible to suggest that centres of all sizes in western Europe shared a common urban identity. This can be illustrated by comparing two Italian urban centres, Venice and the Sicilian town of Gangi, which, while not quite at the opposite ends of the urban spectrum, are usually considered to belong to totally different spheres. Gangi had a population of some 4000 in the mid-sixteenth century. Two-thirds of its inhabitants were engaged in agriculture. The others were artisans, shopkeepers, merchants, servants, rentiers and members of religious orders. At the height of its prosperity at the end of the sixteenth century, on the other hand, Venice had a population of 190 000. It was a major international trading centre, supported by a substantial industrial sector, and was the capital of an extensive maritime and land-based empire. It had a significant number of merchants, rentiers and professionals among its permanent population. As a point of departure for pilgrims and a point of arrival for tourists, it also functioned as a centre of hospitality. Servants and others engaged in the business of food, drink and hotels swelled the already large numbers who worked in the households of the permanent residents. In spite of these substantial contrasts, both Gangi and Venice shared the basic economic functions and the social and cultural indicators that have already been discussed. Both functioned above all as centres of exchange, which linked their rural hinterlands to long-distance trading networks. Gangi lay on the old Roman road between Palermo and Messina and was an important centre for the export of livestock and wine. Venice's strategic location at the head of the Adriatic enabled her to link the Levant and the western Mediterranean with the producers and consumers of central Europe. It was also a centre of exchange for goods emanating from all over northern Italy. Each town had its important public buildings and churches, a central square and large houses belonging to an élite. Each had its cultural identity. Comparisons of a similar kind could be made from any region of Europe. Differences in scale were important, of course. They explain some of the diversity in the urban experience that is discussed later on in this book. On the other hand, the Venices, Lübecks, Rouens and Amsterdams of early modern Europe need to be seen as part of an urban continuum in order to be fully understood, and it is in this light that they and other larger centres are the focus of most of the discussion that follows.

Table 1.1 shows the distribution by geographical area (expressed for the sake of convenience in terms of modern political entities) of urban centres with at least 10 000 population in 1500, 1600 and 1700. While the figures for the lowest category (10 000–24 900) are understated in the case of Germany, France, Italy and Spain because of the lack of reliable demographic data for many towns that were probably in that category, the available figures do suggest that there was considerable diversity in the distribution of large towns in the various regions of Europe and in the rate at which they grew. As in the Middle Ages, there was a sharp contrast between the number of very large towns in the Mediterranean area and in the rest of Europe. In 1500, there were only four towns with a population of over 80 000, of which three (Venice, Milan and Naples) were in Italy. Paris, at 100 000, was

Table 1.1 Distribution by country of urban centres with over 10 000 population

	10 000–24 900	25 000–39 900	40 000–59 900	60 000+
1500				
Germany	17	2	–	–
France	13	5	2	1
Italy	29	4	4	5
England	4	–	1	–
the Netherlands	12	–	–	–
Spain	9	–	1	–
1600				
Germany	10	10	–	–
France	12	5	4	2
Italy	34	9	7	6
England	5	–	–	1
the Netherlands	15	–	–	1
Spain	6	5	3	2
1700				
Germany	9	4	1	–
France	8	9	2	4
Italy	45	9	3	7
England	3	2	–	1
the Netherlands	11	5	2	1
Spain	7	3	1	3

Source: Based on data in J. de Vries, *European Urbanisation 1500–1800* (London, 1984, 269–78)

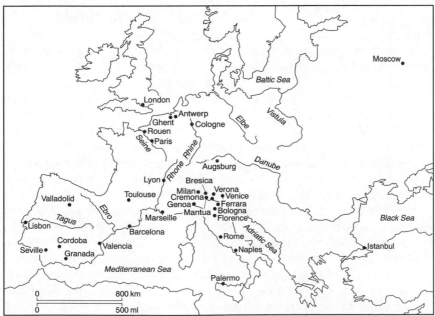

Fig. 1.1 Large urban centres in western Europe *c.* 1550

the only large city in the north. In 1600, the ratio was 7:2. This time, the Italian towns had been joined by two Spanish cities (Seville and Granada), but it is also significant that two of the three largest towns of all were now located in the north: London, with a population of 200 000 and Paris with 220 000. By the end of the seventeenth century, this pattern was even more pronounced. While most of the largest centres were still in the south, they were markedly outstripped in size by London (575 000) and Paris (510 000) and largely overtaken by Amsterdam (200 000), reflecting the definitive movement of the economic centre of gravity between 1500 and 1700 from the Mediterranean to north-western Europe.

Within this broad European picture, there were also several other important patterns. One was the diversity of urban density from one country to another. This remained unchanged throughout the period. There were far more large (10 000+) urban centres in northern and central Italy and in the Netherlands than elsewhere in Europe. (The figures for Italy are understated. De Vries lists at least 18 other Italian centres which were probably in this category in 1500.) In other words, more of the total population and more of the urban population lived in large urban centres in Italy and the Netherlands than elsewhere. Urbanisation levels in the northern Netherlands provinces rose from 30 per cent in the first quarter of the sixteenth century to 45 per cent in 1675. This also gave a particular flavour to the operation of regional networks, whose conventional shape was distorted by the presence of so many highly developed urban centres in close proximity whose hinterlands overlapped. At the turn of the sixteenth century, there were 18 centres in the Netherlands with a population of between 10 000 and 40 000. Most of them were concentrated in an even more limited area stretching no more than 60 kilometres from the coast.

In contrast, areas such as England, France, Spain and most of Germany offered an alternative kind of urban network, which was only occasionally marked by large centres. England is the classic case, where around one in five of the population lived in an urban centre, but only six towns exceeded de Vries' threshold of 10 000. With the exception of London, only Bristol and Norwich had a population of over 25 000 in 1700. For most of the period, London was the only centre to do so. The striking dissonance between the very large (and growing) population of the capital and a countryside, most of whose regional centres scarcely reached 8000 in size, appears to make England something of an exception in Europe, but that reputation is only partly justified. In many ways, the English experience was typical of most of western Europe; an urban network of middle-sized centres fulfilling the economic needs of an extensive hinterland. It is important here to compare like with like. Although the boundaries of modern nation states are a convenient way of organising information about the distribution of towns in early modern Europe, they do not fully reflect the regional hierarchies within which towns operated. England was the one area in which there was the closest overlap between political and regional boundaries. The urban distribution to be found in England corresponded to one of the regions of France, Italy or Germany, rather than to the countries as a whole.

The position of the largest urban centres needs to be considered separately. Their unusual size was not driven exclusively by economic factors. It owed a great deal to their position as capital cities or the location of viceregal administrative centres in the Spanish empire. This pattern was constant throughout the period, although the number of centres whose population exceeded this level rose in line with general demographic trends – quite sharply between 1500 and 1600 and less substantially during the seventeenth century. The seven centres over 60 000 in 1500 were all Mediterranean capitals of some kind (Genoa, Granada, Florence, Paris, Venice, Milan and Naples). Their numbers had nearly doubled by 1600, but only three of the newcomers were not capitals (Rouen, Seville and Amsterdam). By 1700, there were 17 in this class, 11 capitals and six ports (Amsterdam, Hamburg, Rouen, Marseille, Lyon and Seville).

Demographic trends

By comparison with the twelfth century, the early modern period was not marked by a substantial increase in urbanisation, nor was the experience of urban economies a uniformly positive one. The networks of urban centres that had emerged by the end of the twelfth century remained the basis of urban location until industrialisation generated new economic forces requiring large concentrations of manpower. They were joined by relatively few new towns during the sixteenth and seventeenth centuries, and the small minority of new towns that did survive economically in the long term, such as Whitehaven on the English Cumbrian coast and the new capital of the Palatinate at Mannheim, did little to alter the existing urban network. Other artificial implantations, such as the new town of Richelieu built on the borders of Poitou and Touraine in 1631 on the Cardinal's orders, failed to attract enough new inhabitants in order to function effectively.

In the absence of large numbers of new towns, most urbanisation in early modern Europe took place in established centres. This general statement needs some qualification. While many towns grew in size during the sixteenth century, in particular, they only did so in proportion to general population trends. Spectacular demographic expansion of the kind experienced by London, Amsterdam, Antwerp and Seville was far from typical and owed a great deal to the leading part that each played in linking Europe with the world economy.

The general pattern of urbanisation was not so clear-cut. While the overall demographic and economic growth of the sixteenth century was constrained by the slowdown of economic activity in the long seventeenth century, different European regions experienced sharply contrasting demographic fortunes.

The pattern of urban demographic change in Spain set it apart from most other regions of Europe because of the way in which the sharp population decline between 1600 and 1650, which had followed widespread expansion in the second half of the sixteenth century, persisted during the second half of the 1600s. This led to severe urban depopulation. Baeza declined by 43 per cent in the first half of the seventeenth century and by a further 42 per cent in the second, Jerez by 37 per cent and 26 per cent, and Segovia by 43 per cent and 50 per cent. Even Seville, which had expanded by 150 per cent up to 1550, only grew by 39 per cent from 1550 to 1600 and by a further 6 per cent in the 1600s. Madrid and Cadiz were the only major exceptions. Neither had been an important part of the medieval urban network. Madrid owed its demographic impetus to the whim of Philip II, who decided that it should become the permanent seat of government in 1561 (165 per cent growth between 1600 and 1650). Cadiz relieved the gloom of the Spanish economy in the second half of the seventeenth century through a revival of the Americas trade. The number of inhabitants rose from 7000 to 23 000.

The shift in commercial prosperity from the Mediterranean to north-western Europe also affected urban population levels adversely in Italy. It was most evident during the first half of the seventeenth century, during which deurbanisation for economic reasons was compounded by the effects of a disastrous plague epidemic in the 1630s, but some of the signs of turbulence could already be seen in the first half of the sixteenth century. Growth of 41 per cent in Naples and of over 50 per cent in Venice, Perugia and Catania was paralleled by demographic decline in Milan (31 per cent), Florence (14 per cent) and Rome (18 per cent) and, while each of these three cities recovered during the next 50 years, only Rome experienced any real expansion. In the second half of the seventeenth century, the losses experienced by most Italian towns during the first half were largely compensated for, but there was little, if any, growth.

German urban centres also experienced variable rates of expansion in the sixteenth century and a mixture of contraction, stagnation and rapid expansion in the seventeenth. The rapid growth of Hamburg, Augsburg and Magdeburg, which all more than doubled in size before 1550, was not sustained in the second half of the century. Elsewhere after 1550, Frankfurt am Main, Dresden and Leipzig showed early signs of their eventual importance, but, with the exception of the northern ports of Hamburg and Lübeck, the whole region suffered very severe depopulation during the Thirty Years War. Magdeburg lost almost 90 per cent of its inhabitants following the siege of 1631. As in Italy, much of the growth registered by German towns in the second half of the seventeenth century was compensation for the losses of the first half, but the period did witness the emergence of Berlin, Dresden and Leipzig as new economic and political forces in the region.

Berlin grew from a nadir of 12 000 in 1650 to 55 000 by the end of the century, while Dresden, its fellow capital, which had never ceased to grow, rose from 15 000 to 40 000.

To the extent that population figures alone can be used as an accurate measure of economic health, France was much better off throughout than its southern or eastern neighbours. In spite of all the evidence of falling rents, agricultural prices and land values in the seventeenth century, French towns reflected the downturn in the economy by reduced growth rates rather than by stagnation or an absolute loss of population. (The decline of 39 per cent suffered by La Rochelle was the main casualty of Huguenot emigration and the consequent loss of skills, manpower and investment.) Those towns for which there are figures for the first half of the sixteenth century grew less strongly in the second half, always excepting Paris, which more than doubled its growth rate, and Bordeaux, which doubled its size. In contrast with Spain and Italy, French towns expanded most during the first half of the seventeenth century, although the 88 per cent increase in the population of Lyon has to be seen in the context of its sharp decline during the Wars of Religion. After 1650, growth rates slackened. Paris grew by only a further 19 per cent and Marseille by 14 per cent. Only the towns along France's eastern border (Strasbourg, Metz and Besançon) continued to expand.

The provinces of the southern Netherlands were among the most prosperous and heavily urbanised areas of Europe at the close of the Middle Ages. In the long term, this dense urban network and its strategic location at the mouths of the Rhine and the Scheldt opposite the British Isles was to provide a solid basis for economic recovery in the later seventeenth and eighteenth centuries. In the short term, the impact of internal conflict, religious persecution and occupation by a Spanish army brought about substantial falls in the urban population in the second half of the sixteenth century. Before the outbreak of disturbances in the 1560s, the population of the towns of Flanders and Brabant had been growing, albeit slowly, with the exception of Antwerp, whose position as the major link between Spain, the Americas and northern Europe brought it a 125 per cent increase in numbers. By 1600, the population of Antwerp had fallen by 47 per cent, Mechelen by over a half and Bruges by 23 per cent. Only Lille and Brussels continued to grow. The data for the seventeenth century confirm that many of these losses were temporary and that economic activity resumed after the end of the fighting. In spite of strong competition from Amsterdam, which had replaced it as the major European entrepôt port, Antwerp's population grew by 49 per cent in the first half of the century. Louvain, which had been in decline throughout the sixteenth century, grew by 44 per cent and Ghent and Antwerp by 48 per cent and 49 per cent, respectively. Brussels, which had remained the capital of the Habsburgs, grew to become the region's largest urban centre, outstripping Antwerp by 10 000 by the end of the century.

The experience of the northern Dutch provinces scarcely mirrored that of their cousins to the south. The region displayed some of the most rapid urban growth of the early modern period. Its concentration in the sixteenth rather than the seventeenth century is a reminder that most urban expansion in Europe was a consequence of general population growth rather than regional economic prosperity. Many smaller Dutch towns more than doubled their size between 1500 and 1600. Alkmaar grew from 5000 to 11 000, Zaandam from 7000 to 16 000 and Enkhuizen from 4000 to 17 000. Rotterdam and Amsterdam began their upwards trajectory. The static population figures at Nijmegen prefigured its gentle decline in the seventeenth century. The minority of centres that grew even faster in the first half of the seventeenth century encompassed those towns that were the real dynamos of Dutch expansion: Amsterdam, Rotterdam and Leiden – two international ports and an industrial centre – and The Hague, which took on the role of a capital city. By 1650, Dutch urban expansion was over. Many centres were in decline, while others grew no more.

English urban growth followed an idiosyncratic pattern. The dominance of London, both in terms of its size and the speed with which it grew, created a distorted urban network. Whether or not the provincial centres, which were so much smaller, were in a state of crisis in the first half of the sixteenth century, few showed any real signs of expansion until the second half of the seventeenth century, the point at which London's growth curve fell quite steeply. There were exceptions. Bristol and Norwich took advantage of new overseas opportunities to the west and the east after 1600, and the rapid growth of the new manufacturing centre of Birmingham from 1000 in 1550 to 7000 in 1700 was a precursor of the way in which older provincial centres were to be outstripped in the eighteenth century by Leeds, Manchester and Liverpool.

Comparisons of differential rates of urban development in the different regions of Europe leave three conclusions.

- As a whole, urban economies in early modern Europe were not marked by their consistent dynamism. Each region, with the exception of England, which stagnated in the first half of the seventeenth century, experienced a substantial fall in the numbers of the urban population, and much of the growth that followed this only compensated for these losses.
- The sharp fluctuation in urban populations placed considerable stresses on local resources and the nature of the local urban economy.
- While commercial success continued to be the main motor for economic development, some of the most consistent urban growth took place in administrative centres, such as Madrid, The Hague and Turin.

Migration

Migration was both a symptom and a cause of fluctuations in urban prosperity. Increased population flows into or out of towns took place as a result of both push and pull factors. When the prospect of employment, protection or greater prosperity beckoned, individuals and families travelled to settle in the town. A slowdown in the urban economy had the opposite effect. Historians are still undecided whether migrants were primarily drawn to towns or whether towns offered the best prospect to migrants who had no choice but to leave the land or smaller towns.

While the usual distinction between those people who came to a town in order to survive and others who made the journey to improve their standard of living remains valid, it masks a much more complex series of migratory movements, all of which had their own impact on the urban economy, and many of which were only temporary in nature. The least important in the long term was what might be termed 'crisis migration', the large-scale movement of people from the local countryside who sought shelter in an urban centre when their livelihood was threatened by famine, disease or warfare. The town represented their only hope of protection, shelter and nourishment. Their presence in the town was usually only short term, and their impact on the health of the urban economy was negative (see Chapter 7). There was also an annual migration cycle to towns related to the cycle of agricultural production. The urban population was swelled during the winter months by farmworkers in search of temporary employment or relief and reduced by their departure in the spring as demand rose for short-term intensive tasks, such as planting and harvesting. Life-cycle servants came to towns for longer periods of time. Given the paucity of sources, it is very difficult to know if migrants ever intended to remain in a given town or not. As one moves up the social scale, there was a greater likelihood that, whatever their initial intentions, many found themselves in a position in which they were integrated into existing urban communities, from which there was little incentive to leave. Apprentices, at least in theory, received a training, which would ensure them of a skill and conditions in which to practise it. It is debatable whether this latter group come to the town in order to raise their status. While many apprentices came from outside the town in which they were trained, it is less clear that they were typical countrymen. There is some evidence from Germany that many boys who were sent for apprenticeship came from the ranks of rural artisans, where they already had some rudimentary skills. Others were the younger sons of prosperous yeomen and townsmen elsewhere, whose status can scarcely have been below that of a journeyman. It is difficult to place trained artisans who moved in search of work from one town to another as 'betterment' migrants. Certainly, they were far from the vagrants that the Elizabethan authorities suspected them to be when they were arrested on the open road and were able to prove their bona fides through their ownership of the tools of their trade. On the other hand, their migratory patterns differed from most of those that have been discussed so far in that they moved from one town to another rather than from countryside to town. In many ways, their movements were among the most significant, for it was their arrival in large numbers that permitted industrial expansion to take place and, equally, their large-scale departure from towns, such as Hondeschoote, Medina del Campo or late fifteenth-century Coventry that were suffering from unemployment, which signalled the decline of such economies.

In the case of the young men who trained as merchants, travel to another, usually larger, town was almost obligatory. Raymond Moulins, one of the leading merchants in the seventeenth-century Languedoc town of Clermont-de-Lodève, trained with Louis Durand in Lyon, where he spent 30 years, before returning home to set up his own business. As a younger son, he had to look further afield for a career. Heinrich Wedemhof, who became an influential merchant member of the patriciate in seventeenth-century Lübeck, settled in the city after growing up in a similar high-status family in Münster.

Other migratory patterns are important. While most migration seems to have been rural–urban, the movement of journeymen, merchants and professionals was a strong reminder that some of the most significant migration in terms of skills and capital took place between one town and another, usually from a smaller urban centre to a larger one. It also took place over significantly greater distances than rural–urban migration. Three-quarters of all immigrants to Beauvais in the seventeenth century came from within a radius of 20 km. Sixty-six per cent of all Sheffield immigrant apprentices in the sixteenth century came from within a radius of 20 miles. Even in the case of very large centres, such as London, half of the apprentices in the mid-sixteenth century had travelled no more than 90 miles. Only extreme poverty seems to have encouraged much longer journeys, such as those from the mountains of Friuli to Venice, from Brittany to Paris, from Corsica to Marseille and from the Languedoc to Madrid. A census of all 240 Madrid taverns in 1665 established that 15 per cent of all their customers were of French origin, mostly employed in low-grade occupations, such as pedlars, water-carriers and knife-grinders.

Immigrants had a threefold impact on the towns that were their destinations: demographic, economic and sociocultural. (The last of the three lies outside the present discussion and will be discussed in Chapter 2.) There is a general consensus that towns would not have been able to maintain their population levels, let alone increase them, without the aid of immigrants. Thanks to the work of Allan Sharlin, it is now clear that the immigrants' major contribution to the size of the urban population was to swell the labour force rather than to enhance the birth-rate. Most of the natural increase in early modern urban populations remained the responsibility of the established population rather than of newcomers, most of whom were not in a position to marry and have families. On the other hand, it was the increased flow of inhabitants from elsewhere that led to urban expansion on the scale that can be seen in Table 1.1, and the slowdown in the rate of immigration that caused such growth to level off, as in the case of London and Amsterdam, in the later seventeenth century.

It is not easy to judge the impact of in-migration on the economies of individual urban centres. There is an almost complete absence of information about migration by women, for example. Circumstantial evidence suggests that most female immigrants came from rural backgrounds, were unmarried, moved short distances in their late teens, took up unskilled employment, frequently as domestic servants, and did not settle permanently in the town. While the presence of immigrants did swell the market for goods produced in the town and elsewhere, their strongest impact as consumers was limited to items of food. It was the small minority of migrants who brought skills and capital with them that contributed most to economic expansion. Amsterdam is probably the most striking example of the way in which an economy that was already developing rapidly during the sixteenth century received an additional boost from the arrival of religious and economic exiles from Antwerp in the latter part of the century. These men and their sons were to go on to play a significant part in the development of the Dutch East India Company and in the port's overall expansion. A similar contribution, but on a smaller scale, was made by the great Italian merchant families, such as the Bonvisi, who settled in Lyon in the sixteenth century, and Carlo Diodati, César Balbani and Francesco Torrettini, who jointly ran a highly profitable silk business in Geneva at the turn of the sixteenth century.

Economic organisation

A variety of economic activity took place in towns. Common to them all were trade, production, both agricultural and industrial, and some kind of associated services, whether inn-keeping, domestic service, fetching and carrying, prostitution or the professions. On the other hand, the prosperity of towns and their inhabitants was also closely linked to more passive sources of income, such as investments in municipal funds, rents from houses and the ownership of property outside the town.

Three of the five economic functions that we have identified as distinguishing towns from the countryside were concerned with the exchange of goods. Towns were centres of exchange; they had regular links with other centres of exchange and thereby facilitated the movement of both staple and luxury goods over long distances. Finally, their markets constituted an essential mechanism in the economies of their rural hinterlands.

In general terms, little changed in the course of the sixteenth and seventeenth centuries. Towns continued to fulfil these basic functions. The scale of commercial activity, measured in terms of volume, range of goods available for exchange and the distance over which goods were sent, varied according to the position of each town within its own regional hierarchy. Specialised entrepôt ports acted as large-scale storage, exchange and redistribution centres. Within each regional hierarchy, there was some movement up and down over 200 years, particularly at the bottom, where some market towns became deurbanised in the face of local competition. Others expanded, particularly where trade was associated in part with industrial expansion.

Two important changes took place at the top of the European hierarchy. Both affected entrepôt ports, which until then had been among the largest urban centres. First, the pack was reshuffled. Ports, such as Lübeck and Venice, which had been dominant forces in the medieval economy, were overtaken by others as trade routes shifted in response to new sources of supply and demand, benefiting first the Iberian peninsula and the southern Netherlands, where Seville, Lisbon and Antwerp experienced relatively short phases of expansion up to the turn of the sixteenth century related to the development of trade routes across the Atlantic and round the Cape of Good Hope. The rise of London and Amsterdam from the early seventeenth century subsequently shifted the centre of gravity of the European economy to the north-west. The consequent movement of overland routes through central Europe from a north–south to an east–west axis had a knock-on effect on many of their urban staging posts, such as Augsburg, Nuremberg, Frankfurt an der Oder and Erfurt. The direction of trade in this area in particular was modified by important changes in urban demand. This represented the second major change in the status of large commercial centres. The growing demand for luxuries among the wealthy was particularly evident in the new princely towns in Germany, such as Mannheim and Dresden, where demographic expansion outstripped the older commercial centres, leaving them to stagnate, but it was also to be seen elsewhere. Rouen is a case in point. It lost its position as France's second city during the second half of the seventeenth century as a result of the development of Marseille and Bordeaux, but some of the most rapid growth in commercial activity took place in Louis XIV's administrative and judicial centres, such as Dijon.

Within each urban centre, the organisation of commercial exchange responded only slowly to expansion and contraction. At the lowest levels, which were common to towns of all sizes, most retail sales and purchases were carried out by women from market stalls. Products on sale ranged from foodstuffs to goods produced by artisans. Some of the stall-holders lived some distance from the town but were generally at a disadvantage as the urban authorities often set prices in favour of local consumers. Many peasants were obliged to bring grain to the urban market as soon as the harvest was over, a time when prices were particularly low. The larger the centre, the more likely that goods would be sold in a variety of specialised markets, spatially close but functionally distinct. Mid-seventeenth-century Newcastle upon Tyne had four markets on the streets ascending from the river. Fish was sold in the Sand Hill. Milk, eggs and butter were sold around the market cross in The Side. Barley (bigg) and oats were sold in the Bigg Market, which still bears this name, and wheat and rye in Pilgrim Street. This was mirrored by the distribution of markets in Lübeck, where the general market for foodstuffs in the centre of the city was complemented by markets for timber, salt, wine and iron.

Two connected developments took place in the retail trade as demand rose. When commercial activity spilled over into other locations beyond the jurisdiction of the guilds and market authorities, the latter made attempts to regain control. The earliest expansion took place within the market area itself. Stall-holders were complemented by numbers of itinerant pedlars. In Spain, they could be found selling figs, dried meat, fried fish, sausages, cheese pasties and fritters from baskets. Others sold patent medicines, perfumes and trinkets from benches within the market-place. Ben Jonson's *Volpone* was not the only man in Venice who tried to make a living as a mountebank. The phenomenon of overcrowding in market-places by shacks and stalls put up wherever possible was already a source of concern in fifteenth-century London, Paris, Genoa, Venice and Nuremberg. The records of the urban authorities in our period are full of complaints about the threats to public order and the orderly functioning of the market posed by unregistered sellers. As one London pamphlet of 1691 protested,

> there are a sort of people called by the name of pedlars, hawkers and petty chapfolks, who, contrary to the lawe, do carry out, dispose and sell in all cities of this kingdom very great quantities of several sorts of goods ... They multiply daily and have within a few years trebled their number ... in some by-parts of this nation several persons are induced to bring in many prohibited commodities to the ruining of many handicraftsmen.
>
> (J. Thirsk and J. Cooper (eds), *17th-century economic documents.* Oxford: Clarendon Press, 1972: 417)

Unregulated commercial exchanges of this kind were paralleled on a larger scale by merchants who found it more convenient to do business outside the market-place in inns and taverns, where the number of rooms attested to the range of clientele who came into town to do business. Thousands of pounds are reputed to have changed hands every Friday at the Bear Inn in Exeter. Elsewhere in England, the backyards of inns served as unofficial livestock marts. It is not surprising that the mercers of York were so alarmed in 1603 by these developments that they banned all their members, their servants and apprentices from going to any inn frequented by unofficial purchasers.

The rise in the volume of food imports in particular led to the development of practices intended to escape municipal control. In sixteenth-century Lyon, the official sales of grain in the market of La Grenette were circumvented by private deals between carters and merchants before supplies reached the market. Such 'forestalling' and 'regrating' (the resale on the official market of goods obtained in this way) also became increasingly commonplace in seventeenth-century England in spite of frequent government attempts to bring it under control.

The most successful attempts to reform the growing chaos of urban retail markets were those that concentrated on improving conditions for large-scale exchanges. The classic example is the creation of a new 'market island' at the Rialto in Venice, where all major commercial activities, both wholesale and retail, were concentrated after a fire in 1554, but the development of Les Halles in Paris and the new market square in Antwerp may be seen as part of the same process of making commercial exchanges more efficient. On a smaller scale, many of the town halls, which were remodelled in the course of the period, incorporated covered accommodation for retail sales on the ground floor.

The diversity of the import and export trades ensured that no single model of organisation and finance evolved during the sixteenth and seventeenth centuries in response to the increase in commercial activity. The most evident forms of commercial capitalism developed, as might be expected, in north-western Europe during the course of the seventeenth century. The establishment of public banks in Amsterdam, Rotterdam, Middelburg and Delft in 1609, in Hamburg in 1619 and in London in 1698 used techniques evolved in the Mediterranean to facilitate the finance of large-scale, long-distance trade, as well as supplying political entities with a means of underwriting their debts. The parallel growth of joint-stock companies in the same geographical area provided focused financing of ambitious overseas ventures, which recycled both earlier commercial profits and new venture capital from country investors.

The control of a substantial degree of long-distance trade in urban centres by groups of foreign merchants was far from a new phenomenon. Merchants from the cities of the Hanseatic League and from the cities of northern and central Italy had long played an important role in the imports and exports of London in the fourteenth and fifteenth centuries. As trading patterns shifted in the sixteenth and seventeenth centuries, however, so did control of long-distance trade. English and Dutch merchants trading largely, although not exclusively, from London and Amsterdam took over a large share of the most profitable trade in both the Mediterranean and the Baltic. This included a significant part of the coasting trade as well. The efforts of local merchants were increasingly directed towards regional markets, which were still extensive and a source of substantial profits, but were not on the same scale as before. Merchants from outside also exercised a growing influence on the urban economies of inland towns, particularly when the latter were centres of textile production. In the Netherlands, the growing concentration of exports through a small number of ports led to the creation of partnerships of merchants from different towns who jointly freighted ships and bought up local urban production. The expansion of Lyon as an export and silk manufacturing centre in the seventeenth century effectively stifled the commercial and industrial independence of neighbouring centres, such as Grenoble and Geneva. By the turn of the seventeenth century, Lyon merchants controlled much of the Dauphiné urban iron industry and Grenoble glass production. The introduction of these new dominant relationships did not represent a shift within individual regional urban hierarchies so much as a reorientation of economic relationships at a higher level.

However much evidence there is of large-scale capitalist investment in long-distance trade during the early modern period, it was limited to relatively few large entrepôt ports and was a response to the new requirements of commercial expansion. Elsewhere, the pattern of short- and middle- and long-distance trade in other towns retained most of its characteristics. In conditions of commercial decline or stagnation, there was no reason to change established practice and, even when individuals were able to take advantage of opportunities to establish enterprises on a substantial scale, such as Pedro Gutierrez in sixteenth-century Valladolid or Henning Parcham, the Lübeck merchant and landowner who established a charitable foundation upon his death in 1602, they rarely raised additional capital by joining with others. Small family partnerships were common. The Paris grain trade in the seventeenth century was in the hands of some 20 companies whose partners were brothers, cousins and nephews. Much of the long-distance trade carried out in German cities was in the hands of family groups belonging to the élite, such as the Pirckheimer in Nuremberg and the Rodde in Lübeck. Short-term partnerships were also common, either bringing unrelated merchants together or uniting men with capital and men with commercial expertise, where the latter worked for the company in return for a share of the profits. It is significant that all three types of partnership, the familial, the mixed and the semi-capitalist, co-existed in sixteenth-century Lyon.

If the exchange of goods lay at the heart of all urban economies, productive activity, including the cultivation of the land and the keeping of livestock, came a close second in importance.

The occupational structures of towns of all sizes were marked by the proximity of the land. In the middle of the sixteenth century, agricultural workers were the largest occupational group in both Aix-en-Provence, which had a population of at least 10 000, and the Sicilian town of Gangi with 4000 inhabitants. Fifteen to twenty per cent of the population of seventeenth-century Vienne in the Dauphiné worked on the land, mostly in vineyards. Most of the houses in the French textile centre of Clermont-de-Lodève were constructed with outbuildings intended to accommodate livestock. The market gardeners and fishermen of Strasbourg had their own guild. The suburbs of Paris in the 1550s were populated by peasants and vineyard workers. Even in early modern Naples, more than one per cent of those recorded in the marriage registers had agricultural occupations.

This strong agrarian element in the urban labour force was neither new nor surprising. Most of the subsistence migrants who moved to towns brought agricultural skills with them. Demographic growth did not necessarily enhance the distinctions between town and countryside. Indeed, the growth of suburbs beyond city walls and the decay of fortifications in areas no longer considered to be in danger from military attack increased the physical connections between towns and the fields in which they were set. Many burghers owned small plots of land close to the city walls or even within the city walls as an additional source of food and income. Probably one out of every five or six heads of families in sixteenth-century Lyon and at least half the inhabitants in the towns of the Dauphiné owned a minimum of one field. Nor was urban agrarian activity so easily distinguished from occupations that are more commonly associated with the town. Many of those who worked on the fields in and around towns combined this activity with others. Working the land was only one of the ways used by the poor to scrape an income. There were seasonal rhythms. Many commentators noted the way in which towns were virtually deserted at harvest time as the local residents left to attend to their own land or to return to their native villages in order to help to bring in the crops. The Besançon city council even suspended its regular meetings for this reason during the grape harvest. Towns were the main source of the substantial increase in the labour force needed at harvest time.

At the beginning of our period, towns could confidently lay claim to a reputation as centres of industrial production and, while the expansion in rural proto-industrialisation during the sixteenth and seventeenth centuries modified this claim, urban centres retained both the greatest concentrations of the industrial work-force and the greatest diversity of productive occupations. Their presence offered both a wide range of products to the local urban and rural populations and tied the urban economy to exports, with all that this implied in fluctuations in demand.

In principle, the number of occupations in the urban economy was directly related to the size of the town and its position within the regional hierarchy. In seventeenth-century Dauphiné, an area not noted for the prosperity of its economy, most towns had at least 25 occupations, but Grenoble, the provincial capital, had over 80. In sixteenth- and seventeenth-century Strasbourg, there were 99 individual occupations in which at least 10 people worked. In the same period, Paris boasted 112 occupations, including soap-makers, rope-makers, well-scrapers and cauldron scourers, while sixteenth-century Norwich is said to have had 223 occupations, including upholsterers, clock-makers and sugar-bakers.

In spite of the range of occupations to be found in early modern towns, most employment was concentrated within a limited number of sectors, which varied little from one town to another. Sixteenth-century Leicester, with a population of between 3000 and 5000, was a typical example. Well over half of the taxpayers were engaged in activities associated with clothing, footwear, the preparation of food and drink, household goods and building. In a limited number of large specialist export production centres, most of which concentrated on textiles, the occupational structure of the artisan population was even more skewed. Almost a quarter of all tax-payers in Augsburg on the eve of the Thirty Years War were weavers, and more than a fifth of the population of Florence worked in the textile industry in 1631.

The presence of the court and of other wealthy patrons in the largest cities encouraged the expansion of luxury and decorative trades, setting a trend for expanding urban centres lower down the scale. The development of Dijon as an administrative centre in the second half of the seventeenth century created a new demand for locally produced luxuries among wealthy office-holders. There were significant increases in the numbers working in the luxury trades in contrast to the textile industry, where numbers remained static.

As the demographic figures suggest, many urban economies experienced sharp rises and falls in demand, both within the locality and in the broader market. These changes were experienced particularly in the textile industry but also worked their way through other parts of the sector. Taken as a whole, the experience of urban industry in early modern Europe was largely a negative one. By the end of the seventeenth century, many of the textile centres in particular were in decline. Even where they were not, there were strong forces in favour of restricting innovation and retaining, if not increasing, the regulation of production, wages and quality. The paradox lies in the contrast between the stagnation of much urban production and the flexibility with which a small number of urban employers regulated a new, large and low-paid labour force in the surrounding countryside.

As a rule, craft production was small in scale and remained so throughout the period. Contrary to the impression left by reading guild statutes, the production of items for sale involved more than master craftsmen, journeymen and apprentices. Unskilled labour was also necessary in some crafts in order to do the necessary fetching and carrying and to complete simple tasks. This was particularly the case in the printing and construction industries, but it is abundantly clear that the division between the workshop and the master's household in most trades was a fluid one. Masters' wives and female servants moved easily from one sphere to the other, particularly in the food and drink and textile industries, where women carried out gender-specific tasks, such as preparing slaughtered meat, unwinding silkworm cocoons or preparing thread for bobbins. The work of the Venetian servant, Cecilia Campana, moved easily from domestic to industrial tasks. As she stated to the courts in 1660, she served Domenico Condulmero for 10 months, washing yarn, stretching cloth, spreading it on the balconies over the piazza, waiting at table, drawing wine, cooking on occasion and serving the signora outside the house.

More generally, masters' wives took on an important retail role, selling goods and keeping accounts. These transferable skills were so useful that they enabled masters' widows to apply them to other crafts when they remarried. The participation of female workers in craft workshops, whether or not they had been trained and recognised by a guild, became the focus of antagonism from many journeymen in the course of the period. This led to the gradual exclusion of women from this kind of work. Two factors appear to have given rise to this antagonism. The contraction in demand for goods led to greater competition for work among journeymen. Female helpers were perceived as a threat. The status of journeymen declined as their working conditions worsened and their chances of rising to economic independence as masters were restricted by a cartel of existing masters and their sons.

Even in the textile industry, the size of workshops remained relatively small, in spite of the general rise in demand for textiles. At the very end of the seventeenth century, 68 per cent of all master weavers in Beauvais declared that they had one or two looms in their workshops, while only 6 per cent had five looms. Only 7 per cent of masters employed more than 18 workers each. More than three-quarters employed 10 or fewer, and just under half of this group had a work-force of fewer than six. In other words, about a quarter of all the workers declared worked for only six masters. The distribution of the labour force was just as skewed. Twenty-four per cent worked for six masters, compared with the 58 per cent who were employed by 50 masters.

Figures such as these from Beauvais are far from accurate. They do not include female spinners, for example, but they do reflect a hierarchy of masters within the textile industry, which was repeated elsewhere. Legislation that limited the number of looms per workshop (six in Venice, four in Valladolid, two in Lille) was a vain attempt to control the activities of a small number of masters who wished to maximise production to meet rising demand. Some of these masters worked closely with export merchants. Others combined production and diffusion in a single enterprise. The cost of raw materials was such that often small-scale masters were unable to afford to stay in business without working in association with entrepreneurs. Two or three pounds of raw silk in sixteenth-century Lyon cost the equivalent of a loom, in itself a substantial investment for an artisan. The Genevan entrepreneur, Elisabeth Baulacre, developed a business between 1640 and 1693, which supplied gilded silver threads for use in the manufacture of buttons and hat decorations or for incorporation with silk yarn. In the circumstances of economic uncertainty that prevailed, master craftsmen were prepared to sign contracts to work exclusively for Mme Baulacre in return for wages, free lodging, grain, nut oil, charcoal and tallow.

There were limits to this kind of expansion in scale. Where demand fell rapidly, small units proved to be the most resilient. Clermont-de-Lodève was one of the most striking cases in the textile industry. The collapse of its export markets in the middle of the seventeenth century led to the abandonment of large-scale production of standardised cloths. The surviving weavers returned to a form of very small-scale industrial by-employment, in which they combined textile production with other activities, such as repairing fulling mills, working the land and trading in mules. With very low overheads and no additional labour costs, they were able to adapt where entrepreneurs could not.

It is questionable how far the organisation of work during the sixteenth and seventeenth centuries continued to be shaped by guild regulations. The status of the guilds themselves underwent substantial change. In Nuremberg, Frankfurt am Main and Nördlingen, the guilds were dissolved by the authorities for political reasons and were replaced by municipal regulations or by bodies controlled by government appointees. In Turin, where, unlike the Veneto and Tuscany, there was no guild tradition, the establishment of a small number of guilds in the later sixteenth and seventeenth centuries, such as the tailors, goldsmiths, shoemakers and silk weavers, also represented a growth in government control rather than independent decisions by artisans to regulate their own affairs. Granting guild status was a way of transmitting distinctive status to limited groups within a tightly controlled framework of craft associations.

In the majority of towns, where guild organisation was the norm, the extent to which their activities were controlled varied considerably. There was little direct intervention in the workshop itself. The quality of goods, the way in which they were produced, specific forms of training within apprenticeships and relations between masters, journeymen and apprentices were generally left to the guilds themselves. On the other hand, the freedom with which guild officials were able to operate was subject to a range of controls. The registration of guild regulations and their modifications by the authorities gave them the potential to make the guild elders into their agents, a source of power that was enhanced by a gradual shift in the way in which these elders were elected. Some elections maintained the fiction that guild elders were chosen by their members or at least by the master craftsmen but, in reality, these elders could not take their place until their names had been ratified by the city government, a process that encouraged the candidature and election of candidates known to have government approval. In other towns, the selection of elders came to lie entirely within the hands of the government. In due course, the transformation of such positions into venal offices by the monarchies of France, Spain and many Italian states reinforced the role of the guild elder as an agent of outside authority, in this case, one with a much wider jurisdiction.

The more tightly controlled the guilds, the more likely that regulations combined with unfavourable trading conditions to place producers at a disadvantage in what was becoming a world market. The largest Italian textile centres suffered in particular. At a time when Dutch and English ships were bringing low-price, low-quality, highly coloured cloth into the Mediterranean, the statutes of the Venetian wool-weavers' guild continued to require its members to produce 'Venetian cloth of the old standard'. By the time these rules were revised in 1673 to enable Venetian artisans to compete, it was too late. It was only by developing silk production that the Florentine economy was able to compensate for the decline in the traditional wool industry. Significantly, most of the work was undertaken by women outside traditional guild controls. In the 1660s, they constituted 84 per cent of all silk workers.

Elsewhere, attempts to expand and change working practices within a framework of rigid guild controls led to substantial strains, which the urban authorities were not always able to resolve. Relations between the butchers, tanners and shoemakers of Bologna broke down in 1637 when the butchers secretly set up tanning sheds of their own. This enabled them to break the tanners' monopoly and to extend the range of their own business. In Strasbourg, there were major tensions within the coopers' and the market gardeners' guilds between small-scale producers and merchant members who used their superior resources to take control of the labour market and dominate exports. The poorer market gardeners complained in 1615 that the onion export market to Frankfurt am Main was now in the hands of only four men. The *roperos* of Valladolid sold footwear and trousers more cheaply than those made by the guild of the *calceteros*. By the 1570s, there were more tallow-sellers in London outside the Tallow Chandler's Guild than within it. In Dijon, journeymen were making unofficial working arrangements with employers that circumvented guild restrictions. There were major disturbances in late seventeenth-century Lille, when a small number of cloth manufacturers attempted to introduce different and larger-scale production 'in the Valenciennes style', claiming that existing guild regulations did not apply to them because this was a new product.

Town and countryside

An important and growing contribution to the urban economy was represented by the profits from external investment. There had always been an element of rentier income among the wealthier members of the population, derived from the ownership of houses, land and municipal bonds. The purchase of land by wealthy townsmen had helped to facilitate the extension of territory by city states in Germany and Italy. Elsewhere, the ownership of land by the municipal authorities themselves, by wealthy townsmen and by religious institutions helped to sustain the power of medieval towns over their hinterlands.

If this pattern was well established by the beginning of the sixteenth century, the level of land acquisition was to rise over the next 200 years as townsmen purchased more land and more townsmen than before entered the land market. Not only were they in a position to afford more land, the increasing availability of land on the market enabled them to switch funds from other investments. Land became available for a number of reasons. The rise in indebtedness among landowners both large and small during the sixteenth and seventeenth centuries placed the land that they used as surety at risk if they were unable to fulfil their commitments. Much of it came into urban ownership as sureties for unpaid loans by urban creditors. As M de Croissey of Geneva wrote in 1696, 'the inhabitants of the Gex borrow money easily in Geneva, which is an opportunity for the Genevans to make themselves masters of this little area without anyone noticing'. [Quoted in A-M. Prinz, Les relations économiques entre les villes et les campagnes dans les sociétés pré-industrielles. In F. Bayard *et al.* (eds) *Villes et campagnes, xve–xxe siècles*, Lyon, 1977: 33. (Author's translation)] The rest was sold off in order to repay loans and came into the hands of townsmen who played an active part in the land market, both near to their towns and further afield in the case of men of great wealth, such as the Fugger family of Augsburg, who purchased estates in several parts of Swabia. The land market was also enlivened by properties sold as the result of inheritance divisions, through the release of church property, which was not exclusively related to expropriations during the Reformation, and as a result of land sales by monarchs and republics alike to meet spiralling government costs.

A more complex series of approaches to the land developed, some of which were market- or investment-related, including the increasing deployment of certain kinds of industrial production among the rural labour force, while social and cultural factors played a more important part in others.

Townsmen entered the land market for a number of reasons. Land was an important source of food and drink to supplement what could be bought on the urban market. In the Mediterranean area, for example, an urban family could expect to use grain, olive oil and wine from their landed properties, all of which could be stored privately, as a cushion against bad harvests and rising prices. This was seen as a universal benefit. Land included in marriage contracts was frequently valued in terms of both the food it was expected to yield and the annual rent income. Certain urban occupations bought land in order to cut out the middleman in their search for raw materials. Brick-makers bought up land for its clay. Bakers and brewers valued land for its cereals, as did inn-keepers, who had an interest in both wine for their guests and oats for their horses.

Among the wealthy, the acquisition of land offered a new dimension to their leisure activities. As urban populations grew and the environment became more crowded and unpleasant, gardens close to the city walls to be used on a Sunday afternoon or in the cool of the evening came to be at a premium, to be succeeded in charm by houses to be used as places for escape in the summer heat. The Regents of Amsterdam bought up farmhouses in the Vecht valley and the Isle of Walcheran. The burghers of Lucerne did the same. Wealthy Venetians gradually transformed quite simple summer residences into sophisticated homes and villas in which they spent longer and longer periods away from the city.

The slowness with which land was perceived to change in value by comparison with the price of other commodities also made it a secure investment, both when urban prices were rising and when they were falling. The Genoese Doria family purchased the estate of Montaldeo in 1566 because the inflation in agricultural prices promised attractive returns without additional investment. The burghers of York, on the other hand, were active on the local land market in the same period because they wished to compensate for declining opportunities in trade. Even in favourable commercial conditions, merchants gradually added land to their property portfolios during their active life-cycle in order to assemble dowries for their daughters, finance their sons' advancement and to prepare for retirement.

The pattern of land acquisition varied according to the wealth and aspirations of the purchaser and also according to the kind of land for sale and the income-producing opportunities that it offered. Where the land bore feudal rights, income from rents could be supplemented by feudal dues with a minimum of effort. In the area around Amiens in 1674, 82.8 per cent of all fiefs were owned by townsmen or urban institutions.

Ambitious landowners were able to assemble estates through the careful choice of loans and purchases, as long as they were ready to return to the land market to sell in order to round out a parcel that could be leased out. They might begin with a little farm but, in time, this building became the core of a complex of fields, vineyards, pastures and ponds for Friday fish.

With the exception of poor-quality land bought for its investment potential after drainage, most land that came into the hands of urban owners was treated as a reliable source of income, which could be endangered if changes were introduced. Large-scale urban consortia were formed in the Netherlands and on the Venetian mainland. In the case of the latter, the project failed in the long term because the high costs of maintenance reduced the rate of return on their investment to the point at which the investors withdrew and the land returned to its original condition. Other urban landowners were more concerned with conserving their investment than with enhancing it. Many French urban landowners wrote clauses into rental agreements limiting innovation. The Netherlands was an exception to this pattern. The high level of urbanisation encouraged more concentration on specialised dairy farming and horticulture in the northern provinces. There is no real evidence that urban landowners initiated these changes.

It is far from easy to judge the impact on the urban economy of the increase in landownership by the urban population. As far as poorer landowners were concerned, the land offered them a kind of cushion against adversity, an independent source of food and drink and a supplement to other kinds of income. Revenue from the land may also be seen as a cushion in other terms. As it increased, it came to represent a major share in the incomes of the wealthy and, consequently, an important contributor to the fiscal income of the urban authorities. While the rate of land acquisition declined during the 'long' seventeenth century when many urban economies went into decline or stagnated, the presence of relatively secure rentier incomes, of which feudal dues and rents from land constituted a significant part, enabled the wealthy families in urban society to sustain their standards of living and, through their spending, to cushion some of the overall effects on the urban economy of declining profits from trade and industry.

Expanding and contracting economies

Earlier in this chapter, we concluded that urban economies in early modern Europe were not marked by consistent dynamism. They experienced sharp fluctuations in population levels, and much of the growth took place in administrative rather than in commercial or industrial centres. Why did some urban economies survive the period relatively unscathed, others experience substantial expansion and an even larger number experience decline?

It is customary to dwell on the economic successes of the period, Seville and Antwerp, London and Amsterdam, Hamburg and Bremen. Their experience was exciting and stimulating, incorporating very substantial increases in population, in the range and volume of economic activity and in the social and cultural changes that this brought about. As such, it should not be discounted, nor should the factors which led to this success, but it was far from typical of urban economies as a whole. All of them experienced some demographic expansion as part of the overall increases in the population of Europe in the sixteenth century, but this growth was not sustained and, in central Europe and the Baltic and Mediterranean areas in particular, whole regions experienced urban economic decline. Elsewhere, the success of single large cities contributed to the decline of their neighbours. There is little to celebrate here. Changes in the organisation of trade and industry were relatively small, and changes in levels of activity often signalled contraction or stagnation rather than expansion. Even the growth in new demands for luxuries among professionals and administrators did not benefit the local economy. Such products were usually imported from much further away.

There is some justification for looking in greater detail at the causes of urban decline or stagnation than at those of expansion. Each urban economy in decline had its own chronology and its own local factors. By the end of the fifteenth century, Aigues-Mortes was already in decline. Access to the port by larger vessels became impossible as channels silted up and were no longer dredged. It had been France's premier Mediterranean port in the Middle Ages. Located at one of the mouths of the Rhone, it accommodated all the traffic from the Rhone valley, as well as imports from the Levant. Along with Venice, it had been an important departure point for the Near East. By the mid-seventeenth century, Aigues-Mortes was more famous for the malarial swamps that surrounded it than for any international economic activity. Political, rather than economic, change lay at the heart of its decline. Its success had been based on a lack of competition for the French Mediterranean trade. Transfers of trading privileges to Lyon at the end of the fifteenth century, on the one hand, and the incorporation of Marseille and the rest of Provence into the French crown, on the other, provided alternatives, which could offer more than a harbour. Marseille already had thriving commercial connections in the western Mediterranean. Lyon was well positioned both as a major distribution point for south-eastern France and as an industrial producer in its own right. At the other end of Europe, Lübeck was experiencing economic decline from the mid-sixteenth century. In this case, the consequences were not as dramatic as in Aigues-Mortes. Lübeck remained a middle-ranking Baltic port with a static population around a mean of 25 000 throughout the seventeenth century. On the other hand, it was unable to compensate fully for the loss to the Dutch of its traditional role as the middleman between the Baltic and the North Seas or the erosion of secondary routes to southern Germany and Scandinavia. Significantly, the decline in the Lübeck shipbuilding industry reached such a stage in terms of loss of labour and expertise that when new opportunities arose, such as the short-lived participation of north German merchants in the Iberian and Mediterranean trade at the end of the sixteenth century, it became necessary to buy ships from elsewhere.

Two-thirds of the houses in the district of Valladolid which included both commercial and industrial activity were destroyed by fire in 1561. Rebuilding took place, but the inability of the city to regenerate fully after this disaster owed a great deal to the absence of the royal court, which, after using both Valladolid and Toledo as peripatetic capitals, moved south definitively to Madrid. Further north, Medina del Campo lost its position as a commercial and financial centre on a European scale. Its regular fairs had attracted merchants from all over the Iberian peninsula and beyond. Population levels began to fall from the 1560s, even earlier than in other Spanish centres as business fell in reaction to the rupture of trading relations with the Netherlands after the area was affected by war. By 1561, its entire population was smaller than the number of tax-paying households in the 1530s. As in the case of Valladolid, the growth of Madrid to the south created an alternative economic focus, which drained business away. Weakened by its inability to call in international debt payments, Medina was unable to compensate for the removal of its fiscal privileges by the Spanish monarchy.

Each individual account bears testimony to external circumstances over which neither those who worked in nor those who governed these towns had any real control, changes in trade routes, shifts in political frontiers, the relocation of a royal court and the absence of visiting merchants. They ignore the more widespread circumstances, which contributed to their economic difficulties. In the end, however, what distinguished the majority of economic centres that stagnated or declined from that minority which expanded was not the fact of decline or expansion, but the extent to which urban communities and their governments were able to adapt to changes in circumstances. One of the strengths of the city of London was the way in which its merchants were able to overcome the difficulties posed towards the end of the sixteenth century by the breakdown of its traditional commercial links with the Netherlands. Hamburg, too, overcame the threats posed by the breakdown of the Hanseatic League and the growing confidence of the Dutch, who had succeeded in capturing an ever-increasing share of the traffic that passed through the Sound of Scånen. Between 1600 and 1650, the tonnage of shipping operating from the Elbe port doubled, largely because Hamburg became the German redistribution centre for goods from the Levant and the East Indies.

The contrast with the experience of centres such as Aigues-Mortes, Lübeck, Valladolid and Medina del Campo is striking. When faced with threats from competitors, each of these centres showed that they were unable to adapt to these circumstances. They lacked the necessary capital reserves to be able to do so. Their geographical location, which had been the source of much of their earlier strength, was now a handicap. Lübeck's position upstream along the River Trave from the Baltic coast, for example, had offered safe haven, extensive commercial services and warehousing and overland links to Denmark and south Germany. Once Dutch ships had taken control of the Baltic–North Sea trade, there was no reason for them to make the journey upstream. Something similar took place in Venice. Once direct trade routes in spices were developed between the East Indies, the Indian coast and north-western Europe, the routes between the eastern Mediterranean, the Adriatic and the transalpine market, which had contributed so much to Venice's prosperity during the Middle Ages, became secondary.

Lack of capital and a less advantageous geographical situation were compounded both by the actions of the authorities and by the regional impact of war. In the face of declining trade, most urban authorities responded by introducing or extending policies of protectionism. The contrast between Hamburg and Lübeck is instructive. Hamburg, like Amsterdam, and, to a lesser extent, London, benefited from the arrival of foreign merchants with additional capital, expertise and contacts. The city council in Lübeck, on the other hand, attempted to restore the port's fortunes by returning in vain to the medieval formula that had ensured its success. In 1602, it decreed that all goods that passed the mouth of the River Trave must be transported to the city and sold to local merchants before they could be transported further. Without the naval power to enforce this rule, such a policy was counterproductive, driving away trade in foreign vessels that might have brought business to the port. Protectionism in favour of locally produced textiles contributed to the decline of many industrial centres in the Mediterranean. With the enthusiastic support of the master craftsmen, whose self-esteem was associated with the belief that they alone were capable of making traditional products of high quality, the council at Cordoba, a major wool and silk textile production centre, delayed until the last part of the seventeenth century before trying to match the type of goods and production methods that had allowed northern merchants to penetrate the local market with such success. By that time, it was too late. Even with the help of foreign craftsmen, who were brought in to train locals in the methods of the new draperies, the city lacked the financial basis upon which to build a successful industry.

While the impact of warfare was not responsible for economic decline as such, it did contribute substantially to the economic difficulties of many urban centres. In addition to the direct problems posed by the severance of important trade routes or the catastrophic impact of sieges, the fiscal cost of warfare placed a major strain on urban finances and acted as a deterrent to economic regeneration. Germany suffered the most direct economic damage from warfare. In the Rhine valley, the number of taxpayers in Mainz dropped from 1240 in 1629 to 668 in 1650. Its overall population fell by 60 per cent during the same period. Attacks by the French destroyed almost all the most important towns in the Palatinate in the 1690s, requiring major incentives to bring in immigrants on a large scale. The economic costs of attacks such as these were all the greater because they were recurrent. The German town of Stade on the lower Elbe became the capital of two Swedish provinces in the second half of the seventeenth century. Nine bastions were built, with Dutch-style outer fortifications and water-filled ditches between 1645 and 1712. It had been captured by Imperial troops in 1632, recaptured in 1645, blockaded in 1662, attacked in 1675 and finally besieged in 1712. By the time Stade capitulated, one quarter had been burned down.

Higher taxation to pay for fortifications and the billeting of troops (which had its own particular costs in human terms) or, in some cases, to finance bribes to foreign armies to stay away, reduced potential investment margins, encouraged the emigration of skilled workers to rural areas not under urban jurisdiction and placed an increased individual burden on those who stayed. When these higher fiscal costs were introduced in towns that were already suffering from long-term indebtedness, the economic consequences could be grave. Even in Hamburg, which experienced substantial growth in the later seventeenth century, debt levels of 60 marks per head of the population in 1600 were worsened as military expenditure rose by 50 per cent during the first decade of the Thirty Years War.

The role of fiscality as a restraint on economic development was particularly evident in France, Spain and Lombardy, where the territorial state had largely succeeded in removing the autonomy of municipal government. In Spain, the weight of taxation introduced before the Iberian economy went into rapid decline in the early seventeenth century must have been a contributory factor. In Seville, the tax burden rose by seven times between 1590 and 1650 as the result of increases in taxes on wine, oil, vinegar and meat. The fall in the living standards of the artisans was a strong incentive to move to nearby villages, which were exempt from such taxes. Over-taxation by the Spanish authorities in the Lombard cities of Milan and Cremona had a similar effect on the contrasting experiences of town and countryside. The conflict between the fiscal demands of the French state under Louis XIV and the attempts by Colbert to revive the French economy are equally well known. Fiscality won the argument.

|2|

Government

The German free imperial city of Lübeck was located on a promontory of land between the Rivers Trave and Wakenitz. The Trave curved around two sides of the settlement, and it required little ingenuity during the city's period of great economic and political development during the thirteenth and fourteenth centuries to dig a channel to enable the river waters to act as a natural moat. The city itself was built on ground that sloped down to the water on all sides, leaving a narrow plateau in the centre, which widened out into an open space, occupied by the main market and bounded on two sides by Lübeck's two most important buildings, the *Rathaus* and the *Marienkirche*. Three key institutions were concentrated here in one compact area, the centre of exchange, the town hall and the church of St Mary's parish, the area that was largely inhabited by both the economic and the political élite of the city.

The town hall was far more than the meeting place for Lübeck councillors, just as the councillors themselves did far more than meet together to discuss matters of policy and make new laws. (As a free imperial city, Lübeck owed allegiance only to the Holy Roman Emperor and had the right to pass its own laws and collect its own taxes.) The town hall housed the chancellery, which collected taxes, and a secretariat, which registered a wide range of legal matters from the sale of houses and property and the settlement of debts to the appointment of guardians and executors, the settlement of disputes between burghers and, after the Reformation, the appointment of parish clergy. The councillors sat as the city's law court, judging criminal and civil cases. They set wage levels and the price of bread. They organised the food and commodity markets, were responsible for the cleanliness of the streets and for defending the city against attack by soldiers and disease. They undertook to keep good order. The town hall housed an apparatus of government, which, even at the beginning of the sixteenth century, was complex, wide-ranging and under the control of a group of men whose interests were closely identified with the city's economic well-being and who worked very hard to ensure that this continued.

It would be unwise to take Lübeck as a complete paradigm for urban centres throughout western Europe in the sixteenth and seventeenth centuries. With a population of around 25 000, it was smaller than the great cosmopolitan centres in the Mediterranean but substantially larger than many urban centres all over Europe. As a free imperial city, it was, in effect, a city state, to be considered alongside Venice, Nuremberg or Geneva, and, in consequence, its government exercised powers that were not subject to the same restraints as urban governments in the territorial states of England, France or Spain, where only the largest of urban centres had exercised even relative political autonomy during the Middle Ages, and the majority of towns had always functioned under the control of one or more external authorities. On the other hand, the business of government in Lübeck closely resembled that of urban centres elsewhere, and it does represent the way in which burghers' lives were strictly circumscribed by rules and regulations, which were interpreted and applied locally, in terms of both how they lived and worked and how their incomes were constrained by the requirement to make a fiscal contribution to the costs of government.

This chapter is less concerned with the operation of urban government than with the changes in the distribution of authority both inside and outside towns, which affected how government worked. It is intended rather to provide a framework for the more detailed discussion of the operation of urban government in later chapters devoted to religion, planning and the urban fabric, poor relief and to questions of order and disorder.

These changes in the distribution of authority took place at different speeds in different urban centres, but several were so widespread that they lend themselves to more general discussion. In spite of the retention of older constitutional forms, authority was increasingly concentrated in the hands of a political élite, and burgher participation in decision-making consequently declined. Lawyers supplanted or displaced merchants and artisans as decision-makers. External forms of authority in the emerging territorial states played an increasing part in determining who held office in urban government and how much autonomy remained for those in office. On the other hand, the slow and difficult process of state-building created conditions in which the relationship between urban governments and the central administration was more of a wary partnership for much of the time rather than one of dependence on external authority.

The experience of city states such as Lübeck stands somewhat apart from the changes in the exercise of authority experienced by urban centres in the territorial states but, in the new political climate in which territorial rulers disposed of growing fiscal and military resources, the city states were obliged to adapt the way in which they governed in order to survive. Some did not retain their independence, and the ways in which they were absorbed by larger territorial states are a useful point of comparison with the experiences of the towns that comprise the greater part of this chapter. It seems appropriate, however, to begin with the city states.

The city states

City states were few in number by 1500. Most of the medieval city states had become independent because their economic strength had enabled them to take advantage of a temporary political vacuum in the area. They were among the largest cities in Europe and counted as the nodal points of the late medieval economy. The size of the territories and the political organisation of the city states also varied widely. Here, there were important geographical differences. By the beginning of the sixteenth century, most surviving Italian city states ruled over substantial areas of territory incorporating subject towns of their own and requiring considerable complexity of government, not only at the centre, but also in the localities. The most powerful of all, the Venetian Republic, possessed a colonial empire, which stretched between the shores of Lake Maggiore, the Dolomites and the Adriatic as well as a long strip of land along the Dalmatian coast and numbers of maritime colonies on the islands of the eastern Mediterranean. The *Serenissima*'s form of government, therefore, reflected the diverse needs of the city, mainland provinces and maritime outposts. The three were inseparable.

In Switzerland, Germany and the Netherlands, on the other hand, the amount of territory ruled over by city states varied according to the circumstances in which they had been granted the privileges of extended political autonomy. None could compete with the Italian states, which now controlled subject towns of considerable size themselves. The larger northern and central European cities, such as Geneva, Zürich, Nuremberg and Lübeck, possessed a limited *contado*, which bore little relation to their economic prominence. A traveller could cross from one side of Nuremberg's territory to the other in two days. The protected political status of some independent cities, mostly in southern and central Germany, was not necessarily matched by economic importance on an international scale. As free cities of the Holy Roman Empire, small centres, such as Schwäbisch Hall, Kaufbeuren, Dinkelsbühl, Ravensburg and Biberach, owed their independence to their location on imperial territory. They had very little hinterland and did not stand out as centres of production. Like their larger German counterparts, the great Netherlands trading cities of Bruges, Antwerp, Amsterdam and Rotterdam enjoyed an influence that was quite out of proportion to the size of territory over which they had jurisdiction.

In political terms, the majority of city states in existence in 1500 retained their independence throughout the next 200 years. Indeed, their numbers rose. Hamburg escaped from the overlordship of the king of Denmark to become an imperial free city in 1618. On the other hand, the constitutions of Ulm, Strasbourg and Augsburg, Protestant cities in southern Germany, were altered by imperial fiat in 1547, which represented a substantial reduction in their freedom of manoeuvre. A small number of cities, including Strasbourg, Metz and Besançon, were transferred to French sovereignty in the later seventeenth century. In the Netherlands, the events of the Dutch Revolt brought tighter controls over towns in the south and greater independence within the loose framework of the United Provinces to towns in the north.

Two developments took place in Italy. Both were an extension of a trend that had already been developing in the fifteenth century. Many city states in the classical sense, independent political entities ruled over by their citizens, had already become the nucleus of a territorial state ruled over by a single dynasty, such as the Este in Ferrara and the Bentivoglio in Bologna. Others, such as Florence, lost their autonomy in the early sixteenth century, and the extension of territorial control by their ruling families altered their status to capital cities. Milan, already the centre of a hereditary duchy, fell to the Spanish in 1540. Only Venice, Genoa and a few minor city states remained relatively free from outside influence to survive into the eighteenth century.

The experience of continuing independence from outside authority did not leave urban government untouched in the city states. The intensification of oligarchical government in the free imperial cities never quite rivalled the self-confidence and power of the urban ruling élites in Italy, but it did give rise to an absolutist ideology, which differed little from the beliefs of the princes. The rulers of Frankfurt am Main, Lübeck, Hamburg, Augsburg and the others saw themselves increasingly as *Herrscher* (lords) and the other citizens as *Untertanen* (subjects). Attitudes in both Italy and Germany towards subject cities also seemed to parallel the behaviour of the territorial states. Just as royal officials abounded in the French towns, every Venetian subject city (Brescia, Padua, Vicenza, Verona, Treviso, to name only the most important) had its own *podestà* to ensure that the interests of the urban authorities did not run counter to the state.

The need to defend their independence from the depredations of neighbouring jurisdictions and the increasing presence of foreign armies in both Italy and Germany during the early modern period led to a rolling programme of fortification by the city states. With little more than a small hinterland as territory, the imperial free cities concentrated on making their walls as impregnable as possible, not so much to withstand a siege as to deter potential enemies from attempting a siege at all. The complicated networks of bastions projecting from walls graced with massive earthworks to withstand the impact of any known projectile served their purpose. Few sieges of the kind that left Magdeburg razed to the ground during the Thirty Years War were attempted by any of the armies that criss-crossed Germany during the later sixteenth and seventeenth centuries. On the other hand, the cost of such success placed almost unbearable strains on the cities' fiscal systems, both in terms of the construction and renewal of modern fortifications and of the indemnities that it was often necessary to pay passing armies to avoid even the possibility of a siege.

The experience of those cities that lost their independence to outside powers was not entirely negative. The conquests of Louis XIV were located in sensitive border areas, and the rapid construction of fortresses within the urban area fulfilled the dual purpose of supervising a population of uncertain loyalties and defending key routes in and out of the kingdom. The site at Besançon, captured by the French in 1674, was ideal. Vauban constructed an immense and imposing citadel there on the heights dominating the loop of the River Doubs within which the city was built. Lille, which had fallen to the French after a siege seven years earlier, was graced by an even more complex set of fortifications in a marshy area at the north-western corner of the city. The presence of garrisons such as these added a new dimension to urban life, which brought both economic benefits and frequent sources of conflict.

Once the military control of the newly dependent cities had been assured, their princely rulers seem to have taken the greatest possible care to avoid upsetting local susceptibilities. Official documents integrating Lille and Strasbourg into France made great play of the king's respect for local traditions and, while it is clear that steps were taken to integrate both cities into the kingdom, royal representatives were instructed to do so as slowly and quietly as possible. Even contributions to royal defence expenditure were 'negotiated' with some care. This open willingness to respect existing traditions of government was also adopted by the kings of Spain in relation to Milan. In common with the other provinces of the Habsburg multiple kingdom, the Milanese Senate exercised the right to give their approval to decrees signed in Madrid before they could become law. While this changed little in reality, it offered the Milanese government considerable autonomy in its own eyes.

The rise of oligarchy

Urban government in sixteenth- and seventeenth-century Europe was marked by an increasing gap between constitutional forms and the realities of power, a gap that was mirrored by the growing divergence in interests between townspeople and those who governed them. The development of urban autonomy from the twelfth and thirteenth centuries had given birth to a wide variety of constitutional forms, which tended to conform to local practice. Thus, we find a preponderance of single-cameral town councils in England, Scotland, the Netherlands, France, Spain and northern Germany, and a tendency to govern through multicameral bodies in central and southern

Germany, Provence and Italy. At one end of the spectrum, Lille was governed by 33 annually elected councillors, serving alongside seven permanent officials. At the other end, the *Ayuntamiento* of Seville had around 300 members, and the government of Venice, which took responsibility for both the city and its subject territories, comprised all 1500–2000 adult male members of the hereditary patriciate sitting in a great council (the *Maggior Consiglio*) from which members of several subsidiary governing bodies, the *Senato,* the *Minor Consiglio* and the *Collegio* were elected.

The gradual concentration of authority inside urban governments was reflected by the withering away of one of the oldest constitutional forms, the assembly of burghers. Such assemblies had their roots in the communal tradition within which many towns gained their early political autonomy, and the existence of the burgher assembly continued to have resonances for ordinary burghers long after it had ceased to have any practical meaning. Two thousand armed and excited burghers attended the municipal election in Béziers in the crisis year of 1647. Anti-Spanish demonstrators in Naples in 1585 called for the restoration of direct elections to the council through the *Seggio di Sant'Agostino*, the traditional citizen body. But outbursts such as these were far from common. The great council of Strasbourg, comprising 300 men elected by the city's 20 guilds, never met during the seventeenth century. The most important function retained by the 200-strong *Erbare Rat* in Nuremberg was to attend the annual council elections and give its formal assent to the results. The outermost organ of government in the City of London, the Court of Common Hall, had a potential membership of 4000 liverymen. By the end of the seventeenth century, it too exercised purely ceremonial powers.

The decline in burgher influence through bodies such as these was paralleled by a much more serious erosion of power inside the city councils. There was a growing tendency for power to accrue to a much smaller group of men. Outer councils, such as the Great Council in Nice or the 196-member Court of Common Council in the City of London, were too large for effective decision-making. So were some large single-chamber bodies, such as the Frankfurt am Main city council. As the increasing load of administration created the need for day-to-day supervision and decision-making, power devolved to the men with key responsibilities, aided by a small number of councillors. In England, this role was undertaken by the mayor and aldermen, in Valencia and Bordeaux by the *jurats*, in Besançon by the *gouverneurs* and in Lyon by the *échevins*.

While there was no rule that only the wealthiest members of the urban community were allowed to take on such offices, considerable wealth seemed to be a prerequisite for this activity. Attendance at frequent meetings of the council for administrative or judicial purposes required a commitment in time, which could only be taken up by men free from the obligations of running a full-time business. This was one of the reasons why members of urban élites came to rely increasingly on passive forms of income. Men with ambitions to hold high political office did not commit themselves to an active economic life. The presence of wealthy men on the council also corresponded to certain unspoken expectations that they would make substantial personal contributions, if asked, to meet the cost of specific aspects of government expenditure.

Urban oligarchies gradually became self-perpetuating. In Lyon, 82 seats out a total of 220 were occupied by members of 26 families between 1520 and 1539. In the next two decades, 31 families occupied over three-quarters of the seats. In Bordeaux, the mayor was elected biannually by six *jurats* who all appointed their successors, as well as the council of 24 *prudhommes*. In sixteenth-century Aberdeen, real power was in the hands of a dozen or so dynasties. In Paris, seats on the council became hereditary during the seventeenth century. (The social implications of the development of political élites are discussed at length in Chapter 3.)

Elsewhere, the process of election was modified in order to ensure that only the names of those men who were approved of by existing members of the urban government would be put forward by 'electors' who represented, in theory, a much broader constituency. As Christopher Scheurl wrote in sixteenth-century Nuremberg, 'We admit no one onto our Council, excepting the eight Commoners already mentioned, whose parents and grandparents did not also sit on the Council' [Strauss, 1976: 61]. Such an explicit statement of oligarchical power was rarely committed to paper, but the signs of political expectations at the time of elections were clear to read, whether an urban constitution required all its councillors to step down after a short period, as in Newcastle upon Tyne, Bordeaux or Chartres, or whether councillors were elected for life, as in Lübeck or the cities of the Netherlands' provinces of Holland, Friesland, Zealand and Utrecht.

The aggrandisement of political power through the control of electoral colleges can be illustrated by the case of Chartres, where it was customary for two *échevins* to resign from the council each year and for elections to be held to fill these vacancies. Although assemblies were held in each parish in order to elect delegates, they were far from representative of the population of burghers. On some occasions, they were selected by the notaries organising the elections. On others, they were self-selected 'notables', who understood what kind of candidates they were to put forward. In principle, the new candidates had to be of the same status or occupation as those whom they were replacing. If the names were unacceptable to the government, they could be rejected.

Conflicts with burghers

The growth in oligarchical government gave rise to a variety of responses from the rest of the burghers. There appear to have been few signs of constitutional conflict in England. When they did appear, this was largely in the context of the general upheavals in the 1640s and 1650s when groups of men who had felt themselves excluded from power by the existing political élite strove to replace them under the flag of king or parliament or, as in the cases of Thomas Cliffe and Ralph Gardner in Newcastle upon Tyne, they took to the courts to try to break the economic monopoly that underlay the power of the Company of Hostmen whose members dominated the city's government. It is not easy to compare these manoeuvres with events in France or Germany, in which more serious constitutional issues were in dispute. The relative quiescence of the English owed much to the absence of any substantial urban autonomy in the fourteenth and fifteenth centuries and the relatively easy relationship with the monarchy for most of the period under discussion.

Constitutional conflict in France was rarely articulated in exclusively urban terms either. The positions taken up by different parties in opposition to the ruling élites from the mid-sixteenth century had as much to do with the resistance to the monarchy by the Huguenots across the country as a whole as they had with particular conditions in each town. There is little evidence, for example, that the short period of Huguenot rule in Lyon in the 1560s represented a less oligarchical form of government. If anything, the exigencies of defending a fairly precarious political position made the Huguenots' grip on the city tighter than that of their predecessors.

In the free imperial cities of the Holy Roman Empire, deep constitutional issues arose precisely because their governments had a much wider role than those of towns in the territorial states. In some towns, such as Lübeck, constitutional tensions arose during the Reformation, when artisans and others who had been increasingly excluded from real political power articulated their discontent by supporting evangelical preachers against an oligarchy closely associated with the existing church and its institutions. In others, such as Frankfurt am Main, constitutional issues developed later as citizens experienced increasingly damaging economic pressures for which they held their governments responsible.

One central constitutional issue predominated. No one disputed the right of the councils of the free imperial cities to rule. This was their function; they had a responsibility to the emperor to do so. On the other hand, the older concept of government as the joint responsibility of the elected council and the burgher community had been eroded both in practice and in theory. Attempts were made in several cities to incorporate into the burgher oath the idea of obedience to the council as 'lords', and much play was made by the councils during these largely bloodless conflicts of the idea that the other burghers were their subjects. By the end of the seventeenth century, these newer theories of control were reinforced by the growing identification of the political élite with members of the local gentry. In the long term, the power of government remained dominant in the German free cities, but the tradition of an older, more broadly based constitution remained and continued as a potential source of dispute into the eighteenth century. Both Hamburg and Frankfurt am Main experienced major difficulties in the early 1700s, and their autonomy was severely strained by the need for imperial arbitration.

Changes in the organisation of government

The absence of change in outward forms of urban government in the early modern period masked considerable changes in the sources and concentration of authority. The same could be said about the actual practice of government. On the face of it, there was a great deal of continuity between the subjects discussed in council meetings in the seventeenth century and those on the agenda 400 years earlier.

The urban authorities continued to legislate about the conditions under which markets were held, the level of taxes to be raised and the ways in which this could be done most effectively, and the nuisance of clutter in the streets. Even the crises that they faced periodically remained very similar: the threatened outbreak of the plague, the approach of an army, the implications of food shortages after a bad harvest, even the presence of unexpectedly large numbers of beggars.

On the other hand, early modern urban governments were faced with unprecedented levels of immigration, economic fluctuations of some scale and a whole host of external preoccupations related to the extent to which control was passing to higher authorities. Some of the ways in which these problems arose and attempts that were made to resolve them are discussed in later chapters. At this stage, it is important to note two important trends in the way urban administration was being organised: the increasing importance of lawyers and the creation of specialised bodies to deal with individual aspects of government.

Lawyers were first employed by the urban authorities in the later fifteenth century. By the end of the seventeenth century, men with legal training had come to dominate many urban governments, particularly in Germany. In Hamburg, there were demands in 1669 that not only should three out of the city's four mayors be lawyers, but also half the remaining councillors. Lawyer councillors averaged between 10 per cent and 12 per cent of the government in seventeenth-century Cologne. They also occupied at least half the seats in mid-seventeenth-century Barcelona.

Lawyers were involved even earlier in urban government as permanent officials. As syndics, protonotaries and town clerks they brought erudition, literacy and, above all, a range of experience in government to the increasingly complicated demands of urban administration. There was nothing specifically urban about this development. Indeed, the very fact that lawyer administrators could move so easily from town to town and from princely or episcopal court to urban government and back again was an advantage to their urban employers in their dealings with the outside world. It was also an ingredient in the decline in urban autonomy in the sense that even when legally trained officials were not acting as the direct representatives of some outside authority, their experience and attitudes helped to bring in some of the political values from outside, which diluted all sense of local particularism. In time, some of these lawyers went on to become councillors or royal officials or both.

The growing importance of lawyers in urban government should not be interpreted as the displacement of older families by new men from below benefiting from increased access to university education in the liberal professions. Most lawyers already came from high-status families in urban or rural élites. Nor did they have a monopoly of administrative posts in urban government. In both north-western Germany and the Netherlands, administrators with legal training worked alongside men with more traditional backgrounds.

The division of responsibilities for specific areas of government varied from one town to another. In some cases, the work was distributed among mayors and aldermen according to seniority. In Antwerp, the senior mayor represented the city at the Estates of Brabant, took responsibility for matters of security and commanded the urban militia, while the second mayor presided over all civil and criminal court cases. Elsewhere, certain responsibilities were given to named officials, such as the *racional* appointed in Valencia every three years by the king to administer finances or the *rewart* in the towns of Flanders, who held the keys of the city, was responsible for defence and order and settled minor cases in law.

The committee structure set up to deal with specific aspects of urban government, on the other hand, was largely new to the early modern period. Seen in its most graphic form through the group portraits of the regent magistracies of Amsterdam, it was to be found in all sizeable centres by the end of the seventeenth century. In Italy, these were magistracies with legal powers, such as the Venetian *Signori della Notte*, who exercised police authority over the city and its activities at night. In every major Italian centre, magistracies were established to prepare for the eventuality that there might be food shortages. In both northern and southern Europe, the new forms of social policy to deal with the poor spawned a whole army of overseers and almshouse-keepers, under the supervision of boards appointed by the local government. Even matters of such local concern as the construction of the canal from Exeter to the sea had its own committee.

The use of specialised magistracies enabled urban governments to handle complex areas more effectively by building up expertise. There was also potential for the abuse of power, as no one outside these committees was in a position to know in detail how and why decisions were being taken. Ultimately, the committee structure offered princely authority a useful way into urban government. By imposing a common policy on poor relief, for example, on all towns under his control, a prince could ensure that this was being carried out by exercising tight control on nominations to the appropriate magistracy. In other words, the more complicated urban government became, the less it could be controlled by a small independent group of councillors.

Relations with central government

The relationship between towns and their territorial rulers during the sixteenth and seventeenth centuries should not be seen necessarily as a power struggle between them. In many ways the rulers of the larger territorial states had already asserted their position *vis-à-vis* their powerful subjects during the course of the fifteenth century. What took place during the next 200 years could be regarded as the effects on urban governments of the expansion of activity by central government. It was in the smaller, newly emergent territories of Italy and Germany that urban governments experienced severe losses of autonomy.

When comparisons are made between the experiences of towns in different parts of western Europe, it is important to take into account the uneven way in which the power of territorial states developed. Within the British Isles, English towns experienced the growth of royal power from the early sixteenth to the mid-seventeenth centuries, with a hiatus of some 20 years before the restoration of the monarchy in 1660. In Scotland, on the other hand, it was not until the 1560s, with the accession of James VI, that one may confidently write of a growth in royal power.

Early attempts at royal expansion under Francis I and Henry II of France ceased during the second half of the sixteenth century, when the Wars of Religion gave many towns an opportunity to reassert their political autonomy to a degree that had not been known for at least a century. Huguenot centres, such as La Rochelle, Toulouse and Nîmes, ran their affairs without recourse to royal authority throughout the period of warfare. Even Catholic centres, such as Marseille, had become so accustomed to running their own affairs by the end of the century that the monarchy was obliged to undertake extraordinary measures to bring the city back under control. Such experiences may indeed have helped to fuel a royal policy towards the towns in the seventeenth century, which ultimately left them very little room for manoeuvre.

The great towns in sixteenth-century Castile led by Valladolid, Salamanca and Toledo lost most of their privileges following the defeat of the *Comuneros* in the 1520s. Nor was the failure of the rebellion of the *Germanías* in Aragon over the same period any more favourable to the continuation of urban freedoms. In contrast, the towns of Catalonia and Granada remained much more independent until the reign of Philip III in the early seventeenth century.

In the Holy Roman Empire, urban freedoms declined at different times from the mid-sixteenth century onwards. In some cases, it was the towns that found themselves on the losing side in the religious wars, which were exposed to attempts at greater control by an outside ruler. In others, the decline in local autonomy was the direct result of attempts by local rulers to impose their authority on towns in their territory. The timing varied from place to place as it did in the constituent parts of multiple monarchies, such as Milan, Naples and the Netherlands' provinces of the Habsburgs.

The imposition of centralised authority on Italian towns by their lords had already begun in the fifteenth century. The pace of change speeded up rapidly during the sixteenth century when the intermittent warfare that affected most of the northern and central parts of the peninsula gave numbers of petty rulers the opportunity to remove existing urban privileges. The replacement of the Florentine republic by the Grand Duchy of Tuscany was only one example of a much broader phenomenon. Thanks to the writings of Stefano Guazzo, we know of the sense of outrage felt by the citizens of Casale di Monferrato when it was taken over by the Duke of Mantua in 1567.

What is the evidence for the case that territorial rulers deliberately set out to reduce urban power? In the smaller territorial states, such as Mantua, there seems little doubt that this was the case, particularly when the ruler had soldiers at his disposal to enforce his new authority. Other rulers, such as the Prince-Bishops of Münster, set out to extend their power over their urban subjects but were prevented from doing so because of lack of finances. Thirty years were to elapse after the recapture of Münster from the Anabaptists in 1535 before the composition of the city council was to the bishop's satisfaction.

In the larger territorial states, the presence of urban autonomy in individual centres did not present as much of a direct threat as in Mantua or Münster. Where royal power did become increasingly prominent in the towns, this was rather the long-term outcome of a number of actions taken to secure the power of central government. If anything, the changes in power took place as a result of internal modifications to the existing structure of government than in the form of far-reaching constitutional change. At the end of the seventeenth century, most towns in territorial states were governed by the same conciliar bodies as before, exercising not only the same functions as their predecessors, but undertaking even more responsibilities as need dictated. The changes that had taken place lay in the selection of government personnel, the source of their status and in the origin of their policies. Changes like these were characteristic of the way in which new centralised governments used older constitutional forms to suit their needs and overcome obstacles.

To the territorial ruler, many urban privileges were obstacles to the efficient functioning of the law and the rapid collection of taxes. As the chancellor to the Elector of Saxony told the town of Freiburg im Breisgau in 1573, many towns had gross and unreasonable legal customs, which would never have been granted by earlier princes if they had been as well informed about the law as they were now. Several of the king's advisors in mid-sixteenth-century France stated that many urban privileges were contrary to the good *police* of the state. There was nothing new about reforming urban charters. As the source of a town's privileges, a territorial ruler was able to alter them at will, although some pretext was necessary in order to justify an outside intervention of this kind to a citizen body, which was often very sensitive to constitutional change. Such interventions often took place in response to extreme circumstances, such as the reinstatement of imperial power after the Peace of Augsburg of 1555 in towns that had chosen to become Protestant. Changes of this kind were used as short-term expedients. After its recapture from the Anabaptists in 1535, the Prince-Bishop of Münster was able to suspend the constitution of his city entirely for six years. Henry IV of France suspended elections in Marseille in 1607 to avoid conflict between two factions. Elections to the municipal council were suspended in Aix-en-Provence from 1631 to 1638 after both the councillors and the local *parlement* had done little to quell a major revolt against the crown. The same action was taken in Narbonne in 1632. While full constitutional rights were eventually restored in each case, the ruler had made his point; no city could act as if its privileges were irrevocable.

The actions of English rulers took a slightly different direction. English towns had never been given the same range of privileges to which their continental counterparts were accustomed, both because the power of the English monarchy had become relatively centralised at a very early stage and because even the larger English provincial centres were much smaller in size and influence than continental cities. Many English towns did not receive charters at all until the sixteenth century. When they did so, this became a useful source of income to the government but did little to increase the real power of the towns to which they were granted. These charters had little in common with grants of privileges to medieval towns. They were much closer in kind to the empty privileges granted by Louis XIV to bolster towns' sense of self-importance when most of their real power had withered away. The relative newness of many English borough charters proved a fragile blessing. As the events of the 1680s during Charles II's reign proved, charters could be modified and restored at will in response to national political changes. The new conditions for municipal elections drawn up to smooth the way for Charles' Catholic heir, James, were replaced almost immediately by William III, after James' abdication in 1688.

While such direct attempts by territorial rulers to modify urban constitutions were only patchy and short term, other developments were far more effective. In France, the introduction of *intendants* from the early seventeenth century created a new channel of communication between the towns and the monarchy and enabled the monarchs to side-step many of the constitutional privileges that had hitherto stood in their way. The *intendants* were initially appointed to co-ordinate military provisioning and tax collection but rapidly extended their role until they became the effective rulers of many large towns, much as the *corregidores* had become in Castile. It must be stressed that they were not appointed as urban overlords. Their area of responsibility covered a region of France, centred on one of the large towns. Much of the *intendants'* influence in French urban government rested on their increasing control of urban finance, a development that was motivated both by a wish to circumvent the unwillingness of the urban authorities to contribute to a rising curve of French royal expenditure and by the latter's inability to control their fiscal systems.

The chaos in urban finances that had aroused so much concern in royal treasuries was also a symptom of a number of other developments, which enabled the central authorities to extend their power over their urban subjects. Many urban governments found it increasingly difficult to pay for their own expenditure let alone meet the rising fiscal demands from the centre. They were caught between rising local expenditure and falling incomes. Whether the rise in costs resulted from putting costly poor relief legislation into practice, dredging harbours and river access or financing major improvements to fortifications, the effects were the same in the light of falling incomes. Industry and long-distance trade were no longer as lucrative as before. Local fiscal income also suffered from a growing tendency for townsmen with rentier incomes to seek tax exemption by purchasing patents of nobility from the monarchy. It is significant that one of the few towns to resist the French monarchy in the early seventeenth century, La Rochelle, had an unusually strong economy based on long-distance trade.

It would be too charitable to ascribe the weakness of urban finance entirely to the scissors effect of rising expenditure and falling incomes. Some of the corruption of which urban governments were accused was not far from the truth. In late sixteenth-century Gloucester, for example, aldermen appear to have sold off ale-house licences, minor administrative posts and leases for town lands. Nor were morally irreproachable activities any less damaging to urban exchequers. The reconstruction of town halls to the latest designs at great expense can be seen as a final expression of urban autonomy. By the end of the seventeenth century, most large official buildings constructed in the towns of western Europe were being financed from the centre.

In many towns, territorial rulers were able to extend their jurisdiction because of the presence of a number of important institutions, such as major law courts and provincial representative assemblies, which either operated in parallel with the urban authorities or carried out functions from which the urban authorities were excluded. Royal law courts were held in both capital cities and major regional centres. The presence of such institutions not only constituted a mark of status, bringing in very considerable material benefits to the towns in which they were held. They also represented the importance of outside authority in a way that ran parallel to, rather than contrary to, the town's own areas of jurisdiction. In France, the presence of the *parlements* (royal courts with specific responsibility for registering new legislation) in Paris and in important provincial centres, such as Toulouse, Rennes, Dijon, Rouen, Pau and Grenoble, enhanced the position of towns, which were at the head of regional urban hierarchies. At the same time, the urban authorities in these centres were fully aware that they had little control over a national judicial network, and that the presence of *parlementaires* in the town itself constituted a threat to their authority. In the middle of the seventeenth century, there were more than 100 *parlementaires* in Toulouse, men who outranked the *capitouls* and demonstrated this symbolically by walking ahead of them in civic processions. At times of crisis such as during outbreaks of plague, the *parlement* of Toulouse took control of local government.

Just as some of France's major towns played host to provincial *parlements*, large towns all over Europe were selected as the meeting places for provincial and national legislative assemblies, such as the English parliament, the *Reichstag* of the Holy Roman Empire, the *Cortes* of the Spanish kingdoms and the Estates Generals of France and the Low Countries. Once again, these meetings brought material benefits to their hosts, enhanced their own prestige in relation to their local rivals, but also brought the focus of royal attention to bear on them even when no meetings were taking place. No territorial ruler was prepared to risk holding an assembly in a town in which there had been major internal unrest or that had gained a reputation for resisting or prevaricating about requests from the centre.

The functioning of urban government was increasingly dependent upon representatives of external authority. From an early stage, territorial rulers appointed men to attend, or indeed to superintend, important aspects of urban government. The presence of such officers subsequently eased the further extension of central power in the towns. The Scottish kings appointed lord provosts to oversee matters in royal burghs, such as Edinburgh, Dundee, Perth, Glasgow and Stirling. In Valencia, the town's finances were administered by a *racional*, chosen every three years by the king. In Castile, Queen Isabella extended her influence in cities in the late fifteenth century by appointing increasing numbers of men as *corregidores*, as tax collectors, overseers of the city walls and appeal court judges. Similar functions were carried out by the *gouverneurs* and, later on, by the *intendants* in France and the *amman*, *schout* or *bailli* in the Netherlands. The presence of representatives of outside authority was equally common in smaller states, such as the Duchy of Savoy. In Nice, the deliberations of the city council were not officially recognised unless they took place in the presence of the prefect or the lieutenant.

Central authorities were also able to use their influence in urban government more extensively by the twin policy of ensuring that their nominees were elected to urban administrations and that councillors, however they were elected, were given royal office, which strengthened their links with the prince. The first strategy was closely associated with the growth in urban oligarchy. The mechanisms developed by members of urban élites to ensure that 'undesirable' men were excluded from power and that their friends and relatives were guaranteed a share also played into the hands of territorial rulers, who, in turn, found among the urban élites the very individuals with whom they wished to co-operate. The Prince-Bishop of Wurzburg required the council to submit a short list from which he selected names to fill vacancies. From 1548, the Spanish viceroy in Naples ordered that henceforth the *Seggio di Sant'Agostino* had to present him with a list of six names for each vacancy. In sixteenth-century Ghent, the entire council was filled with princely nominees. Elsewhere, while the names of candidates for vacancies in urban government did not necessarily have to be submitted to the ruler for approval, men were chosen of whom the ruler would approve. Once again, there was considerable congruity between the wishes of the ruler and those of the ruling élite.

The appointment of councillors to the service of the ruler was an equally effective way of creating a culture of dependence among the urban élite. Although the rapid extension of royal offices is usually presented as a continental phenomenon, this functioned equally well in England, where the minor judiciary was a particularly effective mode of extending royal power. In both urban and rural areas, men were appointed as magistrates as members of the Commissions of the Peace. As Justices of the Peace, it was their responsibility to keep order and to punish infractions of the law. In the larger English towns, many of the JPs were appointed from among the mayor and aldermen and carried out instructions from the centre.

A problem arises when considering the effects of central government on capital cities themselves. During the sixteenth and seventeenth centuries, the end of the peripatetic court and the growth in the numbers of permanent administrators altered the existing relationship between rulers and their capitals. The period also witnessed a number of further changes in the status of capitals. Some cities, such as Milan, which were accustomed to function as capitals of independent states, lost this status when their territories were taken over by some greater power. Others, such as Florence or Turin, which had once functioned as the capitals of republican city states, were forced to adapt to a new role when their state became the core of a hereditary duchy. In the case of Florence, the city became the capital of the new Medici Grand Duchy of Tuscany in the 1530s. Others, yet again, such as Madrid and Vienna, were selected as permanent capitals by rulers who had moved between several centres. The selection of Madrid in 1561 by Philip II of Spain not only posed problems for the governors of the new capital but left an enormous gap in

Valladolid, which had frequently been used as a capital. New building in the latter came to a complete end. Many of the most recently constructed houses were abandoned.

The cases of London and Paris exemplify the unusual effects of the presence of central government in a capital city. In one sense, the City of London was not a capital, for while kings of England had maintained residences within the walled city, the area with which they identified most completely in the sixteenth and seventeenth centuries lay around the abbey of Westminster, a mile or so to the west and outside the jurisdiction of the city. This was where meetings of parliament took place and the monarch's administrators carried out their work. The presence of the royal court was a powerful magnet, and there was considerable building along a line stretching from the city's boundary to Westminster and beyond. The absence of one single jurisdiction over the entire metropolitan area represented a constant problem for the rulers of the City. Ultimately, the Privy Council took unilateral responsibility for problems that affected the whole of London, such as uncertainties over food supplies in times of dearth, but then refused to bear the costs of their actions on the grounds that this was a local matter.

The organisation of government in Paris was in sharp contrast to the autonomy of the City of London with its own charter and elected organs of government. Paris was ruled by the *bureau de la ville*, headed by the *prévôt des marchands*. The latter was appointed by the king, and a prominent section of the city councillors was drawn from the Paris *parlement*. Without a charter, the city had to follow royal instructions and was always the first to apply national legislation when this applied to urban matters. Even when Louis XIV moved his court to Versailles in the last decades of the seventeenth century, Paris remained strictly under royal control. Its size and the volatility of emotions expressed in times of crisis in the past, such as the episode of the Paris Sixteen in the 1580s and the Fronde in the late 1640s, were a powerful reminder of what could happen when royal controls were weak.

Up to this point, our discussion of the relationship between urban government and territorial authority has emphasised changes in political power from the perspective of princely rulers. There is no doubt that such shifts in power contributed substantially to the growth of territorial states in the early modern period. But it would be misleading to present urban government as a tool of central authority under constant supervision and direction from the centre. There are times when the great mass of instructions sent out by Louis XIV's minister, Colbert, to his *intendants* in the later seventeenth century leave such an impression. With so much information at the king's disposal and such a detailed interest in the affairs of each major town, one wonders whether French urban governments had any freedom of manoeuvre at all.

Most recent studies of the landed nobility in the territorial states now accept that they continued to maintain their local power because of their high social status and wealth and that this was in many ways enhanced by their new position as royal office-holders. Although they were no longer capable of resisting royal authority individually by military force, their importance in the political and social structure of the new territorial states gave them substantial opportunities to interpret princely authority as they wished.

There are close analogies between the position of the nobility and the towns in the new territorial state, not least because most of the towns in southern Europe were by this time ruled by members of the titular nobility. As we have already suggested, the relationship between towns and their rulers in England, France and Spain in the fifteenth century was already one of dependence. The changes in princely authority during the next 200 years changed the rules of the game and not only to the advantage of the princes. Royal patronage reinforced the position of urban élites within their own societies and enabled urban governments to enforce their own authority over the rest of the urban population. It also encouraged urban governments to compete with one another for royal favour in order to protect their privileges, gain advantages over their rivals and protect themselves against the dangers of new taxation, just as the nobility learned to do at court.

When a new ruler came to the throne, he or she was lobbied either directly or indirectly to ensure that privileges granted by their predecessor would be upheld. The leaders of the English port of Chester engaged in an elaborate game with the new king, James I, and his minister, Salisbury, in 1604 in order to make the point that, without the tax exemption granted to Chester by Elizabeth I, the town's economic difficulties would prevent its leading citizens from being able to pay. Unlike the *jurats* of Bordeaux and the *échevins* of Lyon, who both employed professional lobbyists to press their case with the French kings in Paris, the councillors of Chester were far more circumspect. They avoided any charge of opposition to royal authority by complying with Salisbury's request to arrest the merchants who had not paid their taxes, and then found a string of excuses – the severe weather (it was January), the state of the roads, the ill-health of the prisoners – to delay sending them to London in order to gain time to petition for the reconfirmation of tax exemptions.

The choice of lobbyists was largely determined by local circumstances. In Castile, urban governments often used the *corregidor* to lobby on their behalf. As a royal official, he was well placed to do so and, as part of the lobbying exercise was intended to gain advantage over towns' economic rivals, such aspirations fitted in well with the patronage policy of the Spanish monarchy. *Gouverneurs* were used by French towns for the same reasons, but it became clear that this level of political influence was only effective in specific cases and after a great deal of groundwork had been done. In Lyon, the *consulat* developed a whole army of representatives in Paris from the middle of the seventeenth century, lobbying royal officials, sending back information about changes at court and generally making sure that new fiscal policies were not applied disproportionately to their city. English towns also supplemented the traditional delegations of mayor and aldermen by using members of the local gentry to lobby on their behalf at court and as their MPs in the House of Commons. The relatively weak position of towns in England required them to turn to alternative sources of local power to work on their behalf. In return, their gentry representatives were rewarded by additional influence in the towns that they represented and by certain emoluments. The leading merchants of Exeter in the middle of the sixteenth century forged a strong alliance with the Russells, Earls of Bedford. The second earl lent them his support in the search for a royal charter for the city's Company of Merchant Adventurers.

At one remove from the business of making a case at the centre was the need to come to terms with the new power relationships at a local level. Once again, we must avoid making too rigid a distinction between members of urban governments, on the one hand, and members of the local gentry and aristocracy, on the other. There was a strong trend towards the social and political fusion of the two groups (see Chapter 3). Marital relationships and individual business and patronage links between members of the urban and rural élites often made the exchange of information and the use of influence much easier. This also meant that, in times of economic difficulty, members of urban governments knew that while they did not have much freedom of action themselves, they could have recourse to much more extensive help from outside. What had once affected a town was now seen to have implications for the whole area.

By comparison with the beginning of the sixteenth century, the range of activity by urban governments and their capacity to touch the lives of residents had grown in inverse proportion to the degree to which the latter were involved in decision-making. By the end of the seventeenth century, the men who took decisions when faced with the crises and problems of urban life did so in the context of their membership of a narrow political élite, which owed its status as much to external patronage as it did to internal prestige.

|3|

Urban élites

The central role of the political élite in government and the substantial opportunities that participation in decision-making and the judicial processes offered to its members have long been seen to be one of the most important characteristics of early modern urban history (see Chapter 2). The vocabulary used by contemporaries in both medieval and early modern towns to distinguish men who were in some way set apart from the rest of urban society indicated general qualities of excellence and wisdom. Ingrid Batori lists among others *maiores, optimi, honorabiliores, sapientores, discreti* and *die Wisesten*. In fourteenth-century Cologne, they were known as *de besten von der Stat* (the best of the town). Ignace Chavatte, a master weaver in late seventeenth-century Lille, referred to the élite in his town quite simply as *messieurs*. There was also an increasing tendency to refer to the small group of families that generally provided members of town councils in Germany as *ratsfähige Geschlechter* (families capable of providing members of the council), *Ratsgeschlechter* (council families) or simply as *die Geschlechter*. Candidates to the council in Nuremberg were only acceptable if they 'led an honourable life, were wealthy, sound and were kin to other Council families' [Christoph Scheurl, *Concerning the polity and government of the praisworthy city of Nurenberg*, quoted in Strauss, 1976: 61]. Candidates for the *échevinage* in Chartres were required to be selected from royal officers or merchants or, should none be forthcoming, from among 'the most notable of the parish'.

Jurists, such as Charles Loyseau and Sir Thomas Smith, writing in late sixteenth-century France and England, respectively, acknowledged that there was a social hierarchy among burghers but confined their criteria for high social status to the holding of civic office. They chose to distinguish only townsmen in high office, such as mayors or aldermen. Smith identified 'citizens and burgesses' as 'such as not only be free and received as officers within the cities, but also be of some substance to beare the charges'. [Thomas

Smith, *De republica Anglorum*, London, 1583 (facsimile edition, Menston: Scholar Press, 1970: 29]. This approach was also adopted by the growing stream of urban histories, which glorified in the lists of the great men (office-holders) of their town.

The decisions taken by the political élite, their activities and attitudes exercised a strong influence on both the physical shape of their towns and the quality of life of its inhabitants. No definition of an urban élite could possibly exclude the tenure of high political office. This remains one of the most important criteria for the measurement of élite membership and is indeed the definition used by many historians in studies of urban élites. Members of political élites are a particularly rewarding subject for study. As serving members of city councils, their identities are not only recorded at the point of election but are confirmed in a whole range of legal and other sources because of the practice of referring to them by their status as *Ratmann*, *échevin*, councillor, etc. Such sources have been used to trace their business interests, their dynastic planning, their cultural involvement and their religious commitment and, by extension, to measure the collective influence of the political élite within the society of their town. The resulting monographs have proved to be of considerable interest and value in understanding the history of individual urban communities.

The *vroedschaps* of Rotterdam and Amsterdam, the mayors, aldermen and councillors of York, Lübeck or Strasbourg, the *eletti del popolo* of Naples or the *échevins* of Amiens, Lyon or Rouen did indeed fulfil many of the criteria for élites. They were few in number. Twenty-four councillors ruled in Exeter, 24 in Schweinfurt and 33 in Lille. They controlled the appointment of their successors. At all public ceremonies, it was the magistrates and councillors who took precedence over other burghers. Their wealth placed them among the ranks of those who contributed the most both individually and proportionately to the fiscal income of their town.

On the other hand, as a complete definition of the élite, the group of men in office remains far too narrow. It is doubtful whether political power was limited to office-holders. In some towns, such as Bruges, Lille, York or Aberdeen, councillors were not elected for life but took their places for a limited period. Former council members constituted a valuable reservoir of experience and influence and retained a leading position in society. In many territorial states, too, the presence of royal officers and judges in certain key towns came to create a complementary source of political power, which was widely recognised within urban society.

It is also debatable whether the exercise of political power and office, even by a wider circle of men, was enough to explain the leading position occupied by urban élites in their own societies. This chapter is based on the rather different assumption that the men who held political office at any time in an individual urban centre were only part of a much more complex phenomenon, which we may call the 'social élite'. The social élite may be defined as a cohesive social group with leading positions in a broad range of activities: politics, wealth, culture, ideas and the practice of highly regarded professional occupations, such as the law, education or administration. It was not necessary for any highly placed individual to excel in all these areas, as long as the élite did so collectively. Nor should this definition be applied exclusively to adult males. Even if the high status of élite females and children within society was based on their relationship to élite males, they had an important part to play in ensuring both the cohesiveness and the continuity of the élite, a function that extended far beyond childbearing and marriage. S. F. Nadal wrote:

> in order for a group of people with high status and a superior position in society to be considered as an élite, it must have some degree of corporateness, group character and exclusiveness, and its superiority must be of a very general kind.
>
> (S.F. Nadel, The concept of social elites.
> *International Social Science Bulletin*, 8(1956): 415)

When this definition is put to the test in the towns of early modern Europe, it becomes increasingly clear that, while there was considerable diversity in the structure and composition of urban social élites in different regions of Europe and the character of such élites changed over time, each urban society was dominated by a small group of individuals and families, whose status set them apart from those below them.

This enhanced social position was tacitly recognised by four groups. Members of social élites themselves identified each other by associating with them in business, politics, cultural activities and, above all, by choosing them as relatives by marriage. Marriage had both symbolic and real significance. In symbolic terms, it signalled that the two families involved were either of equal status to begin with or reached equal status as the result of the new relationships created by the marriage. In real terms, a marriage created a new set of relationships and responsibilities. Kinship by marriage put an individual, usually but not exclusively a man, in a position in which he could be called upon to be a godparent, guardian or executor of members of the élite. Marriage also implied the transmission of goods and status by inheritance to future generations. It is easy to see why only a small minority of outsiders were permitted to join the élite. Their capacity to upset the delicate balance that kept the élite together was considerable. It was only in extreme circumstances, such as the losses caused by the plague of 1630 in the small Tuscan centre of Poppi (seven of the 22 families that had held most of the offices between 1556 and 1633 were completely wiped out), that male outsiders were imported on a large scale. The men who married into the Poppi élite were rapidly absorbed within it. They moved to the city, benefited from their wives' inheritances, were granted citizenship and gradually took on political office.

The presence of the élite was validated just as much by those who wished to join it. Aspirants to high status, in other words those who considered themselves or their children as potential members of the élite, did all that they could to cross the largely unwritten boundaries that separated them from the élite. Their presence permitted élites both to renew their membership when families either moved out of town or became extinct and to reinforce social barriers in order to protect their monopoly of high status positions in society, but the process was neither easy nor rapid. Two examples from early modern Lübeck suffice to tell the tale. Dietrich Tünemann joined the merchant brotherhood of the *Kaufleutekompanie*, one of the major groups in the Lübeck élite, in 1587, after a career that had taken him from the boats of the Elbe basin to a variety of commercial activities in ports stretching from the Mediterranean to the eastern Baltic. His ascent into the élite was sealed by marriage to the sister of one of the city's mayors. She, however, was only persuaded to marry him with difficulty, for she disliked both his age (he was 52) and his rough manners.

In the next century, Thomas Fredenhagen broke into the élite largely because of his exceptional commercial success. At the time of his death, contemporaries compared him with 'the ancient merchant princes of Tyre'. Unusually, he did not marry into any of the élite families (he had married the widow of a retail merchant who belonged to the circles just below the élite) and, like Tünemann, Fredenhagen only entered the political élite comparatively late in life.

The third group who recognised the existence of an élite were the majority of townspeople, who were under no illusions about their ineligibility to join it. In some medieval French towns, the élite were known as *les gros* (the fat ones), a pejorative term, which reflected both the recognition that there was a concentration of power and wealth in which they could not hope to share and the envy of the poor for the rich. Although the social gap was considerable, the spatial confines of the towns of early modern Europe and the public civic and ecclesiastical ceremonies frequently brought élites and the rest of urban society together in a way that emphasised the former's distinction.

The growing network of office-holders and bearers of titles who owed their own position to the patronage of territorial rulers also recognised the presence of urban élites, not as a group of people whose prestige was on the decline in proportion to the loss of urban autonomy but as a collection of social equals with whom they wished to be associated and from which, increasingly, they came.

The balance of this chapter is devoted to an analysis of three main themes: 'closed' and 'open' élites; the changing role of artisans, merchants, lawyers, rentiers and royal officials; and the élite and noble status. In keeping with the intention of using the early chapters of this book as a framework for a discussion of change and continuity in the urban experience, no attempt has been made here to examine the wider role of élites within their own urban societies.

Closed élites and open élites

In his comparison of seventeenth-century Amsterdam and Venice, Peter Burke makes the very useful distinction between 'open' and 'closed' élites. He contrasts the formal status groups in cities, such as Venice or Genoa, with informal status groups in an 'open society', such as Amsterdam. In these terms, Venice and Amsterdam can be seen as two extremes on a spectrum, in which urban élites were relatively open or relatively closed and were constantly evolving during the sixteenth and seventeenth centuries.

Burke's distinctions obscure the fact that there were at least three different kinds of closed urban élite in early modern Europe:

- statutory élites established during the Middle Ages, which continued to hold power exclusively into the eighteenth century;
- statutory élites established in the course of the sixteenth and seventeenth centuries;
- exclusive groups established during the Middle Ages, which failed to retain their monopoly of high status.

By the end of the seventeenth century, Venice was the only major city to have retained full statutory divisions between the élite and the rest of society, and even the Venetian patriciate cannot be said to have survived the period unscathed. Its importance in this context lies more in the way in which it perpetuated a model of urban society that had been far more widespread in the Middle Ages but was being modified elsewhere under pressure from political and economic change. The roots of the Venetian legislation that established the hereditary distinction between the *nobili* (patricians), the *cittadini* (citizens but, in reality, semi privileged merchants, notaries and servants of the state) and *popolani* (the people), lay in the political uncertainties at the turn of the thirteenth century, which were resolved by the inclusion into the political élite, the members of the city's great council, of a number of wealthy families. A line was drawn under the list of families whose male legitimate members would henceforward have the exclusive right to belong to the government and hold offices in it. In spite of this legislation, the size of the patriciate, which numbered some 2000 adult male members at the beginning of the sixteenth century, and growing confusion about who had the legal right to enjoy the privileges of patrician status led to a refinement of membership criteria and of the mechanisms by which these were tested and confirmed. A century and a half later, the drain on finances brought about by the need to protect the key island of Crete from a Turkish occupation led to the introduction of legislation to allow new families to buy their way into the élite, although the changes to the composition of the élite implied by these purchases were much more limited than the detractors of this legislation feared.

The new legislation introduced in Venice in 1506 to refine claims to élite membership coincided with a much wider range of changes in many of the cities of northern and central Italy and in at least one centre in southern Germany. The *libro d'oro* (golden book), which was opened in Venice in 1506 became the model for others (Brescia in 1509, Genoa in 1528, Vicenza in 1567, Bologna in 1567–90, Jesi in 1575, Cremona in 1576, Carrara in 1595, Padua in 1623 and Lucca in 1628).

These golden books were often an attempt to clarify rules drawn up long before. One of the chief purposes of the Genoese golden book, for instance, was to establish a single order of nobility, which excluded all persons who were not known for 'their dignity of life, integrity of behaviour, long residence by their ancestors... or believed by public testimony to be worthy of nobility' [*Instruzioni, Norme e regolarmenti sulla Nobiltà e Ascrizioni* (compiled *ca.* 1675). Quoted in M. Nicora, La nobiltà genovese del 1528 al 1700. *Miscellanea Storica Ligure*, 2, 1961: 223. (Author's translation)].

Anxiety about status also motivated patrician families in Nuremberg, whose solution to the problems of distinguishing those with a right to rule from those without it owed less to abstract ideas about nobility than to a very real sense of how élites worked. In 1521, the Nuremberg council passed the *Tanzstatut* or Dance Law. According to this legislation, only the 43 families named in the statute and their legitimate male descendants could in future be invited to take part in the dances held in the vaults of the Nuremberg Town Hall. The exclusion of everyone else created an enclosed environment in which business deals were struck, marriage alliances arranged and political strategies planned. It also undermined the élite aspirations of several other families whose growing wealth had posed a threat to the existing élite.

A similar concern to define the urban patriciate in terms of noble status arose in newly emergent territorial states, such as Tuscany, Milan and Aragon. In contrast with the social uncertainties in city states, such as Venice and Nuremberg, this new emphasis on establishing a statutory élite came from outside the city, even though it met the aspirations of high-status families. The new dynastic rulers used it to establish a new framework of privileges, which did much to enhance their own power, while appearing to meet the anxieties of families insecure about their own status. In Florence, the new Medici duke reassured members of the city's existing élite by giving them and their descendants the right to call themselves *patrizii*, but he also allowed more recent families appointed to high office to register their names in the Florentine golden book. In Milan, the process of shifting the source of high status from the city to the territorial ruler was confirmed towards the end of the seventeenth century by the requirement that all new aspirants to élite status in the city must demonstrate their nobility before being accepted, a requirement that was willingly supported by existing members of the élite. In common with high-status urban families all over Italy, no matter what the form of government within which they functioned, social anxieties in

Milan were confronted by a growing emphasis on the distinctiveness of nobility, honour, civility and a complete absence of any association with the vile and mechanical arts. Nor was this development restricted to northern and central Italy. In Barcelona, specific families were named as *custodens honrats* by Ferdinand of Aragon as part of a growing association between the local landed nobility, who were moving into the towns to take up royal offices, and the older families of the urban élite with whom they merged.

Many medieval German societies had been characterised by the presence of a strong hereditary élite. By the sixteenth century, however, members of most well-defined hereditary groups were only a remnant of their former selves and had been supplanted by others. The closed brotherhood of the *Theodori-gilde,* founded by the salt merchants of Lüneburg in 1461, only allowed in 17 new families during the next 140 years. These newcomers were all required to be salt merchants and to have close family ties to existing members. Patrician families in Brunswick controlled their position through the exclusive *Lilienveste,* founded in 1384. In Göttingen, the government was dominated by members of the *Kaufgilde* until the early sixteenth century. Similar brotherhoods dominated medieval society in Ulm, Augsburg, Frankfurt am Main and Strasbourg. But, with the exception of Frankfurt am Main, where members of the *Limpurgergesellschaft* still occupied around half of the seats on the council in the seventeenth century, and the Lübeck *Zirkelkompanie*, which, despite a pause of 45 years after the Reformation, succeeded in remaining a powerful economic force because of their continued presence on the council and their virtual monopoly of the landed estates around the city, none of these hereditary brotherhoods sustained the numerical strength that would have assured their continued dominance in the early modern period. The number of old patrician families in Ulm declined from 13 in 1505 to eight in 1545. Only seven of the 21 families that were members of the Augsburg patriciate in 1383 remained in 1538. The numbers of the Strasbourg brotherhood of the *Constofler* fell from 315 in 1392 to 35 in 1535. Given these small numbers, none of these groups were comparable with the hereditary élites in northern and central Italy.

The co-existence in the Lübeck élite of a hereditary group like the *Zirkelkompanie* with others, such as the brotherhoods of long-distance merchants (the *Kaufleutekompanie* and the various *Fahrerkompanien,* such as the *Bergenfahrer*, the *Spanienfahrer* and the *Novgorodfahrer*), lawyers and *rentiers*, is a reminder that many open élites contained elements of older privileged groups, whose prestige and wealth might not have been enough to guarantee the continuation of their political power but was still strong enough to ensure their continued presence on a plane slightly apart from their fellow members. It is also evidence of the way in which many élites were experiencing a slow process of evolution in the course of the sixteenth and seventeenth centuries, during which the external form and functions of the élite remained virtually unchanged, while its composition altered significantly.

This raises the question of the openness of 'open élites'. Burke uses the phrase to make a contrast with an urban élite whose composition and outer limits were controlled by legislation. Where no specific legislation existed, it is possible to write of an 'open élite', but the term is entirely relative. Any group that was small enough and compact enough to exercise power on a wide range of fronts had at its disposal a whole battery of unwritten rules, prejudices and agreements, which provided a semi-permeable barrier for those below them in society. On the other hand, there were substantial contrasts between those urban societies in which the economic bases of élite power remained fairly constant and those in which the volatility of the economy brought about substantial change, and between those societies in which a largely mercantile élite remained in control and those in which the merchants were supplanted by lawyers, rentiers and office-holders.

Changes in composition

There seems to be a close correlation between economic stagnation and the relative lack of change in the nature of urban oligarchies. When cities went into sharp economic decline, for example, members of the élite were often among the first to leave a town in search of prosperity elsewhere. Coventry at the turn of the fifteenth century is a case in point. Following a sharp downturn in the city's textile industry, many of its leading families departed, to the extent that their absence caused major damage to Coventry's fiscal income. A similar, if less drastic, process affected many German towns, such as Regensburg and Breslau, where wealthy families chose to leave their native town in search of service among the local nobility.

Economic stagnation, on the other hand, encouraged social stagnation. In the absence of the expansion of existing trade and industry or the introduction of new sources of wealth, there were few opportunities for a substantial group of outsiders to make enough money to challenge and open up the existing oligarchy. Instead, a small number of individual recruits were able to slip easily into place in the élite when gaps appeared. Many of them came from a similar social milieu in another town and found little difficulty in being accepted by the élite in centres such as Lübeck, Lindau, Lille or York. After all, they often married into families whose members had taken a similar path a generation earlier.

When economic circumstances did change for a generation or so, most 'open' élites were flexible enough to absorb an increased number of newcomers before closing down again when the short-lived wave of expansion had passed. In Lübeck, the decline of the Hanseatic League in the late fifteenth and early sixteenth centuries brought about all the symptoms of commercial stagnation, declining export industries, a sharp reduction in shipbuilding, fiscal difficulties exacerbated by the cost of new fortifications and a well-established oligarchy determined to retain power at all costs. Yet, for a period of 22 years between 1590 and 1612, half the seats on the council were occupied by newcomers to the élite. This period corresponded almost exactly with the great expansion of seaborne trade between north Germany, the Iberian peninsula and the Mediterranean, and this trade was indeed the reason why so many new men enriched themselves so quickly. The opportunities for profit offered by this new trade were so tempting that even old-established Lübeck families took part in the race for shares in ships trading with the south. Once the Spanish trade fell away, the recruitment of newcomers also declined. However, because the traditional recruitment mechanisms of marriage and business association continued to function smoothly, the oligarchical position of the élite remained untouched throughout.

The case of Lübeck once again illustrates clearly the ways in which the interplay between economic change and social structure resulted in fewer changes to the composition of the élite than might have been expected. Even in urban economies in full expansion for most of the period, such as Amsterdam, Seville or, on a smaller scale, Newcastle upon Tyne, the rapid generation of commercial profits only opened up the urban élite for a relatively short time. The potential for political and economic power represented by an expanding economy led to a rapid closing of the ranks among the most successful merchants. They employed the same strategies as élites elsewhere in order to maximise their individual and collective positions – intermarriage, business partnerships and control over the membership of urban government. In Newcastle upon Tyne, the rapid growth in coal exports in the sixteenth century brought to prominence a number of families with rights to export coal along the River Tyne. Although their monopoly was only confirmed by royal charter in 1600, members of the Hostmen's Company had already acquired leading positions on the city council and had created a network of marital and business links with other Newcastle merchants, which assured their social and economic dominance until the early eighteenth century. Outsiders who benefited from successive phases of economic growth, particularly in the second half of the seventeenth century, were unable to break the Hostmen's monopoly and join the élite.

The growth in the social exclusivity of the Newcastle merchants and the exclusion of members of craft guilds from political and social prominence was matched elsewhere. The political and social importance of master craftsmen in medieval towns had been emphasised by the large number of urban constitutions that contained at least a quota of seats on the council for guild representatives, often a direct consequence of social upheavals in the fourteenth century. By the early sixteenth century, such arrangements no longer corresponded to social changes, and certain anomalies resulted. As all members of the city council in Strasbourg were required to be members of a guild, many of the wealthy sons of élite families chose to join the poorest guilds, the fishermen and the gardeners, in the expectation that they could join the council as their representatives. None of their working members could have afforded to take part in the costly and time-consuming business of government.

The exclusion of artisans from urban élites and the gradual disappearance of artisan councillors was also a reflection of changes in the status of master craftsmen. Economic growth enabled a small number of them to establish larger workshops and to extend their economic activities. Pedro Gutierrez, a master furrier in the Castilian city of Valladolid in the sixteenth century, was both a manufacturer and a merchant and appears to have had a virtual monopoly of the supplies of skins produced in the regions of Salamanca, Siguenza, Soria and Almazar. Some of these skins were re-exported, others were given to artisan outworkers to be tanned or made into finished goods. In 1573, the known value of Gutierrez' operations was nearly 300 000 *maravedis*. The real value must have been much greater. The growing range of operations of the more successful master craftsmen, such as Guttierez or Daniel Wörner, the textile entrepreneur of sixteenth-century Nördlingen, placed them beyond the traditional guild framework among the ranks of the wholesale merchants.

The position of artisans in urban élites was also undermined by the external political forces that effectively removed them from many town councils during the sixteenth century. Interventions of this kind were most frequent in the Spanish Empire, France and the larger towns of southern Germany. Part of Charles V's political strategy in the free imperial cities that fell to him after the Peace of Augsburg was the reform of electoral practice to ensure that a Catholic oligarchy could not be challenged by artisan councillors with Protestant sympathies. Far from being an artificial imposition, however, these constitutional revisions reinforced the trend of upward social mobility by a minority of master craftsmen. After two generations, it was difficult to tell their descendants apart from the sons and grandsons of merchant members of the élite.

The growth in importance of mercantile élites in many urban centres was only a temporary phenomenon. By the end of the seventeenth century, lawyers and rentiers were taking an increasingly important part in government and society, in some cases displacing the merchants entirely from government, if not from a high social position. This took place in towns of all sizes. Peter Burke's study of the Regents of Amsterdam demonstrates graphically how one of the most open élites in western Europe came to follow the general trend. Early seventeenth-century Amsterdam experienced rapid commercial expansion. As a result, many new men entered the élite, combining an active involvement in long-distance trade with government responsibilities. By mid-century, however, this enthusiasm had waned. Entrepreneurs had been succeeded by rentiers. Burke cites a sour contemporary comment that 'the regents were not merchants. They did not take risks on the seas but derived their income from houses, lands and securities' [Quoted in Burke, 1974: 104]. Such comments need not be taken entirely at face value, of course, any more than the observation of the Münster clothier, Johann Wedemhove, in 1580 that:

It is daily experience which has made me aware that our times are no longer the same as in years past, and now there is a different deceitful world, one in which no tradition exists between men. Thus we have given up trade and are now taking up planting and sowing.

(Quoted in Hsia, 1984: 109)

But these complaints were a sign of important changes in investment patterns.

There were a number of reasons for this increase in the number of rentiers in the Amsterdam élite. The Dutch economy did not expand as rapidly in the second half of the seventeenth century as in the first, so there were fewer incentives to invest exclusively in trade. Established families looked for more secure sources of income to pay for an increasingly expensive and luxurious lifestyle. We should not be entirely persuaded by the formal group portraits of the regents that they consisted of sober, abstemious men living in strict conformity to the tenets of Calvinism. Like their counterparts elsewhere, they encouraged their sons to study at university, to go on the Grand Tour and to buy land. Even in mercantile Amsterdam, the influence of a wider aristocratic culture did not pass unnoticed among the élite. There was also a very practical reason why members of the Amsterdam élite preferred to seek an income from passive sources. Participation in government, either in Amsterdam itself or on one of the committees of the Dutch Estates General, was costly and time-consuming. Men could no longer afford the time and effort represented by heavy involvement in trade. Living off rents and investments was an ideal solution. Conversely, this development excluded many active merchants from reaching the highest levels of the élite but offered a way in for their sons and grandsons.

The movement towards a rentier élite in mid-seventeenth-century Amsterdam (and Rotterdam) was unusual only in the comparative sharpness of the contrast with the élite's earlier involvement as merchants. By the middle of the century, this had also become the norm for the older established families in Lübeck. The members of the *Zirkelkompanie* set the tone from the beginning of our period. As major owners of land and real estate in and around the city, they eschewed trade as unnecessary and inappropriate. It is interesting to see that they came to be joined in the Lübeck élite by other rentiers from outside the city, such as Thomas van Wetken and Adrien Möller, who never traded, and that investments in houses (land was in short supply around Lübeck) came to represent an increasing proportion of the income of even the merchant families in the élite. Although it had been customary for older merchants to spread their investments in this way, there was a clear trend in the course of the seventeenth century for men to turn to passive sources of income at a much earlier age.

In other parts of Germany, rentier interests among the élite surfaced much earlier. The great merchants of Nuremberg gained a reputation for their involvement in high finance. Like the Fugger of Augsburg, the Imhof, Paumgartner, Immel and Welser loaned large sums to European rulers in the sixteenth century. Members of the élite in early sixteenth-century Strasbourg invested heavily in land around the city and counted members of the local nobility among their creditors. So did leading burghers in Freiburg im Breisgau.

In France, the movement towards rentier incomes seems to have coincided chronologically with the experience of the Dutch towns. By the mid-seventeenth century, the most important families in Beauvais derived more than half their incomes from land and between a fifth and a quarter from loans. The same took place in Amiens.

There is conflicting evidence from the larger Italian towns. One interpretation suggests that the movement out of trade into land and rents took place very early and was encouraged by a long-standing tradition of combining membership of an urban élite with substantial landholding outside the city, by the adoption of a more aristocratic ethos and by the rapid decline in the commercial fortunes of centres such as Florence, Venice, Milan and Genoa, during the sixteenth century as a result of the movement of international trade routes away from the Mediterranean.

Recent studies do suggest, however, that some members of Italian urban élites continued to invest in trade in spite of their rentier interests and increasingly noble way of life. Commerce does not appear to have been a source of derogation to the noble merchants of early seventeenth-century Genoa. On the contrary, they justified their activities on the grounds that they were essential to international trade. In spite of the encouragement of noble values by the Tuscan state, important Florentine families remained active in trade throughout the sixteenth century. Few of them joined the prestigious order of San Stefano, which required its members to renounce trade.

Even in Venice, which had seemed for so long to epitomise the abandonment of trade in favour of the land, there is evidence that even the wealthiest of patrician families retained an interest in trade. While patrician investors tended increasingly to withdraw into the background and leave the day-to-day running of their business affairs to others, as was also the case in Florence, the continued buoyancy of the trade in silk, timber and olive oil encouraged continued investment. As late as the 1640s, Marin Tiepolo di Francesco owned a silk shop in Venice at the sign of the column. His close relative, Almoro Tiepolo di Domenico, who was wealthy enough to purchase the high office of Procurator of St Mark's, established a company trading in silk in 1660, linking suppliers from Reggio Emilia with customers in Hamburg. The Tiepolo family was also actively engaged in timber trading until well into the eighteenth century.

According to the Elizabethan traveller, Fynes Moryson, 'The doctors of civil laws in Germany live in great estimation. No profession is more studied and followed by young gentlemen of the better sort.' [F. Morgan, *Shakespeare's Europe*, London, 1943: 303]. His observation could have applied equally to any of the states of western Europe. Well-qualified members of the legal profession played an increasingly important role in urban élites everywhere. By the late seventeenth century, at least a quarter of the councillors in the minor English provincial centre of Gloucester came from legal families. The location of provincial *parlements* in important French centres, such as Toulouse or Rouen, introduced a major legal element into the local urban élites. Lawyers were also heavily represented in Spanish centres, such as Valladolid and Barcelona. In Lübeck, three of the four mayors serving in the 1660s were members of the legal profession. The list is endless.

The evidence for the rise of the legal profession in urban society should not be taken to suggest that one social group was being displaced by another. Except in the very early stages of the rise of the legal profession to social importance, the lawyer members of urban élites owed their position less to their profession itself than to their social origins. Most high-ranking lawyers came from élite families, either in the same city or in another. Legal practice was a notoriously peripatetic occupation and, in those parts of Europe where the opportunities for employment at princely courts rivalled those in the cities, little prevented lawyers from moving on in due course. This alone does not explain why the law should have become such a valued source of status, often in places of long-distance trade. The increased litigation of the time offered greater financial rewards than before, but it was above all specialised legal advice that was in great demand on town councils and at princely courts alike. Legal training was also an essential prerequisite for office-holding of the kind that became endemic in French, Italian and Spanish towns. As an occupation in which the practitioner did not sully his hands, the law also became an attractive way of rising to noble status.

In certain cities, religious changes acted as a catalyst for changes in their élites. Leaving aside temporary upheavals, such as the Wullenwever uprising during the Reformation in Lübeck or the Anabaptist occupation of Münster, both in 1535, which led to the short-term departure of high-status families, élites in many parts of Europe were opened up by the impact of the Reformation. The Revolt of the Netherlands loosened the oligarchy in Amsterdam and the other Dutch towns during the later sixteenth century as a result of emigration by Catholic families. Religious changes in Germany after the Reformation and the Religious Wars also led to enforced changes to the élite in the long run on religious and political grounds. The Prince-Bishop of Münster introduced a deliberate policy to exclude Protestant sympathisers from the élite after the defeat of the Anabaptists and the reversal of the earlier Lutheran regime in the city. In the end, this paid off but only at the price of a generation of uneasy relations with both Catholic and Protestant members of the élite.

Office-holding

The gradual loss of urban autonomy to the forces of the territorial state had an important effect on the nature and composition of many urban élites. The distribution of offices by territorial rulers in order to extend their control over the affairs of their urban subjects rapidly became a source of patronage, status and income for resident townsmen and for members of the local nobility, who came to live in towns in order to exercise their new functions. In France, the process began earlier than elsewhere, in the fifteenth century, but the growth in importance of office-holding as a determinant of élite status became widespread throughout the period in Spain, Italy and in the towns of the princely territories in the empire. Only England and the Netherlands seem to have followed a different path.

The importance of office-holding was enhanced by the policies of venality practised by territorial rulers in order to raise money; policies, which in turn generated aspirations among the wealthy both inside and outside urban élites. The venality of office allowed office-holders to tighten their grip even further by making the offices hereditary. The northern textile centre of Beauvais was dominated by 46 families in the seventeenth century. Comparisons of the family origins of the officers of the *baillage* and the *bureau de finances* in Amiens between 1620 and 1640 and between 1700 and 1715 show a strong tendency towards an hereditary caste. The numbers of office-holders in the *généralité* of Montpellier, which included the town, rose fourfold between 1500 and 1600. Here, too, the office-holding élite became a self-perpetuating group.

Venality of office was only one aspect of the growing influence of royal power on élites. Kings of France took an increasing interest in the nomination of town councils during the seventeenth century in order to ensure that men whose loyalty was beyond doubt were in key positions. After the Restoration of the monarchy in England, English kings also exercised a new influence over the nomination of magistrates. The turnover of men in office in late seventeenth-century Gloucester, for example, rose slightly for this reason. The location in towns of royal officials, such as the *corregidores* in Castile and the *intendants* in France, also altered the character of the élite in the more important centres.

The presence of these officials underlined the decline in status of men whose area of activity was becoming strictly parochial. It is not surprising that enterprising men should have been attracted to the court by this new framework of patronage. Bourgeon's fascinating study of the forebears of Louis XIV's minister, Colbert, demonstrates clearly how the *marchands*, the great wholesale merchant families of Reims, advanced to Paris by gaining appointment to royal offices, acquiring feudal rights through the purchase of land, all in Reims and its neighbourhood, until one Oudard Colbert, Sieur de Villecerf, moved on to Troyes in the late sixteenth century. By 1604, he was in Paris and had been appointed to the office of *secretaire ordinaire de la reine*. Seven years later, he had risen to the rank of one of the 54 *conseillers secretaires du roi*.

The élite and the nobility

The growth in importance of office-holding among urban élites, increased landownership and other forms of rentier income, and the adoption of lifestyles and attitudes designed to set them apart from their fellow citizens all reinforced their separate identity at the head of the social hierarchy. On the other hand, these developments coincided with changes in the territorial aristocracy, which in many ways represented a social *rapprochement* between the two groups.

This poses something of a paradox. How can we refer to an élite whose presence was increasingly felt by the rest of the urban community when, in many ways, that élite had ceased to be distinctively urban and could be said to have become part of a broader territorial or even a national élite? Part of the answer lies in changes in both the urban élites and the rural gentry and aristocracy with whom they were having increasingly cordial relations.

The isolation of towns from their hinterlands by fortifications, laws or mental attitudes had never been fully complete, even in the Middle Ages. Paradoxically, the extension and modernisation of the protective walls of many towns during the sixteenth and seventeenth centuries took place at a time when the number of outside influences on towns was on an irresistible increase.

The relationship between leading townsmen and noble status was a long and complicated one, which varied from one region of Europe to another. In reality, this relationship had more than one characteristic. It was only in the later sixteenth and early seventeenth centuries that these separate characteristics came together in a re-evaluation of nobility, which was defined by territorial rulers rather than according to feudal custom. There is evidence that members of medieval urban élites imitated a noble way of life, not only because this was the only available model of distinctive high social status in the wider society outside the town, but also because feudal relationships penetrated urban society in the form of fealty owed by certain burghers to local lords. In Nuremberg, some members of the élite bore coats of arms and chose to display their high status by hanging their livery in the churches where their members were buried. Tournaments for the élite and visiting notables were held in the city; the earliest was in 1446 and the last in 1561. Emperor Maximilian took part in one in 1491. Fealty sworn to local lords by Strasbourg burghers in the late fifteenth and early sixteenth centuries sometimes created conflicts of interest when those lords were in dispute with the city. This had proved so disruptive in Cologne that the practice was banned by the city council in 1345.

The identification of urban élites with noble status in medieval Italy was even more widespread. Their members referred to themselves as nobles. The roots of this practice lay partly in the movement of members of the landed nobility into medieval Italian towns, although this was not the case in Venice, whose patricians bore the title *nobil huomo*, but these titles were generated locally and had no validity among the territorial nobility outside the towns. They were not granted by any outside authority and did not depend on the ownership of land with feudal rights, a situation that may explain why even the noble patricians of Venice, Florence and Genoa joined the search for more widely recognised aristocratic attributes in the sixteenth and seventeenth centuries.

These strong links between urban and rural élites in the later Middle Ages were maintained or intensified in the sixteenth and seventeenth centuries. A number of new factors came into play in the later period, which both eased the transition from urban to rural élites yet further and increased the fusion between the two, so that it was no longer necessary for a townsman to give up his urban status in order to belong to a broader élite.

By the seventeenth century, there were distinct moves in some areas to give noble status to the entire ruling group in a city. At the end of the century, the Milanese *congregazione degli ordeni* recognised all patrician families as *pro facto* nobles and required all new applicants to show positive qualifications of nobility before they were accepted. The purchase of noble titles and the increasing acquisition of feudal rights linked to estates now in urban ownership enabled members of urban élites to remain where they were while enjoying an enhanced status. In Milan, the assumption of a fief now came to be one of the criteria of patrician membership. In Nuremberg, the gradual acquisition of noble titles by the patrician families named in the *Tanzstatut* was crowned by the right granted to them all by the Emperor in 1687 to be known as *Wohledelgeborene* or *Hochedelgeborene*. All the Lübeck *Zirkelkompanie* families, now only a minority in the élite, were ennobled by Emperor Ferdinand III.

Elsewhere, the introduction of venal offices in the towns initially opened up élites and then gave them an additional hereditary basis. Such offices, as we have seen, were particularly attractive to members of the legal profession, who used them to advance themselves in urban society. The *letrados* of Valladolid did much to even out the differences in power and status with the local nobility. They acquired noble titles through office-holding and increased wealth and influence by becoming creditors to both the local nobility and the Spanish monarchy. In Barcelona, the members of the local nobility, who moved into the city in search of office and income, became closely associated with other members of the élite, whose adoption of noble ways of life (honorific forms of address, the bearing of arms, conspicuous consumption) facilitated these relationships.

All over Europe, the sale of noble titles by penurious territorial rulers offered townsmen a new opportunity to enhance their status. Prosperous burghers in the cities of the Holy Roman Empire queued up to obtain patents of imperial nobility from the Emperor. Between 1519 and 1740, 10 200 individuals were raised to noble status by the Emperor, of whom 273 were councillors in the free imperial cities alone. In France, Louis XIV carefully worded his proclamations offering noble titles by purchase in order to attract members of urban élites. In an edict of 1696 seeking to ennoble 500 men at once, he stated that those would be given preference

> who, by the posts and offices which they have held or hold, have made themselves praiseworthy and worthy of being elevated to this degree of honour and distinction; even businessmen and merchants carrying on wholesale trade, which they will be able to continue without forfeiting the said quality of nobility.
>
> (Edict concerning ennoblement in return for financial contributions from among the most distinguished in the realm, March 1696. In D. and P. Ranum (eds), *The Century of Louis XIV*, New York: Walker, 1972: 347)

Even in the Netherlands, members of the Amsterdam élite were caught up in the search for higher status. In common with townsmen elsewhere, they bought land, built country houses for their own convenience and acquired feudal titles with their estates. Daniel van Hagendorp bought the title of Lord of Moercapelle in 1635, followed by Johan van der Meyden, Lord of Sleesewijck. Other Dutch townsmen who could not afford the high price of patents of nobility imitated the practice of their French counterparts and usurped noble status by adding the name of their feudal estate to that of their own family before quietly dropping the latter a generation or two later.

Movement into the countryside by prominent English townsmen was an even more common phenomenon. By comparison with most of the continental examples discussed so far, English towns were smaller, poorer and far less independent. As a result, the influence of the local gentry and aristocracy on urban élites was correspondingly greater, and there were fewer incentives to stay. The lack of emphasis on noble titles in England also eased the transition from wealthy townsman to landed gentleman and made marriage alliances between prominent urban and rural families, such as the Crouchmans of Cambridge and the Langtons of York, relatively simple. It was not too difficult to call oneself a gentleman if one's way of life and sources of income resembled those of longer established gentry families so closely. Nor could the older families complain if the individual was a close relative by marriage. Mervyn James lists a whole cohort of Newcastle coal-owning families established in the Durham countryside in 1615: Liddell, Tempest, Selby, Mitford, Anderson, Riddell, Brandling, Hodgson, Cole and Jenison.

Further encouragement to urban élites to imitate noble values and way of life was given by the increasing presence of the country nobility and gentry in the towns as visitors. Even outside the capital cities, whose courts were a proper focus of noble interest, the multiple functions of the larger towns attracted members of the nobility to take up residence there for relatively long periods of time. They saw to business, both secular and ecclesiastical, attended law-courts, lobbied royal officials and competed with members of the urban élite for venal office. They also devoted time to shopping, entertainment and to the search for marriage partners for their children. As university education became an increasingly attractive route to social advancement, the sons of both gentry and townsmen mingled at Oxford and Cambridge, Bologna and Padua, Burgos and Valladolid. Patterns of cultural transmission are notoriously difficult to follow, but it does appear that the taste for fine art developed by patricians in the great Italian city states and taken up by princely patrons probably reached the townsmen of northern Europe by way of the royal court rather than the aristocracy. Both urban and rural élites now came to share this court culture. As in so much else, the cultural dimensions of urban life were now dictated by the centre.

How far did this *rapprochement* between urban and rural élites eliminate the differences between them? The experience of individual towns varied a great deal. In brief, most of the changes that have been outlined took place after 1600. Some of them built on social trends, such as urban landownership, which had been in existence for several hundred years. The attractiveness of aristocratic status and culture varied according to a man's wealth and position in the élite, but there was an alteration in attitudes in the course of the early modern period so that, by the end of the seventeenth century, an aristocratic or gentry way of life had become at least an aspiration for all members of urban élites.

On the other hand, while much can be made of the willingness of members of urban élites to move out into the countryside and to develop close social and marital links with members of the aristocracy, those who departed from the town opened up gaps in the élite, which were filled by other lawyers, merchants or professionals only too willing to take their place. Within a generation or two, these newcomers would come to resemble other élite families in their reliance on a rentier income, but their initial rise into the élite was almost always associated with the profits of international trade.

Strangely enough, the processes that culminated in the adoption of an aristocratic lifestyle also reinforced the differences between landed nobility and noble élites. As the prestige of the city was now increasingly identified with its élite rather than with the burgher community as a whole, it is not surprising that members of the urban élite should wish to identify themselves closely with their urban roots.

|4|

Social horizons

There are major pitfalls in writing about European urban society in the sixteenth and seventeenth centuries. The historian is overwhelmed by information about the inhabitants of towns. A great deal is known about their occupations, their households, their customs and their lifestyle. There is considerable visual evidence of how they dressed and the kinds of houses they lived in. Travellers' tales abound in descriptions of their behaviour. Indeed, it is in the very differences between one town and another, which gave rise to comments of this kind, that one can appreciate the pitfalls of generalising about urban society. While it would be an exaggeration to suggest that each urban centre had its own forms of social organisation, there were dramatic differences between urban societies in the different regions of Europe, as well as the social contrasts to be expected between economies of differing size and organisation. There were major contrasts between commercial centres of great size, such as Amsterdam, industrial centres, such as Lyon or Florence, and semi-agrarian economies, such as Embrun in the French Alps or Gangi in Sicily. The social profile of individual centres, such as capital cities, administrative or ecclesiastical centres, was also distorted by the concentration of specialised groups, such as courtiers, lawyers, soldiers, royal officials or churchmen.

While these pitfalls are not to be avoided with impunity and due respect must be paid to different types of urban society and to the changes that they experienced over time, certain key questions relating to an understanding of urban life in early modern Europe need to be addressed. Can we speak of a unified urban society, which embraced all its members and gave them a single urban identity? Ceremonies such as the communal swearing of an oath of loyalty to the city were commonplace in early modern Germany. In theory, they brought together individuals and groups from all levels of society. Public gatherings of this kind were intended to guarantee social and political stability and, indeed, had some part to play in this. On the other hand, the evidence of the increasing concentration of political and social power in the hands of a small minority, which has already been discussed in the chapters on government and urban élites, suggests that the urban community, which was expressed through ceremonies such as oath-swearing, civic processions and royal entries, was more of an élite construct than a social reality. It masked many complexities, the most important of which was the exclusion of important categories of the population – women, the poor, immigrants, members of religious minorities, the clergy and members of religious orders – from contemporary images of who was included in urban society. Any social categories used by contemporaries, which did recognise the subdivision of urban society, suffered from their rigidity. They were based on models that took little or no account of social changes. To have done so would have suggested an element of social instability, which few were ready to admit. Precedent and familiarity were the cement which held their social picture together.

This chapter has been organised in such a way as to cut across these difficulties by examining the nature of urban society less from the outside in than from the inside out. By using the concept of social horizons, it still proposes to address the extent to which urban societies cohered together as single communities. It assumes that each individual living in a town belonged to a series of overlapping groups with whom they had frequent contact, to whom they related and which, to a certain extent, helped to create their own public identity. These groups varied in importance and number. For many, the most important context for urban life was their membership of a household, supplemented by a kinship network. Beyond these horizons, the possibilities were potentially endless but, in reality, were strictly circumscribed by neighbourhood, occupation, wealth and gender, as well as by the individual's position in the life-cycle. The cohesion of any urban society depended on the extent not only to which each group retained its internal coherence but also how far overlapping memberships of different groups and the relationships between the members of these different groups contributed to a sense of social stability (social order and disorder will be examined in detail in Chapter 8).

The household

More urban inhabitants belonged to households than to any other group within society. The household, rather than the family, may be considered as the basic urban social unit for several reasons. First, it comprised the co-resident domestic group – all those sharing the same hearth, even if they were not related by blood or marriage. Second, it was commonly used as the basic assessment unit for fiscal purposes. As the work of Herlihy and Klapisch-

Zuber on the Florentine *catasto* of 1427 has shown, tax records offer an invaluable picture of the composition of households by age, sex and occupation. Finally, it avoids confusion with what many contemporaries understood the term 'family' to mean, an institution embracing both extended kinship networks and the concept of the lineage in which living members of a family group were seen as part of a social continuum, which included both their ancestors and their putative descendants. Both kinship groups and lineages had their place in urban society and will be discussed in their turn but, as the household was where an individual's earliest and most intense social relationships took place, it requires the most detailed discussion.

The inclusion of servants, apprentices and lodgers in the co-resident domestic group is particularly apposite, given the disproportionate expansion in the number of servants during the later part of the period, particularly in the largest centres, and the distribution of servants among households far lower down the social scale than in the countryside. The higher mean household size of 6.1 for seven London parishes in 1695, compared with 4 in the port of Southampton and 4.5 in the smaller centre of Shrewsbury did not reflect a substantially larger family unit in London, only more servants per household. Population figures for Venice show an increase in the proportion of servants from 8 per cent in 1581 to over 10 per cent in 1642, which was, in its turn, a point on a rising curve well into the eighteenth century.

The fluidity of the market for servants reflected a reality that many servants only stayed in an individual household for few months at a time, not long enough to bond with other members, and the same could be said about lodgers and, to a lesser extent, about apprentices, who, in spite of the length of their indentures, could and did change masters if there was not a meeting of minds. On the other hand, changing masters was far from an easy process, as attested to by the difficulties of Jean Galtié of Clermont-de-Lodève who had been placed with a merchant in Lyon in the middle of the seventeenth century. He had to convince both his father and his elder brother from a distance that he was not at fault when the relationship with his master did not work out, and it was some time before his local sponsor moved him to a partnership that included a cousin by marriage.

The resolution of Jean Galtié's difficulties is a reminder that, for some servants and apprentices, membership of a household was also reinforced by the bonds of kinship, although this was less common in towns than in rural households. For other, non-related servants, long service in a household brought with it a level of familiarity, shared experiences and intimacy, which was frequently rewarded by bequests in their employers' wills. Even when servants left a household after long service, such affective bonds remained and were – a condition similar to kinship. There were similarities, too, between the position of servants in the household and that of children in the family. Both servants and children lived in the household as a phase in their life-cycle. Both owed obedience and service to the head of the household and, in return, were supplied with protection, food, accommodation and training. Servants were required to take part in family prayers. The head of the household acted as a mediator between them and the judicial and religious authorities.

Most urban families living in individual households were closer to a nuclear rather than to an extended model. The rural conditions that favoured the functioning of extended families in which several generations lived together, often including more than one married couple with children, were far from appropriate to the ways in which artisans and merchants lived and worked. In an urban environment, there was no concept of retirement rights, according to which the elderly ceased to work but were cared for by their children in the same household. In spite of the substantial inward migration to towns from the countryside, the predominance of young single men and women rather than entire family units inhibited the transfer of rural family models on a large scale.

On the other hand, it was quite common for the conventional nuclear family of two parents and young unmarried children to include additional members, if only temporarily. In many of the cases in which this occurred, the main reasons were economic. In areas where the eldest son inherited, it was common for the heir to remain at home with his parents, although he had reached the age of maturity, often taking on substantial responsibilities within the household, which extended into family enterprise. After his marriage, the Lyonnais, Vitale Mile, formed a trading company in partnership with his father in which the company's assets included both capital, goods and the contents of the house that they shared. Many daughters brought their husbands into their own families where the latter worked in a common enterprise with their fathers-in-law. In such a case, Domenico Verardo, the husband of the fifteen-year-old Margherita Clemente, joined both the household and the business of her father, a Turin grain merchant.

In any urban society, a certain proportion of households was made up of single people, either living alone or with one servant. They could be said to represent the failure of the family system. Most were poor or relatively poor. The majority were women who had been married, but whose husbands' circumstances had left them without provision to remarry or to live in common with grown-up children. (Spinsters tended to be accommodated in the households of their relatives.) In 1561, the proportion of urban households headed by widows ranged from 15 per cent in Valladolid to 19 per cent in Segovia and 21 per cent in Medina del Campo. One in 10 of all households in the suburb of Boroughside in the area of London that lay across London Bridge were single-person households. Many more of them were female than male.

The presence of extended families in urban societies was largely limited to the élite and was particularly dominant in the Mediterranean area. The reasons for this pattern remain unclear. They developed, in part, from family trading partnerships of fathers and sons or uncles and nephews, who pooled their family patrimony as a basis for raising commercial capital, shared buildings, which served both as living accommodation and as storage, and provided an environment in which wives and children who had been left behind during trading voyages could live safely among their close relatives. The difficulty with this explanation is that, in other parts of western Europe, such as France and central and northern Germany, similar trading partnerships were developed between close kin, but the latter lived in individual households. The key may lie in distinctive rural rather than urban practices. Many of the successful merchant dynasties that developed in Florence and Genoa, for example, had aristocratic origins and retained substantial landed estates in common. The rural model had been transferred to an urban environment and continued to survive there in spite of changes in trading practices and the shift of many of the older families out of trade into investment into land and rents.

Belonging to an extended rather than a nuclear family or one of its variants provided its members with a variety of different experiences. The nuclear family unit is notorious among historians of the family for its instability and lack of permanence. It was brought into being when a couple married and ended with the death of one of the partners. In the demographic circumstances of the sixteenth and seventeenth centuries, it was unusual for a child to grow to adulthood in the company of both of its parents. Living with step-parents or step-siblings was fairly common, with all the tensions and uncertainties that often implied, even if the step-parent was a relative, a neighbour or perhaps a servant working in the same household. For those who lived in extended households, some of these traumas were, if not avoided, at least mitigated by the presence of other kin from whom they could receive reassurance and support without going outside. On the other hand, many of the characteristics of life in extended urban families were shaped as much by the high social status and income levels of the families concerned as they were by the form of the household. This can be illustrated most graphically by the way in which members of an extended family were subsumed into a lineage that stretched both backwards and forwards in time. Wealthy Florentines composed *ricordanze*, books that combined genealogy, family chronicles, details of landholding, inheritance and marriage settlements, which were passed on from father to son and supplemented by those who followed. While part of their function was informative – a married man often only learned of the details of a marriage contract negotiated by his father when a *ricordanza* was passed on to him – their composition and transmission were intended, above all, to exalt the family as the central defining characteristic of its male members.

A similar sense of the need to transmit a sense of responsibility to the family was articulated in the wills of the wealthy, in terms of both public responsibilities and the need to retain the public honour of the family through the careful choice of marriage partners for both sons and daughters.

To be fair, this sense of family continuity across the generations was not limited to members of extended family households. Naming practices were a powerful link between one generation and the next. Among the merchants and lawyers of early modern Lübeck, one son in each generation was given the same forename, Heinrich in the Balemann family, Hermann in the van Dorne family, Paul in the Wibbeking family and Gotthard in the van Höveln family. The choice of baptismal names was more complex than this pattern suggests. They enabled the links between two families created by a marriage to be strengthened yet further by passing on names from the maternal family to the new-born child. Names given to children who died young were frequently given to other children born after they had died, both in recognition that one child was a replacement for one who had been lost and in order to retain the links with earlier generations created when the name had been chosen originally. Godparents allowed their forenames to be used at baptism to underline the link of spiritual parenthood. Some families, usually of high status, transmitted the same unusual forenames in order to serve as a mark of social distinction or translated family names of mothers into forenames for their children. The Venetian patriciate contained many women named Trevisana, Loredana, Giustiniana, Donata, Moceniga or Contarina, whose forenames had once been chosen for this reason.

Beyond the household, the horizons of its members were broadened by their membership of several kinship groups: those related to their fathers or mothers; those to whom they were related by marriage; and those to whom they were related by baptism (spiritual kin). According to the definition of spiritual kin used by the Catholic Church when defining the limits of consanguinity, the latter theoretically extended beyond godparents to anyone fairly closely related to them.

These kinship groups were support networks, operating on the basis of affinity through kinship. They also operated at several different levels. There could be frequent and close association in business, politics or corporate activities, such as membership of guilds, merchant brotherhoods or confraternities, all of which also served to reinforce the strength of kinship links. Frequent visits to one another's houses fell into a similar category. Social visits of this kind were more common between female kin, but this pattern was not exclusive. Domenico da Mosto, a Venetian patrician, used to visit his cousin, Giulio Girardi, a civil servant, two or three times a week after sittings of the lawcourts. He was given very favoured treatment by comparison with other members of the same kinship network, who only had contact with the Girardi household for major events in the life-cycle, such as baptisms, weddings and funerals. These visits fell into the same category of occasional links as actions undertaken to meet unexpected or occasional requests for support, such as being asked to take an orphaned or homeless child into the household, to contribute to the costs of a girl's dowry or to take the place of a deceased father in drawing up and signing a marriage contract.

Numerous studies of kinship attest both to the closeness of bonds between individual members of kinship networks and to the uneven distribution of these bonds. There is no clear pattern suggesting that an individual's paternal kin were closer to him than his maternal kin or that kin by marriage held an inferior position to those of the family into which one was born. Many of these relationships were fostered by personal liking, geographical proximity and, above all, by the capacity to provide support. In spite of little testamentary evidence of bequests to a wide range of kin, the evidence that some of them were called upon to help and were willing to do so suggests that the kinship network did operate as a support group at key moments in an individual's life-cycle, both those that might be predicted, such as the need to contribute to a dowry to give a girl the most favourable conditions in which to make a marriage, and those tragedies that were not predictable but that all families feared: illness, unexpected deaths, homelessness or unemployment.

The importance of the kinship network as a support group seems to have been in direct relation to the length of time a family had been resident in a given town and to their place on the social scale. While the importance of kinship to migrants should not be discounted – many migrants chose to settle in towns where they already had kin whom they knew would give them some initial support – the size of any kin group to whom they could turn was necessarily smaller than those to which longer-term residents belonged. Most commonly, they acquired kin by marriage and, even though they might still have remained in contact with natal kin in their place of origin, this did not contribute to their integration in urban society or to the relationships that linked members of urban society.

Neighbourhoods

In the absence of fully fledged kinship networks for the less well-off and recently arrived migrants, the bounds of urban neighbourhoods represented some of the most important social horizons of the urban population, and one of the most important mutual support groups to which they belonged outside the household. Townspeople belonged to two different kinds of neighbourhoods, official and unofficial. The difference often lay in the extent to which the boundaries that shaped people's social identities were defined from the inside or from the outside.

Official neighbourhoods were made up of overlapping secular and religious units. Sectors, such as the *arrondissements* of Paris, the *sestieri* of Venice, the *Quartier* of many German cities, wards in English towns, the *gonfalone* of Florence and the *piazze* or *ottine* of Naples, were subdivisions of the entire urban area created during the Middle Ages for the purposes of distributing the tax burden, organising emergency services, such as defence, policing and fire-fighting, the distribution of welfare and the organisation of representative assemblies of burghers. Parishes, on the other hand, whose bounds were defined by the ecclesiastical authorities and often cut across secular lines of jurisdiction to include parts of suburbs or even agricultural land, focused on the need to provide for the spiritual needs of the laity within a relatively small area (see Chapter 5).

The dividing lines between unofficial neighbourhoods are less easy to establish, for obvious reasons. It is evident from a whole range of sources that individual townspeople were engaged in a cluster of relationships with their neighbours. Such relationships varied in intensity, and their geographical extent varied according to gender – women tended to travel less far. Often, we only become aware of them when they are placed in juxtaposition with solidarities in other unofficial neighbourhoods, through adolescent gang warfare, for example. The composition of unofficial neighbourhoods also shifted over time in response to changes such as the exodus of the rich to more spacious and modern housing, which liberated accommodation for the less fortunate, the influx of immigrants and the demolition of old housing and the construction of new streets or fortifications (see Chapter 6).

Official secular neighbourhoods provided an important framework for their inhabitants, but this was more significant for some than for others. They had little meaning for women, because both office-holding in the quarter and service in the militia were reserved for adult males. Office-holders owed some, but not all, of their status within the community to their selection as representatives of the quarter, but the power of such offices to confer social status declined as increasing numbers of burghers were excluded from the political process (see Chapter 2). Even militia service, which was often one of the defining characteristics of burgher status, declined in importance in those parts of Europe where the defence of individual towns took on a lower national priority. In some cases, the militia was completely deserted by the wealthy, as in seventeenth-century Amiens. In others, as in nearby Lille, which was in a sensitive military location close to the border with the Spanish Netherlands, the militia became the preserve of the élite. In Frankfurt am Main, on the other hand, the disturbances of 1614 were the catalyst for a reorganisation of the urban militia into 16 quarters. The experience of Frankfurt am Main suggests that, although the old administrative subdivisions had declined in their capacity to reinforce urban solidarities, enough tradition and memories of association remained in order to provide a framework for unrest, as in the case of the disturbances in Hamburg during the Reformation and the uprising of the Paris Sixteen in 1588 (see Chapter 8).

The parish retained far more influence as a focus for association. The parish church was not only the location of spiritual activities, such as attending services, taking communion or going to confession, it was also the symbolic centre of the parish. Parishioners were associated with it at key points in the life-cycle: birth, marriage and death. The bells of the parish church were the voice of the parish. Parishioners met in the church to hear news and to take part in public meetings, to gossip or to court. Individual items or chapels in parish churches were associated with individual families, guilds or confraternities, who consequently experienced a strong emotional attachment to the building. Regular parish processions and festivals reinforced the sense of neighbourhood identity.

For Catholics, the protection offered by the patron saint of their parish reinforced the help individuals expected to call upon from the patron saints of guilds and other occupational groups. In return, they dedicated much of their time and energy to ensuring that the parish church and its ceremonies were decorated and honoured. Ignace Chavatte, the Lille master craftsman and diarist, recorded frequent alterations to his parish church of San Sauveur. The teams of parish clergy, too, did much to draw parishioners together. Their collective knowledge of their flock as a result of meeting them in church, at confession and in their own homes made the clergy an important repository of information, not only about the state of their souls but also about how they lived. It was no accident that the Venetian authorities often turned to the city's parish clergy when they wished to know about the activities and reputation of one of their subjects and their family.

The role of the parish in Catholic urban societies, however, was modified by developments during the Counter-Reformation. New-style lay confraternities offered an alternative focus, which was both devotional and collective (see Chapter 5). While the old parish structure remained and continued to fulfil many of the spiritual and social needs of its inhabitants, the sharper focus of the confraternities offered men, in particular, alternative spatial foci for the expression of their religious beliefs and an alternative social context in which to relate to others.

The changes to the urban parish brought by the Reformation may have removed some of the practical ways in which the communal spirit could be expressed within the parish but, in many ways, parish churches continued to be an expression of collective identity in spite of rather than because of these changes. The early changes introduced by the Reformation in Strasbourg swept away many parish boundaries in an attempt to emphasise the personal nature of worship, but the old parish network was re-established in 1547, and the council appointed officials to each parish to act as a link between parish clergy and their parishioners. Parishioners continued to celebrate their marriages in their own parish church.

Unofficial neighbourhoods frequently overlapped with wards, quarters or parishes, but their composition was organic rather than in any way determined from above. Contemporaries defined neighbourhoods in almost tautological terms. These were the areas within which they considered the other inhabitants to be closer to them than anyone else, people with whom they had a special relationship born of familiarity and knowledge, people with whom they shared their food and drink, people upon whom they depended for mutual support and, above all, people with whom they felt more solidarity than anyone else. James Farr suggests that the neighbourhood was defined by contemporaries by what could be seen or heard from their homes or places of work, a distance of some 50 yards in each direction.

When the assailants of a local youth in the rue de la Porte Guillaume in later sixteenth-century Dijon returned to the site of the murder, they found his armed neighbours standing guard and left at some speed. Agnès, the wife of Louis Cordier of Troyes, testified in 1528 that, while she was preparing for bed on St Andrew's Day, she heard her neighbour, the widow Perette, cry out that a priest who had harassed her earlier had come back. Agnès immediately rushed out to support her, holding her clothes in her arms. When plague broke out in Lübeck in 1639, Elsabe van Wickede, the wife of the absent council secretary, Joachim Carstens, fled across the street with her children to shelter in her brother's house. The birth of a child was of such importance to local neighbourhoods in London that legislation was passed by the aldermen in 1565 curtailing celebrations of births, baptisms and churchings.

The evidence of neighbourhood solidarity is so widespread that there can be little doubt of its importance in the lives of their inhabitants. Witnesses attesting to good character in court cases, prosecutions by the Inquisition or inquiries into the status of women wishing to marry into the Venetian élite all frequently came from the same neighbourhood as the principals in the case. Only they had the detailed information to be able to make these statements. They were the boatmen who ferried their neighbours, the vegetable merchants who supplied their houses and saw them pass by every day, the barbers who came to shave them and the builders who came to repair their fireplaces. Houses were so close to each other that comings and goings were easily observed.

Neighbourhoods were a filigree of debt and credit relationships. Loans were used in many different ways to cement relationships within the neighbourhood. Many were not expected to be repaid directly. Instead, they were used as a way of reinforcing the reputation of the donor within the community as a man of honour and liberality. Who else might one turn to in times of need? These mutual and dependent links were also expressed in other important ways. The neighbourhood was a source of guardians for widows and orphans, of godparents and of witnesses to wills, marriage contracts and marriages.

As the case of Elsabe van Wickede in plague-ridden Lübeck suggests, neighbourly contiguity was often also reinforced by kinship or occupational solidarity, particularly where there was distinct social zoning. Most Lubeck patricians lived in a series of broad curving streets sloping down from the

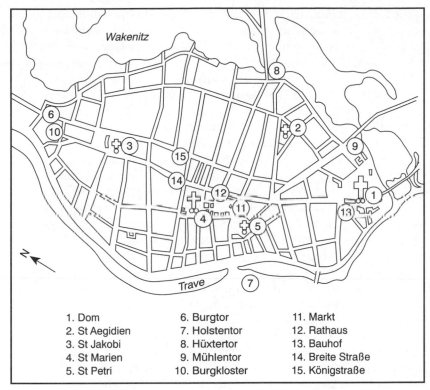

1. Dom	6. Burgtor	11. Markt
2. St Aegidien	7. Holstentor	12. Rathaus
3. St Jakobi	8. Hüxtertor	13. Bauhof
4. St Marien	9. Mühlentor	14. Breite Straße
5. St Petri	10. Burgkloster	15. Königstraße

Fig. 4.1 A plan of Lübeck showing a typical street layout

Breite Strasse (14 on Fig. 4.1) to the harbour on the River Trave. Elsewhere, we find specific concentrations of artisans – coopers in the Jordanwell ward in Coventry, printers and booksellers in the rue Saint-Jacques in Paris, cordwainers in the parish of St-Pierre-le-Vieux in Strasbourg, textile workers in the parishes of St-Sauveur and St-Maurice in Lille, clothworkers in the rue des Tanneurs in Amiens, merchants in the parish of S Vicente in Toledo.

Female solidarities

Far less is known about urban female solidarities than about male social behaviour, but there is growing evidence to suggest that women were engaged in a complex of social relationships with other women that stretched well beyond the household. Few of these relationships took place within publicly recognised frameworks, such as guilds, confraternities and the body of burghers, in all of which female members were treated as honorary men at best and as temporary and not fully qualified members at worst. On the other hand, many of these relationships were work-related because of the way in which women were increasingly engaged either in gender-specific occupations or in occupations in which they represented the majority of workers. Some 84 per cent of all the silk workers in Florence in the 1660s were women. There were concentrations of women in some of the Lyon guilds in the later sixteenth century. Thirteen of the 18 female apprentices in Lyon between 1553 and 1560 were indentured with female masters.

Women were heavily engaged in the retail trades, particularly in the market-place, where they sold food or products made by their husbands. There were so many women fruit and vegetable retailers in mid-sixteenth-century Nuremberg that the council took steps to limit their numbers. Others worked as employment agents, a job that was an extension of the informal networks of contacts that women everywhere used to find domestic servants. As the Venetian servant, Maria Bon, recorded in the mid-seventeenth century, 'when I went to the house, they told me that they needed me to come and so I came' [Venice, Archivio di Stato, *Avogaria di Comun*, *Busta* 108 (author's translation)]. Her employer was pregnant and needed someone else to help in the house. After Martio Fantucci helped Julia Ligia, a widow from northern Italy living in sixteenth-century Rome, with a lawsuit, her daughter Cecilia carried messages between them and subsequently entered Fantucci's household as his servant and mistress. In York, many servants moved from one employer to another within the same parish.

There were important female solidarities at times of pregnancy, childbirth, illness and personal distress. Often the same women were involved. Someone who could help to bring a child into the world was also expected to aid other women in times of personal distress or illness. They functioned as an alternative to the power of the clergy. Julia, a Venetian boatman's daughter, procured a bottle of holy oil from a midwife as a potion to persuade one of her lovers to marry her. A group of women from the Friulian town of Latisana arraigned by the Inquisition for witchcraft in 1591 were found to have used herbs to cure illness. They were well-respected healers within the local community, whose activities embraced matchmaking and the cure of sick children. While official midwives were often registered by the urban authorities, as in Germany, Holland and England, and given an extensive training, which included learning how to carry out emergency baptisms, their numbers were limited. Whether or not they had access to the services of a trained midwife, most townswomen relied on the aid of untrained female neighbours and relatives during the birth, women with whom they had everyday contact, for whom these services were only part of a network of reciprocal aid and support.

Devotional activities were a particular focus for women to relate to each other. In those urban societies in southern Europe, where higher status women rarely left the house without male company, attendance at Mass and participation in the decoration and preparation of the church building were a rare opportunity to meet and co-operate. Elsewhere, the proliferation of

Protestant sects, such as the English Quakers, who developed their own parallel women's organisations, offered women opportunities to meet together to discuss their concerns in a religious context.

This emphasis on female co-operation and networks within urban societies should not mask the fact that such societies were also held together by relations of mutual hostility, rivalry and tension between women living closely together. Whether it was competition for husbands, material goods in shops or status, each woman was well aware of the dangers of calumny and the need to defend their reputation. Sexual morality and local status were inextricably connected, and feeble attacks by women on each other frequently used one to undermine the other. As one married woman stated in a defamation case before the ecclesiastical court in Oxford in 1584, she had been accused of being a bastard and had retorted that her accuser was 'a whore of her tongue'. In seventeenth-century Grenoble, many women accused of prostitution or procuring by their neighbours responded by accusing others of the same activities. Universally, attacks on women's reputation were seen as attacks on the honour of their male relatives, leading to violent responses on the latter's part, a reminder that gender-based neighbourhood relationships were also part of a broader network of status and reputation.

By laying such an emphasis on the neighbourhood, both official and unofficial, as a source of social solidarities, the dynamic elements of urban society at a time of considerable shifts in population are in danger of being played down in favour of the static. Evidence from tax records, parish censuses and rental agreements suggests that it was not uncommon for people to move house when their economic circumstances changed, particularly where there was a strong rented sector. Moving house in a large city could be akin to dropping completely out of sight as far as one's neighbours were concerned. Andrea Andreas di Simon, herb vendor in the Calle Lunga di Santa Maria Formosa in Venice in the later seventeenth century, well remembered his neighbour, the Dutch merchant, Giacomo Stricher. Stricher lived in the same street until he went bankrupt and moved away to another part of the city. Andreas was unable to say where he had gone or what had happened to his family. In another part of Venice, the house of the notary, Martin Corte, was left empty four or five months after his death. The neighbours could not say what had happened to his widow. Rumour had it that she had remarried and left the city.

Cases like these, where individuals changed neighbourhood because of literally life-changing events, such as business failure or remarriage, were only part of a larger pattern of changing accommodation. Comparisons of baptismal records in early modern Strasbourg suggest that around one tenth of all families with at least two children moved from one parish to another. In the London district of Boroughside in Southwark, persistent occupation of housing in the seventeenth century was running at only 27 per cent. Similar trends were to be found in the large artisan parish of Saint-Jean in Dijon. In all three, the same salient features recurred. Movement from one neighbourhood to another was particularly common among their poorer inhabitants. The most stable members of the neighbourhoods, those who were responsible for the strongest links with each other and who defined the character of a neighbourhood, did not move to such an extent. Most movement, contrary to our two Venetian examples, took place within a very limited area, and its effects on the social fabric were consequently less damaging.

Guild solidarities

In a society in which small-scale industrial production was still one of the most common forms of employment, the guild offered men engaged in the same skilled occupation a social world that met many of their needs, one which sometimes transcended the neighbourhood. Economic pressures, political change and the development of new occupations may have diluted the influence of guild membership in some towns, but these were never more than a minority. The corporate guild remained the social model for those occupations that lacked official recognition, those that were carried out by artisans and those, such as the law and medicine, whose prestige required official recognition and protection from competition. In London, the water-bearers, street porters and labourers, none of whom were recognised by the authorities, all formed shadow livery companies. At the other end of the social scale, notaries and lawyers, surgeons and physicians organised themselves into colleges whose membership represented a valid licence to practise.

For most artisans, guild membership gave them a social identity, a meeting place, an institution whose activities were the focus of important male-bonding processes, small-scale welfare support and, before the Reformation and Counter-Reformation, offered alternative outlets, a way of expressing lay piety. Just as the guilds had acted as the intermediaries between individual citizens and the community in the Middle Ages, they continued to fulfil this role by interpreting social norms laid down by the élite and the church and ensuring that they were carried out, not only where their members worked but also in their homes. Although the distinction between merchants and artisans was growing, many guilds continued to have both merchant and artisan members and, where this was not the case, the forms and functions of merchants' guilds or brotherhoods were closely modelled on those of the artisans.

The influence on its members of the early modern craft guild can be seen in the 1536 Newcastle upon Tyne Tailor's Ordinance. Like all other ordinances, these regulations reflected the ideal rather than the reality – this ordinance followed a period of discord – but the practices that it contained continued to provide a framework for the daily lives of its members. An annual cycle of activities was dictated by the church calendar, the civic calendar and the guild's own ceremonial year. The Newcastle tailors were to meet together to take part in the processions on Corpus Christi Day and St John's Day. They would be involved financially and sometimes in person in the occasional presentation of the mystery plays. Attendance at the annual meeting at which guild officers were elected was compulsory, as was attendance at the regular masses, which were to be said 'for the brethren and sisters of the said fellowship, past and present' [R. Welford, *History of Newcastle and Gateshead*, II, London, 1885, pp. 154–7, (reprinted in P. Clark and P. Morgan, *Towns and Townspeople 1500–1760*, Milton Keynes: The Open University Press, 1977, pp. 18 19)]. The collective nature of these activities was reinforced by the requirement to wear livery, not only on those occasions on which the guild showed its solidarity to the town at large but also on those occasions when members came together for internal guild purposes, to feast, to elect officers and, above all, to show respect for the dead. The ordinance required a full complement of guild torches to be carried to the church at a member's funeral and a half-complement of torches when a member's wife died.

Activities such as these were carried out by guilds in towns throughout late medieval Europe. They remained the ideal framework for the next 200 years, but the reality of guild solidarity crumbled under the pressures of a growing division between masters and journeymen, characterised by new rules restricting the mastership to the fortunate few and growing solidarity among journeymen whose status had become devalued.

There is widespread evidence that master craftsmen were bending the rules to ensure that the ownership of workshops was limited to a small self-perpetuating élite, into which only a select number of outsiders was allowed. This was a process that dated back to the fourteenth century in some cases, but the economic difficulties faced by many artisans in the sixteenth and seventeenth centuries persuaded masters to do everything possible to protect their own interests, both by keeping down the total number of masters and by erecting barriers to deter all journeymen who lacked the necessary capital resources or who were unable to obtain exemptions usually reserved for the sons of existing masters. Rules governing the preparation of the masterpiece, the traditional test for journeymen, required more complicated and expensive work than before. From 1565, the journeyman carpenter in Strasbourg who aspired to the mastership was required to make a wardrobe, rather than a folding table, a chest or a window frame. Even if a journeymen had the skill and the means to pay for the materials to pass this test, he was often deterred still further by the knowledge that a new master would have to find the money to pay fees to the guild itself (400 *livres* in Paris at the end of the seventeenth century) and to a whole range of officials and institutions, not to mention the cost of a celebratory feast to which all the other masters were invited. Even where the urban authorities abolished restrictive practices of these kinds, master craftsmen found ways to maintain the status gap between themselves and the journeymen.

This development was advanced yet further by the presence of merchants among the leadership of craft guilds and by the organisational changes in production, which affected those industries most involved in exports, such as the textile industry (see Chapter 1). The distinction between master craftsmen, who were actively engaged in commerce, and merchants, who joined guilds in order to advance their economic interests, is not an easy one to make. Often, members of these groups were linked by marriage. There was considerable intermarriage in the Turin tailor's guild between wealthy master craftsmen and the wool and silk merchants who joined the guild from the later seventeenth century because its judicial autonomy from government interference enabled them to avoid controls on imports and exports. The medieval heritage of a political system in which all members of some city councils had to be members of a guild to qualify for council membership (see Chapter 3) encouraged both merchants and the sons of élite families to join the most unlikely guilds in order to participate in government. The most extreme case in this context was membership of the Strasbourg market gardener's guild which was very popular among wealthy aspirant politicians.

As journeymen became part of larger enterprises, often financed by men who were engaged in both the production and the sale of commodities and subject to quite sharp swings in demand, their conditions of employment became far less secure. Rather than acting as a guarantor of their standard of living, the guild now often seemed to them to be the tool of the interests of wealthy masters, controlling both production and distribution. Relationships between masters and journeymen worsened. Much of the old patriarchalism of masters was slowly replaced by a much more authoritarian position reinforced by revised guild statutes. In the second half of the seventeenth century, the administration of guild confraternities in Dijon became the monopoly of masters. Among the textile producers in seventeenth-century Lille, masters and journeymen, while still sharing the same patron saint, revered him in distinct religious ceremonies.

If the earlier solidarity of guilds was broken down initially by the actions of master craftsmen, it was fragmented yet further by the behaviour of journeymen, who formed parallel organisations outside the framework of the guild (such as the French *compagnonnages*) in order to find accommodation and employment, and whose social bonding came to resemble an extension of adolescence, marked by heavy drinking and an excessive suspicion of the institution of marriage from which their reduced status excluded them.

The anomalous position of women within guilds reflected the constant contrast between the importance of their economic and social functions and the marginal position that they were accorded in terms of institutional status. The existence of regulations permitting, or even requiring, women to become burghers, a prerequisite for guild membership, did not predicate full social acceptance. More than 5 per cent of all Cologne burghers in the first half of the seventeenth century were women, largely widows. Immigrant spinsters and widows were required to buy or earn burgher status in sixteenth-century Munich. Both here and elsewhere, masters' widows could be listed in guild registers as responsible for workshops. Practices such as these were circumscribed by increasing restrictions. Female burghers in Germany could not take part in communal oath-swearing ceremonies. Women were excluded from holding political office all over Europe. At the guild level, too, they did not hold office.

Their position within their guild was often further marginalised by their small numbers, their ranking among the poorer masters and the temporary nature of their status as owners of the means of production. Although 15 per cent of all master weavers in Augsburg around 1600 were women, they only employed 5 per cent of the journeymen in the guild. Widows controlling workshops were subject to pressure from other masters to marry one of their journeymen. These pressures grew as time passed. Transferring the workshop to male control was believed to safeguard future employment. It relieved some of the growing pressure on the mastership from ambitious journeymen who would not otherwise be able to afford the cost of becoming a master. Ultimately, it also answered the misogynistic doubts of journeymen who doubted the capacity of women to control them or manage the workshop's affairs properly.

Burgher solidarities

The legal distinction between burghers and non-burghers was one of the most potent divisions in urban society in contemporary political and social theory. Called variously freemen or burgesses in England, *cittadini* in Italy, *Bürger* in Germany, *burger* in the Netherlands and *bourgeois* in France, these individuals, almost always men, were the officially recognised members of the commonality of their town. Burgher status brought with it a social position that was valid in the world outside the town as well as within the bounds of its jurisdiction. In return for their loyalty, commitment, participation in the militia and fiscal contributions, the town gave its burghers judicial protection in their relationships with non-burghers, economic and political freedoms with the exemption from certain taxes. Burgher status was a prerequisite for guild membership and the minimum requirement for taking part in municipal elections. In Exeter, only freemen had the right to take part in long-distance trade. The citizens of early modern Valencia did not have to pay any tolls on goods disembarked in the ports of the kingdom of Valencia. They also had grazing rights throughout the kingdom, including the right to cut wood, remove stones and sand and make charcoal. Lübeck burghers were allowed to brew beer on their own premises on condition that this was for their personal consumption. The citizens of Paris, who often had land outside the city, were allowed to sell their own wine and grain from home. They were also exempt from military service and the requirement to lodge soldiers.

It is questionable how far burgher status retained its importance as a source of social solidarity during the sixteenth and seventeenth centuries. Other social distinctions among the burghers took on far more meaning. In France, *bourgeois* came to be used almost as a term of abuse among those who subscribed to status distinctions dominated by the all-powering desire to take on noble attributes. In Spain, the search for gentility among townsmen nearly became a crusade in itself. Even where this attitude was less widespread, there is evidence that the old importance of burgher status was being eroded at the top, if not at the bottom. In Amsterdam, where burgher status was transmitted from father to son, the sons of élite families were exempted from registering as citizens on the grounds that their fathers' status was proof enough. Nor were they required to take the burgher oath, a sharp contrast to the highly public ceremonies in early sixteenth-century German communities such as Augsburg, where burghers jointly took an oath of allegiance to the city in the open air. In Lübeck, too, where such traditions might have been expected to continue, a new law in 1586 freed the sons of existing burghers from the requirement to take an oath to the city. There were increasing complaints that the rules about taking up burgher status were not being followed. The insouciance of the many Lübeck residents who were qualified to become burghers but did not take the oath was amply illustrated by the case of Heinrich Balemann, the secretary to the city council from 1702, who neither obtained burgher status nor took the burgher oath.

It was at the outside edges of official urban society that the importance of burgher status remained. It was a screen through which successful immigrants were able to pass and an impenetrable barrier to anyone who did not conform to the criteria of solidity and reliability laid down by the élite – members of religious minorities, potential rivals in commerce, temporary migrants, foreigners. It was not always easy to become a burgher. Outsiders had to find burgher sponsors and demonstrate that they had enough means not to become a burden on the town through indigence. Often they were obliged to find the money to pay for their own equipment as members of the urban militia. In some places, there was a residence requirement, five years in seventeenth-century Bordeaux, 15 in early modern Venice.

In this sense, the distinctions between burghers and non-burghers retained their importance, even if they were sometimes challenged, as in the cases of Thomas Cliffe and Ralph Gardner, two unfree merchants in Newcastle upon Tyne, who conducted lawsuits against the urban authorities during the seventeenth century in order to obtain permission to trade out of the Tyne, or Claude Chéron, whose nomination as a member of the council in Chartres in 1686 was blocked on social grounds. Chéron was said to be 'the son of a peasant and not of a resident of Chartres ... a man who is a stranger to the town, of base birth and base occupation'. [A. Sanfaçon, Organisation municipale, instabilité et tensions sociales à Chartres dans la seconde moitié du xviiᵉ siècle, *Historical Reflections* VIII, 1981: 54. (Author's translation)]

Immigrants

The distinction between burghers and non-burghers took on an additional importance in the light of the social impact of in-migration (see Chapter 1). Such men and women came from very diverse backgrounds, largely but not exclusively rural, and had travelled distances ranging from a few miles to over 1000 miles. They included farm labourers and students, maidservants, artists, merchants, craftsmen, sailors and shepherds. Their arrival constituted both a threat to the social fabric and a source of labour, capital, potential marriage partners and new neighbours.

Migration posed a twofold threat to urban society. The arrival of subsistence migrants was perceived as a threat to the social fabric by the urban authorities, who feared that they would bring disease, unorthodox ideas and behaviour and a potential drain on the resources needed to pay for poor relief and subsidies to keep down the price of food (see Chapter 7). This threat was rarely justified. The presence in a town of people with different cultural backgrounds and expectations also had the potential to undermine existing institutions and solidarities, either by diluting them or by creating parallel interest groups based on groups of immigrants from the same geographical region who kept themselves apart from the host society. The question arises whether official and unofficial integrative mechanisms were strong enough to counteract the destabilising impact of large-scale migration.

Marriage was one of the strongest integrative mechanisms. Two-thirds of all new burghers in Frankfurt am Main between 1600 and 1735 acquired citizenship because they had married the daughters of existing burghers. The two processes, marriage and acceptance as a burgher, were closely linked. The double fee for unmarried immigrants who applied for burgher status was a clear deterrent. One-seventh of all licences to marry in London between 1598 and 1619 were granted to immigrant brides. The marriage registers in seventeenth-century Amsterdam contain a substantial concentration of immigrant husbands. Marriage for both men and women permitted them to enter established circles of urban society. They became members of their spouses' kinship networks, with all that this implied in terms of mutual support, social conditioning and the establishment of a new local identity.

In some cases, the identity of the newcomer was entirely subsumed within that of the family into which he married. The Spaniard, Agostino Suarez, who married into the Fonseca family in mid-seventeenth-century Venice, was rarely referred to by his own name. He was simply known as 'the brother-in-law of the Marchese Fonseca'.

Apprenticeship was an equally potent form of integration for males. Youths who underwent training in one of the crafts lived in their masters' households and worked alongside journeymen, who both taught them the necessary skills and inculcated them into the 'mysteries' of their guild. Later on, guild membership was an important integrating force, both for immigrant apprentices who became journeymen and for journeymen who had been trained elsewhere. In the case of the latter, there were fewer opportunities for personal advancement, particularly where the economy had ceased to expand. Figures for seventeenth-century Dijon suggest a decline in the number of immigrant journeymen who succeeded in finding wives. Similarly, many apprentices in the poorer trades in English towns did not complete their training because of unsatisfactory conditions and an absence of job security.

Immigrant couples with ambitions to establish themselves in the host society imitated their neighbours by creating links through loans and godparenthood, which in turn created conditions for the favourable marriage of their own children to local families, the third stage in the integrative process. Two Flemings, Louis and Catherine Revelois, a court carpet-maker in Turin and his wife, benefited from this activity when their sons and daughter married a few months apart in 1626 and 1627. Clara became the wife of a notary, while Pietro and Marc'Antonio married the daughters of grain merchants.

The experience of long-distance migrants to Turin like the Revelois has been contrasted with a group of families from the nearby Lanzo valley engaged in the provision of food. Many of them retained close links with their place of origin, doing much of their business there and seeking partners for their children among their former neighbours. A similar distinction in behaviour was to be seen in sixteenth-century Aix-en-Provence, where immigrant plasterers and leatherworkers retained close occupational and marital links, which set them apart from Aix society, while the immigrant shoemakers and tailors, who do not seem to have shown much occupational solidarity as a whole, did not.

Immigrant merchants appear to have been in an anomalous position in urban society, particularly when they had travelled long distances. While a certain unwillingness to integrate and put down roots might have been expected from merchants who anticipated returning home after a few years, longer-term immigrant merchants also displayed a certain reticence about becoming fully integrated into the host society. Around 500 English merchants from London and Newcastle upon Tyne joined the brotherhoods of St George and St Martin in the Baltic port of Elbing. A few became burghers, but almost all the cultural activity of the English community remained centred on their warehouse. The Flemings and Portuguese who settled in Valladolid took on charitable responsibilities, as did the Italians in Lyon, where they were leading supporters of the *Aumône Générale*, and yet these same men consistently married wives from Italian immigrant stock.

Did they refuse to join in or were they excluded? The evidence from established economic centres, as opposed to the new foundations such as Mannheim, which offered substantial incentives to merchant and artisan immigrants, suggests a mixture of both. The complexities are well illustrated by the case of Giacomo Stricher, an Amsterdam merchant, who settled in Venice in the mid-seventeenth century. His appointment as consul to the Dutch soon after his arrival suggests that Stricher was highly regarded by the Venetian government, a picture reinforced by his selection to make large loans in ships and materials to support the war effort against the Turks. One of his sons became a priest. Two daughters married Italian husbands, one possibly a member of the Venetian nobility. On the other hand, neither Stricher nor his other two sons ever became citizens of the Venetian republic, his close links with the immigrant Dutch community were reinforced by the marriage of one of his daughters, and his sons eventually moved away to trade in England and the Netherlands. Their continued involvement in international trade was a counterweight to the attractions of total commitment to a society in which their immigrant status placed them at a disadvantage.

Social stratification

How did the multiplicity of groups in urban society whose members' worlds were largely bounded by relatively limited social horizons fit together to make a single urban society? Perhaps the question should be posed in a different manner. Given the presence of all these groups, was there such a construct as a single 'urban society' in any given town? It might be argued that all they had in common was a shared space, which was only shared on the margins of neighbourhoods and in certain places of communal assembly, such as the market-place, and a shared economy in which the actions of production and consumption linked producers and consumers. There is a case, however, for examining at least two of the indicators with which the homogeneity of an urban society can be measured: marriage patterns and deference patterns.

Marriage within a well-defined social group was a way of reinforcing its identity by creating new kinship links, economic links and social links. The more endogamy, the stronger the group and the more detached from other groups in society. The more men and women married outside their own groups, the more we can treat this as evidence of social mobility and an opening up of links between different groups. Marriage had both a symbolic and a real significance. Symbolically, it signalled that the two families involved were of equal status. It created new kinship networks bringing its members obligations – godparenthood, guardianship and the execution of wills. The real significance of marriage, on the other hand, lay in the transmission of goods and status to the next generation.

The evidence for urban endogamy is patchy. Most studies have concentrated on those social groups, such as the élite or other high-status groups of professionals, whose status, small size and relatively complete records enable the historian to conclude that their reputation for endogamy was justified. Lower down in society, the difficulties of gaps in evidence and the scale of such an enterprise would have been enough of a deterrent were it not for the confusion surrounding the classification of different groups. Mousnier's analysis of Parisian marriage patterns in the 1630s offers a useful model, but it is doubtful whether it could be used in other urban contexts without much careful modification.

Endogamy was one of the defining characteristics of urban élites, who not only practised a highly exclusive marriage policy but also used marriage as a mechanism for admitting new members (see Chapter 3). Little dynasties of professionals developed, such as Venetian notaries and high-ranking administrators or the pastors of Lübeck's parish churches, an interesting case of a newly emergent professional group (pre-Reformation clergy were excluded from lay status), which was determined to assert a group identity.

Further down in society, the barriers between one social group and another were more permeable, even though close geographical or occupational proximity favoured a substantial degree of social cohesion underpinned by marriage. Once again, there were contrasts here between rural practice, in which villages were characterised by a very high level of endogamy, particularly if this included marriage to partners from neighbouring parishes, while the more fluid nature of urban society was reflected in much lower levels of endogamy. In one French rural parish south of Paris (St Denis d'Athis), two-thirds of all grooms found brides who lived less than five kilometres away. Altogether, 91 per cent married brides from parishes within a radius of 10 kilometres.

Artisans married each other's daughters, although not necessarily from the same guild. As Claire Dolan points out in her study of marriage among the artisans of Aix-en-Provence, the daughters of artisans often married long after their fathers had died, and their choices were therefore influenced more by the occupation of a brother, an uncle or a step-father than by that of their father. On the other hand, in certain occupations, such as weaving, the inclusion of looms in a girl's dowry facilitated the economic survival of the bridegroom. A poor weaver was unlikely to obtain the tools of his trade in any other way than through marriage or by inheritance.

The growing social gap between journeymen and master craftsmen was enhanced by a form of endogamy, which laid less emphasis on a common occupational background than on common status. In mid-seventeenth-century Paris, 40 per cent of all master craftsmen married the daughters of other masters. Intermarriage between masters and the daughters of other masters in Dijon rose from 36 per cent to 47.8 per cent during the first half of the seventeenth century.

Downward social mobility is less easy to trace, but it too was marked by the choice of marriage partners among the children of those master craftsmen whose enterprises had either been squeezed by their more successful competitors or who had been obliged to drop to the position of journeymen themselves, working for another master.

The growth in marriages between the families of merchants and master craftsmen also underlines the growing gap between journeymen and masters. The dividing line between production and marketing became increasingly blurred, the larger the enterprise organised by the master craftsman. Many were merchants themselves or had close business associations with merchants of a kind that were easily cemented by marriage. This kind of upward social mobility from master craftsman to merchant was paralleled by a growth in marriage between the sons of merchants who had trained as professionals and members of the professional group that they had joined. On the other hand, the process of upward social mobility was qualified by the relative difficulty with which some new lawyers were able to find wives from the same professional circles. In seventeenth-century Paris, many recently qualified lawyers married the daughters of merchants, generally from the circles into which they themselves had been born. On the other hand, the establishment of such a link enabled others who could now claim to be related to a lawyer to take the first steps in moving up themselves.

The relatively few cases of successful upward mobility sealed by marriage represented only one of the ways in which members of different urban social groups were linked vertically rather than laterally. Social obligations, such as acting as a witness to a marriage contract, holding a child at the font, giving or receiving loans, acting as the executor of a will, could and were ways of reinforcing lateral social links, but they were also part of the patterns of deference and patronage by which those of higher status were able to express their social position and develop a reservoir of obligations upon which they could draw should need arise (see the discussion of social order and disorder in Chapter 8). This behaviour can be seen as a pattern of surrogate kinship, one that cut across lateral social relationships but far from replaced them.

In the 1640s, 121 high-status men acted as the godfathers for the children of Dijon artisans, representing the spectrum of high-status men in the city. Over half were nobles or royal officials, almost a quarter were *avocats* and the balance were other lawyers. Leading members of the city council in

Lübeck were frequently requested to act as godparents to families of lower status. It is debatable how far the duties of these spiritual parents extended beyond the baptismal ceremony. Their main function was to be present at the time and to be seen to be publicly linked to the child's family.

The choice of witnesses to marriage contracts conveyed prestige in both directions. In mid-seventeenth-century Paris, it was customary for high-status contracts to be signed by large numbers of witnesses, between eight and 11 per marriage among the nobility, and, while the highest nobility eschewed merchants and master craftsmen as witnesses, lawyers comprised a fifth of the witnesses of second-ranking nobles (*écuyers*) and merchants and *bourgeois de Paris* a further tenth. In return, a small number of nobles, merchants and lawyers acted as witnesses to master craftsmen.

The interplay between different social groups in urban society is far from easy to measure, let alone to summarise. This is a theme to which all the later chapters of this book return.

5

Religion and society

Organised religion was a major part of urban life at the beginning of the sixteenth century. Ecclesiastical buildings dominated the skyline and, in the case of abbeys and cathedrals, dominated the housing around them. Tonsured men were a common sight in the streets. Holy images, primarily of the Virgin Mary and St Peter, adorned coins, doorways to public buildings, bridges, gateways and many private houses. Parish churches were the social and cultural centres of their communities. They were places of meeting for communal discussions, official announcements and banquets. Guild membership combined the association of men belonging to the same occupation with the confraternal worship of patron saints. Much educational and charitable provision was in the hands of the church, particularly among the regular clergy, whose buildings and places of worship lay in or near to the town.

Ecclesiastical bodies formed an important part of the urban fabric in economic and political terms. Land and buildings within towns belonged to institutions over which urban governments had no control. The same applied to members of the clergy, who were exempted from any form of secular taxation. As non-burghers, they were outside the urban body politic, but their presence in the town remained an important constraint on urban autonomy, particularly where a town served as an episcopal seat. As landowners outside the town, ecclesiastical institutions, cathedral chapters, monasteries and convents disposed of a great deal of wealth and economic potential. On these estates, which were outside the jurisdiction of urban governments, they were able to encourage activities which were in direct competition with the work of urban artisans.

Religion shaped the lives of townspeople at every point. Baptism, Christian burial and, to a lesser extent, marriage were key religious ceremonies, without which it was believed that their immortal souls were in danger. Alongside the ceremonial year defined by the rhythm of civic and guild office, the

Christian year gave shape to the succession of the seasons. All the major festivals were concentrated into six months of the year from Advent until Corpus Christi Day and marked by intense periods of spiritual preparation and celebration. Each town, each parish and each smaller grouping also celebrated its patron saint and a host of other minor festivals with services, feasting and more secular forms of entertainment.

By the end of the seventeenth century, the religious landscape of the towns of western Europe had changed. The Reformation and Counter-Reformation between them had brought about major changes in organisation, belief and practice. They had also ended any illusion of a single unified Christian church, even if the majority of towns continued to identify with one of the Christian confessions and to deny the validity of any others. Whether Protestant or Catholic, the organised church and the institutions of urban government worked ever more closely together to assert both a religious and a political orthodoxy, which underwrote the primacy of the élite and of territorial rulers.

The process of change was complex and led to a considerable level of turmoil in the lives of townspeople, particularly in the sixteenth century. Some of this was violent, but much more was present in the mind, when new ideas suggested new possibilities or threats to deeply felt beliefs and solidarities.

There is still a great deal of debate about the strength of the Church on the eve of the Reformation. Expressions of anti-clericalism at the beginning of the sixteenth century in many parts of Europe certainly reflected anger at the apparent wealth and influence of the Church, to which all burghers had to pay tithes and whose institutions were increasingly becoming a source of credit. There is equally no doubt that many of the criticisms of the Church made before and during the Reformation were justified. Absentee bishops and archbishops were common, as was clerical pluralism and concubinage, a relatively poorly trained clergy and a lack of clarity about central points of dogma. All of these were potential sources for dissatisfaction and led to calls for reform. On the other hand, relatively few towns manifested major discontent with the services offered by the Church. In the end, most Protestant regimes were installed from above by town councils or territorial rulers for reasons that were only partly theological and, even when all the German free imperial cities that introduced the Reformation are considered, the fact remains that Catholicism continued to be practised by the majority of European towns.

The Reformation brought with it new challenges to the unity of the urban community, which had repercussions extending far beyond the presence of alternative beliefs and forms of worship. Religious minorities formed new kinds of social solidarities, which cut across those that had existed before the Reformation, and complicated the social relationships that developed later. They also created problems and opportunities for the urban authorities: problems because political control was associated with religious conformity and opportunities because members of religious minority groups often had considerable economic potential.

This discussion of the role of religion in the urban societies of early modern Europe is concerned with far more than matters of belief. Religion was so closely bound up with an individual's personal identity that it exercised strong powers of social unity and disunity: unity among urban communities, which shared the same beliefs, and among separate groups, which co-existed in an atmosphere of religious heterodoxy; and disunity between adherents of the different Christian confessions and between Christians and Jews.

It can be argued that the sixteenth and seventeenth centuries were a time in which, in spite of the presence of more secular authority, religious belief had more influence on the daily lives of townspeople than at any time since the twelfth century and that, although both Protestant and Catholic reforms appeared to give members of both sexes more opportunities to express their religious beliefs in private and in public, this increasingly took place within a framework of strict orthodoxy, in which more popular or individualistic forms of expression were placed under strict controls. In order to explore this, the chapter has been divided into three linked sections: the nature and impact of the urban Reformation and Counter-Reformation; the expansion of urban lay piety throughout western Europe; and the complex impact on urban life of the widespread presence of religious minority groups.

The urban Reformation and Counter-Reformation

The religious experience of townspeople in the early modern period was heavily coloured by the Reformation and the Counter-Reformation. The urban Reformation took on three distinct forms:

- the rejection of the traditional church by the urban authorities and its replacement by some form of Protestantism;
- the reorganisation of worship as a fiat of the territorial ruler;
- the temporary introduction of religious change by a movement that was not strong enough to retain control in the long term.

The first pattern may be typified by the free imperial cities in Germany, such as Nuremberg, Lübeck and Strasbourg, and the cities of the northern Netherlands; the second by German Protestant princely states and by Denmark and England; and the third above all by the French Huguenots, who gained control of a number of important urban centres in the later sixteenth century, such as Lyon, Toulouse and La Rochelle, but were unable to assert themselves within a Catholic French monarchy during the seventeenth century.

The introduction of Protestantism comprised a number of organisational and theological changes. Control of church buildings, possessions and personnel shifted from Rome to the territorial state, the city state, or, in the case of Calvinism, to local and regional consistories. The clergy were given secular status and were thus subject to the same laws and taxation as other members of urban society. They were permitted to marry and, consequently, took their place more fully in the networks of kinship and inheritance to which other townspeople belonged. An officially recognised religious vocation was limited to men, although the early stages of both Lutheran and Calvinist movements gave considerable opportunities for female religious expression. The closure of convents and monasteries and the expulsion of religious orders from Protestant towns not only reduced the numbers engaged in distinctive religious work, it also removed an important dimension from the lives of townspeople, which was only partially replaced by other initiatives, such as poor relief schemes, hospitals and schools. In liturgical terms, the mass was abolished, services were held in the vernacular rather than in Latin and there was more emphasis on sermons and hymns. Images as objects of veneration were removed both from inside churches and cathedrals and from public places. The intercessory role of saints and the Virgin came to an end. Although marriage ceased to be a sacrament, the Protestant churches achieved a determining role in the wedding ceremony.

In the majority of European towns in which there was no Reformation, the presence of Protestantism elsewhere and other initiatives for reform within the Catholic church during the first half of the sixteenth century encouraged equally important changes, which altered both public and private devotional practice. By contrast with the Protestant emphasis on the individual's direct relationship with God, these changes in the Catholic church were intended to renew the central ideas of Catholic intercessory theology, the mass, the sacraments, the Trinity and the saints.

There was nothing exclusively urban about these religious changes. Once they had worked their way through, they affected rural parishes as much as urban centres. On the other hand, much of the impetus for change came from townspeople, its effects were felt more intensively, and the opportunities for religious pluralism were far greater where the population lived in the greatest numbers.

These changes took place during a period of more than a century from the 1520s. Local conditions led to enormous variety in behaviour, organisational change and timing, but many of the changes were equally determined by external political conditions. Even in the free cities of the Holy Roman Empire, in which much of the early momentum of the Reformation was developed, the rate of religious change was strongly influenced by the potential responses of powerful territorial neighbours. Elsewhere, the religious orientation of subject towns depended to a great extent on Protestant or Catholic territorial rulers.

Beginning in the 1520s and 1530s in the Electorate of Saxony and many German free imperial cities, the long-term schism in the Catholic church spread to Hesse, Brandenburg, Brunswick, Württemberg and several German-speaking Swiss cantons. By the end of the 1530s, a form of Protestant church strongly influenced by Lutheran theology had also been adopted by the territorial rulers of Denmark, Sweden and England. The process continued in Germany well into the later sixteenth century – to the extent that many historians refer to a second Reformation.

Whether the Protestant Reformation resulted from popular pressure from below or political direction from above, in most cases the final decision to break away from the Papal church was taken by the secular authorities. There was a great deal of support for Reformation ideas from the wealthy. A petition to invite an evangelical preacher to a larger church in Leipzig in ducal Saxony in 1525 was instigated by the council. Most of its 105 signatories were wealthy. The burgher committee calling for a Reformation in Brunswick in 1528 contained long-distance merchants and members of council families. Jürgen Wullenwever, the leader of the radical party which introduced the Reformation in Lübeck in 1535, was a member of the *Novgorodfahrer*, a leading brotherhood of long-distance merchants. Humanist members of the council in Nuremberg, including its secretary, Christoph Scheurl, helped to usher in one of the earliest urban Reformations.

The degree of support for evangelical ideas by members of German urban élites is less surprising when we consider that many of the lay leaders of the evangelical movement came from the outer circles of the élite and that their position was dictated in part by internal political conflicts with councillors. Some, but not all, councillors continued to identify with the Catholic church less because of religious conviction than because they had vested interests in the patronage network offered by the Catholic church. Conflicts between city councils and the Church or the local territorial ruler also influenced the decision to introduce the Reformation, as in Erfurt, as did the all important need to take control of evangelical movements, which were threatening to bring about a change in the social order, as in Augsburg and Strasbourg.

It is unlikely that the Reformation would have been introduced so widely had there not been support from below. The presence of charismatic preachers drew large crowds to hear their sermons and helped to harness a general antipathy towards the church by spreading evangelical ideas. Pressure to install these preachers as pastors of the city churches became one of the characteristics of the urban Reformation. In many parts of Germany, too, the development of a popular religious movement in the towns was part of a long-term constitutional conflict between the guilds and the élite.

The decision to introduce Protestantism in a town did not necessarily mean that changes in form meant changes in substance. The transfer of power from the Pope to the kings of England had considerable political implications. On the other hand, they did not engender an immediate change in the beliefs and practices of most English townspeople. While there was considerable conformity to changes in government policy, whether it was

the watered-down Catholicism of Henry VIII, the Protestant radicalism of
Edward VI or the renewed Catholicism of Mary, few real changes in religious
sensibility appear to have taken place before the 1580s when the first Puritan
lectureships were established in a number of towns and the policy of the
Church of England itself under Archbishop Grindal took on a more Calvinist
tone.

For every town or territorial state in which a Protestant church replaced
older forms of ecclesiastical organisation, there were many others where
this did not take place. Some of the conditions for the successful introduction
of Protestantism were present in such towns, but their limited scale did not
favour change in the organisation of the church. Individual members of the
Catholic clergy began to include the vernacular in their services and to preach
about justification by faith and the iniquities of a materialist church that
had lost touch with its roots. At the same time, a small number of leading
laymen took an interest in humanist ideas and began to discuss them. As in
the 'Reformation' towns, artisans under economic pressure from ecclesiastical
institutions began to articulate anti-clerical attitudes. And yet, official change
did not take place and, in time, anti-Papal attitudes faded away. References
to developments in Cologne, Duderstadt, La Rochelle and the Swiss cantons
as 'failed Reformations' tend to minimise the fact that there were pressures
for religious change in a much wider range of towns. The geographical
location of such towns in predominantly Catholic areas of Europe, the
absence of an organised movement in opposition to the church and the
absence of support from the ruling élite all created conditions that inhibited
change.

Throughout the sixteenth century, the proliferation of Protestant ideas
among townsmen brought potential religious instability to many parts of
Europe. This took several forms. The circulation of literature and its public
discussion were considered to be heretical and potentially subversive by both
religious and secular authorities, especially in Spain, the Italian states and
southern Germany. In the years after the Colloquy of Regensburg failed to
end European religious disunity in 1541, religious debates flourished among
doctors, lawyers, printers and tailors in many of the towns of northern and
central Italy, as well as among the more intellectual groups of *illuminati*
among the élite and the upper clergy. In Spain, in contrast, the proportion of
cases of Lutheran heresy handled by the Inquisition in Toledo indicates that
Protestantism was perceived of as less of a problem than either Judaism or
Islam, which had been widespread on the Iberian peninsula until recently.

Public actions, such as iconoclasm, demonstrations calling for the closure
of convents and monasteries and the conversion of church buildings for
evangelical worship, brought about open and violent conflict between
opposing groups of townspeople, particularly in France and the Netherlands.
The level of violence spread as religious conflict became associated with
political tensions. The disagreements between Emperor Charles V and the

princely supporters of Martin Luther after the Edict of Worms of 1521 brought about a generation of conflict, in which sieges of towns supporting one Christian confession or the other played an important part. Similarly, but on an even more intensive scale, the two parties in the French Wars of Religion, the Huguenots and the Catholic League, came to be associated with militant Calvinism and militant Catholicism. Levels of ill-feeling and bloodshed exceeded anything known since the suppression of the Albigensians in the thirteenth century. Towns were both the power bases of each party and the centres of conflict in which religious and political control oscillated from one side to the other, as in Lyon. Religious loyalties continued to draw German cities into conflict during the Thirty Years War.

The Calvinists, who played such an important part in European politics from the second half of the sixteenth century, represented the second generation of Protestants. Unlike the supporters of the Lutheran Reformation, they did not come to dominate the official church of many European cities. Geneva, in which Calvin developed many of his ideas and put them into practice, was an exception. Where a Lutheran church already existed, only the accession of a new territorial ruler sympathetic to Calvinism, such as the Elector Frederick of the Palatinate, offered any hope of a peaceful change. Elsewhere, Calvinism grew alongside Lutheranism, as in England, where a modified form of both was present in the Anglican church at the time of the Elizabethan Church Settlement of 1559, or attracted support from those opposed to the Catholic church. In Scotland and Bohemia, a short period of conflict resulted in the establishment of an official Calvinist church. The same was the case in the seven northern provinces of the Netherlands, in which a Calvinist church emerged as part of the long-drawn-out war for independence from the Spanish crown. In France, on the other hand, Calvinists dominated a limited number of towns in the west and south-west between the 1560s and the 1630s before gradually losing the right to religious self-determination during the decades before the revocation of the Edict of Nantes in 1685.

In contrast with areas in which Lutheranism became the official religion, Calvinists were always in a numerical minority, even where they became the dominant political and religious force, as in Geneva, Scotland and the Netherlands. Lutheran cities and territorial states practised the principle of *cuius regio, eius religio*, which became enshrined in the Peace of Augsburg in 1555. In order to be a full subject in a Lutheran state, it was necessary to be Lutheran. Given the Calvinist principle of predestination, which implied that the 'elect' could only be a minority within a population of sinners, and the Calvinists' physical inability to impose their beliefs on the local population, there could be no congruence of religious belief and urban residence.

The spread of Calvinism from Geneva to France, the Holy Roman Empire, Scotland, England and Bohemia was only the most significant manifestation of the fragmentation of Protestantism, which had begun to take place within months of Luther's initial criticisms of the Papal church. Urban centres proved to be particularly fertile ground for the ever-increasing numbers of Protestant sects. The size and openness to immigrants of large maritime centres, such as London and Amsterdam, encouraged the proliferation of sects, but individual sects thrived even where there was no strong immigrant element in the population. In the later sixteenth century, Anabaptists were prosecuted in Cologne and in the towns of Holland and Zealand. Their support came from the same social groups as the men and women who criticised the clergy at the outset of the Reformation: literate artisans who had access to published literature, were increasingly well versed in the Bible and were ready to take on new ideas. Once control of the Lutheran and Calvinist churches had passed into the hands of the élite and a new orthodoxy appeared to have been established, alternative answers to the anxieties of artisans and a small number of merchants had a strong attraction. The millenarian ideas, which were stressed by all Protestant sects, exercised a powerful influence on those who were worried by the pace of political and economic change. Given the negative attitudes towards them expressed by the local secular and religious authorities, which were strengthened by memories of the Anabaptist occupation of the German city of Münster in 1535, members of the sects tended to worship in private, and no accurate figures of their numbers are available.

The religious map of Europe around 1560 shows that, in most areas, the Catholicism of the old Papal church remained the dominant religion. Only in the Netherlands, Germany and central Europe, where political authority was fragmented, was there any evidence of a large Protestant minority or minorities. Sixty years later, the same remained the case, although Calvinism had now spread beyond Geneva into other parts of the Swiss confederation, into the newly independent Dutch United Provinces and, through the decisions of their rulers, into the German states of Nassau, Hesse and the Palatinate.

The organisational changes to the Catholic church embodied in the decisions of the Council of Trent are well known. They were dedicated to removing the kind of abuses and poor quality service, which had left the Church open to criticism from the later fifteenth century onwards. In the towns, better informed and trained priests from the new diocesan seminaries were complemented by members of the religious orders, by the Jesuits in particular, and a renewed alliance developed between the upper clergy and members of the urban élite to whom they were often related.

The presence of Protestant ideas, many of which circulated in various forms much further afield than Germany and northern Europe, also enabled the leaders of the Counter-Reformation Church to counter heresy at home by emphasising the differences between them, while using some of the same techniques that had been proved to be so rewarding to the evangelical movements. Enhanced importance was given to processional celebrations, which enabled the Church to convey several messages at once. By organising processional routes to cover large areas of urban centres while connecting key points of religious significance, they were able to involve large numbers of the community, either as participants or as onlookers. The presentation of key objects of veneration focused attention on them as symbols of central beliefs in order to reinforce their place in Catholic dogma. Finally, the composition of each procession, bringing together different elements of the Church and the secular body politic broadcast the double message that the lay and the ecclesiastical were inextricably linked and that church and urban institutions were in partnership.

Sermons were used increasingly to emphasise the differences between Catholicism and Protestantism. In Augsburg, the Church organised 'controversy sermons' each year to reinforce central Catholic beliefs. By emphasising how the Lutherans decorated their churches by missing out most imagery and by covering their altars with brown cloth indistinguishable from that in everyday use, for example, preachers reminded their audiences how their own church was decorated with all the most important symbols and images of intercessory religion, using vestments for their clergy and luxury altar cloths in order to make the distinction between the holy and the material. A similar kind of thinking underlay the enormous *auto da fe* organised by the Inquisition in Spain, at which those whose faith had lapsed and were to undergo public punishment were confronted by a mass public ceremony asserting the central faith from which they had lapsed. The theatrical nature of such ceremonies as well as the frisson of seeing high-born members of urban society in the procession of sinners drew large crowds on whom the simple message of the *auto da fe* made an immediate and deep impression.

The establishment of new orders, such as the Theatines, the Ursulines, and, above all, the Jesuits, led to the insertion of many new buildings to emphasise the centrality of the church. Jesuit churches rivalling cathedrals in their splendour were built on the edge of Lyon, Cologne and Antwerp. Elsewhere, they chose prime sites for their colleges. The whole of the area behind the Left Bank in Paris was extended by numbers of new buildings erected by the mendicant orders, so much so that the monarchy passed a law in 1620 limiting the use of the land by religious orders for fear that too much would lie under mortmain.

An enhanced spirit of piety and identity with their religion led townspeople to contribute generously to the redecoration and external refurbishment of existing churches and to the construction of new buildings. These churches became the centrepiece of new perspectives set up by new streets. If the reconstruction of Rome was the only example of the wholesale building of churches and other votive buildings, the Counter-Reformation also left its mark on other buildings. Longhena's church of Santa Maria della Salute in Venice, built in memory of the city's survival from the plague of 1630, became the centrepiece of vistas along the Grand Canal, the Giudecca Canal and the Basin of St Mark's and permanently altered the city's appearance as it was approached across the lagoon. Where there was no room for new construction on a large scale, attempts were made to release land around churches to put them in greater relief. The quarter around the church of Sainte-Eustache close to Les Halles in Paris was remodelled in this way in the early seventeenth century.

Changes in the physical appearance of towns were not the only manifestations of the Counter-Reformation. More wayside chapels and votive images were built. Religious painting for private use flourished, and so did meditative treatises. The arrival of the Jesuits offered new educational opportunities. Jesuit colleges were set up in most major towns and, after some initial suspicion on the part of the urban authorities, for the Jesuits owed them no allegiance, their leading role in the Counter-Reformation was recognised and encouraged. As well as being educators, they were to be found in every area of activity in which the Christian ethic could be a controlling influence. They took over the arrangements for welcoming honoured visitors to Lille in the seventeenth century. They organised plays in Latin and German in Bavarian towns and sponsored confraternities almost everywhere. As in the case of the Protestant Reformation, the respective roles played by the ecclesiastical authorities and individuals in bringing about changes in practices are not easy to determine. Suffice it to say that the decisions of the Council of Trent and their implementation would not have been received so enthusiastically by townspeople had a deep sense of piety and wish for change not already been in existence.

The development of the Jesuits was only one manifestation of a substantial inflation in the numbers of the clergy as the result of the Counter-Reformation. The numbers of the regular clergy swelled in particular. In the later sixteenth century, around one-sixth of the population of Cologne were members of the clergy and their households. In the southern Netherlands, the numbers of convents and monasteries in every large town doubled at least. By 1697, 5 per cent of all the population at Mons were clergy. So many monks and nuns were in search of accommodation in Grenoble during the seventeenth century that the inhabitants around the main square became alarmed that the close proximity of nuns would dampen their normal way of life. The rise in the numbers of the regular clergy brought them into contact with lay people even more than before, as teachers, carers for the sick, distributors of charity and takers of confessions.

While the renewed religious enthusiasm of the Counter-Reformation may have been the mainspring for the growth of new religious orders and the increase in recruits to the old, other factors encouraged the rise in the number of nuns, which had less to do with religious conviction than it had with the economics of marriage. Dowry inflation in the later sixteenth and seventeenth centuries among the urban élites and aristocratic families of Catholic Europe directed the thoughts of many a father to the relative cheapness of the spiritual dowries levied on those girls who took the veil and ensured that many girls who had been sent to convents for their education remained there as nuns.

Religiosity in towns

One thread united all the diversity of changes in religious belief and expression witnessed by the towns of early modern Europe. Both the Reformation and the Counter-Reformation represented a process with roots in the fifteenth century, the growth of individual piety. This phenomenon could also could be called the growth of religiosity, for it represented far more than a wish on the part of the individual to express his or her religious beliefs more urgently and more directly than was possible within the confines of the existing church. What characterised the sixteenth and early seventeenth centuries was the strong commitment among a wide spectrum of townspeople to bring about or respond to religious change both inside and outside the church.

Responses differed among Protestants and Catholics. There was a readiness to criticise existing theology and ecclesiastical organisation and an openness to new ideas in pamphlets and sermons among Protestants in the earlier stages of the Reformation, and a general interest in and familiarity with the Bible later on. Members of the Catholic church manifested a renewed identification with the central symbols of their faith by taking part in confraternities and processions. Among both Protestants and Catholics, their new sense of the importance of religious belief promoted both public and private acts of devotion.

In the heat of religious conflict, in which many of the most extreme manifestations of religiosity were expressed, it is not easy to disentangle how far these feelings were overtly encouraged by religious leaders and to what extent they arose from below. Even later on, when religious institutions and secular authorities of all kinds asserted increasing control over popular expressions of religious belief, they were able to harness these intense feelings of religiosity among the urban population at large to the interests of their church. There was widespread popular outrage in Lille in 1688 when two Swiss soldiers were found guilty of having defiled the host, but it was the Bishop of Tournai who took the lead in organising a mass on the next day (a Monday) to reconsecrate what had been profaned.

The religious conflicts in sixteenth-century France were born out of this new sense of religious commitment on both sides, and the effect of confrontation and violence was to deepen these beliefs until they reached a height of fanaticism. Like their co-religionists in England, Scotland, Switzerland and the Netherlands, French Calvinists devoted themselves to private study of the Bible, constantly searching for reassurance that they had been endowed with the gift of grace by God at birth, and attended lengthy sermons and lectures in order to deepen their understanding. Unlike the Catholics, for whom particular places and times had a religious significance, the Calvinists endowed everything they did with the same level of meaning. Their constant awareness of man's sinfulness left them in a never-ending state of penitence and self-examination.

The inner conviction of Protestants that they were right and that it was their task to rescue the Catholics from themselves led to acts of iconoclasm. Contrary to the views of the urban authorities, these were a carefully structured series of actions intended to remove from church buildings anything that might stand in the way of the individual's direct communion with God and to free the Church for 'godly' worship. Images were removed and destroyed throughout the Reformation. Pictures and statues were destroyed by young monks in Wittenberg from 1521. Zwingli had preached against images in Zürich in 1523 before presiding over the methodical removal of images from 15 of the city's churches. In Augsburg, a statue of Christ used in the Ascension Day service was deliberately allowed to smash 20 feet to the floor of the Church of St Moritz in 1533. Calvin wrote critically in *The Institutes* of the veneration of images, and his followers in both France and the Netherlands pursued a policy of iconoclasm. The month of August 1566 was particularly marked by the occupation and 'cleansing' of churches in the southern Netherlands by Calvinists who argued that 'they had preached in the fields long enough'. In later sixteenth- and early seventeenth-century England, too, Puritan-controlled urban authorities supervised the destruction of religious symbols, such as the two market crosses in Banbury, but, unlike Continental cases of iconoclasm, these actions marked a stage in a war against traditional culture rather than against Catholicism.

The response of Catholics to incidents of local iconoclasm was a mixture of horror that anyone could destroy or remove sacred votive images, anger at what had been done and a determination to resacralise the buildings and objects that had been defiled. In Rouen, violent anti-Calvinist sermons in 1561 in the wake of iconoclasm encouraged Catholics to attack houses that showed no decorations for Corpus Christi Day and to hold public meetings to reaffirm their own faith. In one case, feelings ran so high that when a youth refused to genuflect before a statue in front of which bands of children were accustomed to sing *Ave Maris Stella* in the evening, he was attacked with his own tennis racket and had his collar bone broken (see Chapter 8 for a more detailed discussion of confessional conflict as a source of urban disorder).

Added impetus was given to Catholic urban piety by changes in confraternities. These devotional organisations to enable laymen to achieve salvation by gaining merit had been commonplace throughout Europe during the Middle Ages, in both urban and rural communities, but the late sixteenth century witnessed a major change in their nature and operation. There was a widespread move, particularly on the part of the Jesuits, to sever confraternities from occupational groups and from churches and chapels whose patron saints had been a subject of veneration and to focus instead on the central images of the Counter-Reformation Church in a deliberate attempt to counter Protestant ideas. Confraternities took the names of images, such as the Holy Sacrament, the Trinity, the Holy Blood and the Holy Cross. Many focused their devotions specifically upon the adoration of the Virgin. They opened their doors, at least temporarily, to women and became both an important part of the cultural lives of their towns and an alternative focus of social solidarities. Their numbers increased rapidly. The Marian congregation in Antwerp had only 320 married men as members in 1612. By 1637, membership had risen to 700, while in Cologne, numbers of confraternity members doubled between 1608 and 1654. Between 1612, the year in which the confraternity of Santa Maria de Victoria was founded by the Jesuits in the Bavarian town of Ingolstadt, and 1633, the number of confraternities rose from one to six.

Relating the level of religiosity to an individual's social status is not easy. Much of the evidence about the ownership of religious books, votive objects and paintings is provided by inventories, which by their very nature tended to be drawn up only when the property left behind was valuable enough to list. Similarly, the use of religious formulae in the preamble to wills, which has often been seen as a measure of growing piety in the sixteenth and seventeenth centuries, is not as reliable as it seems. With the exception of the wealthy, who were sufficiently versed in the language to impose their own ideas on a will, most testators were more than willing to leave the wording up to the notary whom they had called in for the purpose.

These considerations should not prevent us from asking whether the increase in religiosity extended below the circles of the wealthy. The high level of urban literacy among both Protestants and Catholics gave them access to the Bible and devotional texts. In Montpellier in 1574–76, two-thirds of all artisans could sign their names on notarial documents. In the Paris of the first half of the seventeenth century, 86 per cent of all men and 58 per cent of all women signed their wills. In two London parishes for which there are reasonably reliable figures, there was a literacy rate of 72 per cent. The growing number of religious publications in print listed at the Frankfurt am Main book fair also testified to a growth in urban literacy.

The social background of men and women engaged in Reformation movements or Counter-Reformation movements also indicates a much broader social base. French Calvinism seems to have attracted a wide urban social following. In Lyon, almost every level of society was represented among their ranks, although there was a tendency for Calvinists to be members of newer occupations or of those undergoing change, rather than lawyers and senior judicial officers. Many intermediate office-holders did show some sympathy for Calvinism. In Dijon, the majority of artisans remained Catholics, but there was a clear geographical concentration of Calvinist artisans in certain streets.

Supporters of the Lutheran and Zwinglian Reformations were drawn from an equally wide social spectrum. While merchants, students, printers, clergymen and friars were often among the first to discuss evangelical ideas, they were taken up rapidly by artisans in general. A similar pattern applied to English Puritans. If this term is taken to include everyone who saw themselves among the more committed Protestants in the Church of England in the later sixteenth and seventeenth centuries, then there does not seem to have been any monopoly of these ideas among urban élites, although members of the élite in towns such as Bristol and Salisbury were strongly attracted to Puritan ideas. Once again, the spread of literacy enabled a much broader range of men and women to gain access to religious tracts and to the Bible.

It was only to be expected that the degree of commitment and devotional enthusiasm that marked the sixteenth century during the Reformation and the earlier stages of the Counter-Reformation would wane as religious conflicts and the excitement of the new began to fade away. In almost every urban society, Lutheran, Calvinist, Anglican and Catholic alike, active participation by lay people in religious life at the end of the seventeenth century came to be the preserve of urban élites and those just below them in society. This situation came about chiefly because the authoritarian nature of each official religion was linked to a political authoritarianism, which those lower down in society were unable to share. While the earlier part of the period had seen a flowering of popular religion, once religious organisations became fully established, they created their own orthodoxies from which the faithful were not permitted to deviate.

The religious procession had been one of the most enduring examples of mass participation in civic and religious culture. One description of a procession of the Holy Sacrament held in the Netherlands in the early sixteenth century records that the street surface was repaired and cleaned along the processional route. Houses were abundantly decorated and, during the procession, lighted candles were placed in open doors. The procession itself was headed by the guilds, followed by three girls, representing St Mary, the Magdalene and St Barbara, a young knight as St George in the act of killing the dragon, three militia companies, churchmen, barefoot penitents and a litter carrying the holy sacrament surrounded by the town musicians. The laity completed the procession. Ignace Chavatte's description of the same procession in Lille at the end of the seventeenth century contains some significant differences. The procession was now led by the militia companies as a precaution against violence. They were followed by the guilds, who presented certain tableaux of legendary and biblical scenes, but while these had been complemented in the past by tableaux presented by groups from the quarters of the city through which the procession passed, this role had now been taken over by the Jesuits. The council's restrictions on unruly behaviour suggest that this was becoming quite commonplace and was almost certainly a reaction by the common people to their exclusion from the procession. All people of improper status were forbidden to mingle in the ranks of the councillors and clergy. No drinks were to be offered to those taking part in the procession. Anyone found slowing down or breaking up the procession was to be fined. In mid-seventeenth-century Paris, chains were placed across all streets adjoining the route of the procession on Ascension Day.

In spite of all these restrictions, some degree of religiosity remained lower down in society. It is a measure of the success of religious education that so many confraternities remained in existence for artisans as well as rentiers. Two of the four Marian congregations in Antwerp at the end of the sixteenth century were intended for unmarried artisans and French-speaking artisans, respectively. Ignace Chavatte, one of the poorer master weavers in Lille in the last two decades of the seventeenth century, has left a diary redolent of an active religious life. He not only went to mass on Sunday, he attended Vespers, visited churches in other parishes and attended sermons in the churches of the mendicant orders close to his home, as well as taking an enthusiastic part in his confraternity.

Simon Schama has demonstrated to great effect how the Calvinist church succeeded in transforming Dutch culture in the seventeenth century. Even if this culture may be said to have been transmitted from above, it was fully accepted as part of the identity of all residents of the United Provinces. The culture of the Scottish lowlands was equally marked by the Calvinist tradition, if not to the same degree of artistic endeavour.

One may conclude that the Reformation and Counter-Reformation had far-reaching effects on the culture of European towns and that, even if most people no longer took an active part in thinking for themselves, the intellectual framework within which they acted was clear and influential.

Religious minorities and the urban community

In one way, the Reformation was a failure. In spite of their heartfelt expectations, neither the church based on Papal authority nor any one of the variants of Protestantism that held sway in different towns succeeded in gaining a total European monopoly of faith. Instead, each church was faced with a world in which there was a multiplicity of Christian belief, with which it had to come to terms, and, even more important, many were faced with the presence in their own towns of men and women who did not share the majority religion. Some were Catholics who remained in towns where Protestantism had been introduced. Others were Protestants, who had not been sufficiently numerous or influential to bring about religious change and yet chose to stay on in their native town. In other towns, the economic and political vicissitudes of the later sixteenth and seventeenth centuries had encouraged people to settle in towns whose majority religion they did not share.

The geographical distribution of religious minorities was fairly uneven. In spite of two attempts to draw the religious frontiers of Europe at the Peace of Augsburg in 1555 and the Treaties of Westphalia in 1648, Protestant or Catholic minorities continued to live in many of the larger German towns. In England, few towns outside London contained substantial Catholic minorities; the conditions for open recusancy were more promising under the patronage of influential rural landowners. In France, there was widespread support for Calvinism among the towns of south-western and western France in the second half of the sixteenth century, as well as in Paris. The rapid changes in political control in the Netherlands in the last third of the sixteenth century created a situation in which a Calvinist minority came to rule over a majority of Catholics in the countryside and a minority of Catholics, Lutherans and Protestant sects in the towns. The numbers of Protestant sympathisers in Italy and Spain were very small in contrast. To complicate matters even further, the presence in many towns of Jewish communities as both residents and migrants raised questions about the toleration of religious minority groups, which were both of long standing and, in the light of Christian heterodoxy, quite new.

Religious co-existence, however tenuous, became the hallmark of many European towns in the century and a half that followed the Peace of Augsburg. The existence of religious toleration or at least the toleration of others who did not share the majority religion in a town raises a general question about the extent to which non-religious factors influenced the perception and treatment of minorities by members of the host societies and their governing bodies, and a secondary question about the extent to which these relationships were pacific and co-operative rather than conflictual. An analysis of the experience of four religious minorities in the towns of early modern Europe, Lutherans, Calvinists, Catholics and Jews, suggests that it was not so much the religious beliefs of each minority that influenced their treatment as their social status, economic activity and the extent to which the religious orthodoxy of the host community over-rode other considerations.

These relationships also need to be seen in the context of the religious changes of the sixteenth century. A distinction needs to be made between two phases of religious diversity, a fluid phase and a flexible phase. The fluid phase could be said to be the period of time in which communities were first confronted by the presence of a minority of men and women who actively dissented from the prevailing religious trend. This was an experience for which there were no precedents and, although the urban authorities attempted to contain potential sources of disruption by using well-tried methods of mediation and social control before turning to force, supporters of both confessions at many levels of society became involved in actions arising out of feelings of anger, fear and an intense identification with their religious beliefs.

This fluid phase of religious diversity was relatively short-lived, lasting for years rather than decades. It was succeeded fairly rapidly by a flexible phase, which was characterised by a recognition of the presence of distinct religious minorities in many towns and of the need to formulate strict rules controlling their status and their rights to practise their religion in private and in public. Perhaps 'flexible' is not the best term to apply to a situation in which the authorities belonging to the majority confession came to terms with the presence of religious minorities in their midst. Reading the rhetoric of the clergy about other confessional groups certainly leaves the impression that intercommunal relations were characterised by rigidity, but the detailed experience of religious minorities suggests that the influence of the clergy had its limits when faced by more secular imperatives.

There were substantial Lutheran minorities in many German towns. For much of the second half of the sixteenth century, the Lutherans of episcopal Bamberg remained a significant element in urban society. Although a second attempt to introduce Protestantism had failed in the 1550s, 14 per cent of all householders in the parish of St Martin were still Lutherans in 1596, and 21 per cent of all marriages were either between Lutherans or involved one Lutheran partner. After the early departure of the leaders of the Protestant movement, those of their supporters who remained in Bamberg were allowed to worship freely and even to eat meat on Fridays as long as these activities were carried out in private in order to avoid provocation. In Ingolstadt in Bavaria, which lay close to the border with the Protestant Palatinate, sermons were given in the 1560s in the houses of cabinetmakers, tailors, brewers, barbers and bookbinders. Students appear to have spoken freely about religion in their lodgings and to have eaten meat on Fridays and feast days. There were also constant cases of refusals to take the sacraments. In spite of pressure from the territorial authorities in Munich, the Ingolstadt town council took the line of least resistance until the last years of the sixteenth century, pursuing booksellers while permitting Bible reading in private, and restricting applications for burgher status to Catholic immigrants while allowing existing Lutheran burghers to retain their positions in society.

Similar differences in emphasis between territorial and urban authorities took place in Münster. An archiepiscopal seat, the city had come to European notoriety in 1535 when a Lutheran regime was replaced by a group of Anabaptists before the city was recaptured by Catholic forces. Unlike Bamberg or Ingolstadt, Münster had experienced a Lutheran Reformation, and a substantial minority of Lutherans, including several councillors, returned to the city upon the defeat of the Anabaptists. The failure of successive Prince-Archbishops to remove these Lutherans from positions of influence in Münster until the 1580s was both a sign of their own inability to pay for an army to force their will on the local council and a reflection of the strength of feeling within the community in favour of peaceful co-existence. Protecting the right of Lutherans to live and worship in the city became a watchword for the defence of civic privileges from incursions by the territorial lord. Church services were conducted as a mixture of Catholic tradition and Lutheran hymns. Immigration by Lutheran artisans was encouraged as a way of rebuilding the city's economy.

The ending of toleration in Bamberg, Ingolstadt, Münster and many other German towns in the last 20 years of the sixteenth century coincided with the first effective wave of the Counter-Reformation. The work of the Jesuits, in particular in education, preaching and the general encouragement of Catholic piety, led to an end to open toleration of Lutherans. In Münster, the Jesuits replaced all the teachers at the cathedral school with their own men. Most of the staff had been tinged with Lutheranism, and the Jesuits now introduced a deliberate campaign to win over the sons of Lutherans. On the other hand, the decline in toleration was also closely linked to the decline in the economy. Artisans in competition for work in a declining labour market were all too ready to find fault with non-Catholics.

Even in those cities where strict confessional parity was the official policy of the city council, religious and economic factors worked in favour of Catholics over Lutherans. Augsburg is the best-known example, although the Treaty of Westphalia also recognised parity in Kaufbeuren, Dinkelsbühl, Ravensburg and Biberach. Lutheran and Catholic worship took place freely, and all offices were shared equally or rotated. The result was three overlapping phenomena, parallel religious lives, converging economic activity and a slow demographic erosion of the position of the Lutherans, which transformed them into a minority group. The two communities kept themselves to themselves, spurred on by the presence of the rival confession to find ways of making themselves distinctive. Characteristic first names, separate cemeteries and styles in women's clothing all served to keep them apart. On the other hand, both groups contributed to the city's economy, and it was not unusual to find Protestant goldsmiths and engravers supplying the Catholic community with votive images. Almost imperceptibly, however, the Lutherans found themselves in a minority in the later seventeenth century as the numbers of Catholics were swelled by immigration from a largely Catholic hinterland.

No single pattern applied to Calvinist minorities in European towns. They belonged to three distinct groups, French Huguenots, German Calvinist immigrants and English Dissenters. The Huguenots became an official minority with the passage of the Edict of Nantes in 1598. Calvinist settlement in Germany was also largely a phenomenon of the later sixteenth and seventeenth centuries, while the official exclusion of the Dissenters from the Church of England only dated from the Corporation Act of 1661.

Officially, the position of French Calvinist townsmen was defined by the Edict of Nantes, which was renewed upon the accession of Louis XIII and Louis XIV, before it was revoked in 1685. This was far from a confirmation of the religious *status quo* at the end of the sixteenth century. All buildings and revenues belonging to the Catholic church, which had been taken over by Calvinists during the wars and used as places of worship and sources of income, were to be restored at once. While Calvinists were free to live wherever they wished, public worship was only permitted in a limited number of towns, from which Paris was expressly excluded. They were forbidden to proselytise among children (the same conditions applied to Catholics). Cultural primacy was given to the Catholic church. No Calvinist was allowed to work or open a shop on Catholic festivals – a source of provocation during the Wars of Religion. All Calvinist marriages had to be contracted according to the laws of the Catholic church.

On the other hand, in the spirit of political reconciliation, the Edict banned all discrimination against Calvinists wishing to enter universities, schools or colleges and opened all political offices as well as membership of the *parlements* to all appropriate candidates notwithstanding their religion. Special courts of law were established to try cases involving Calvinists, and the fortifications of towns, such as La Rochelle and Montpellier, which had been at the core of the Huguenot military movement, were allowed to remain untouched. Some of the restrictions on the practice of the Calvinist faith were also mitigated by a series of secret articles negotiated with the Huguenot leaders.

The history of the relationship between French Calvinists and the Crown in the seventeenth century took place less in the context of the Edict of Nantes than in spite of it and was the product of the interplay between local conditions and royal policy. Once their final stronghold at La Rochelle had fallen in 1630, all Calvinist minorities were open to a variety of pressures from the monarchy, local Catholic officials and the Catholic church, a process that has been referred to by one author as 'the time of asphyxiation'. Just as toleration of the Lutherans in German Catholic towns ended in the final years of the sixteenth century because of the resurgence of the Counter-Reformation, Calvinist freedom of worship in France became increasingly difficult in the face of a Catholic church in the full flood of expansion. Sermons were preached against them, encouraging the local populace to disrupt Calvinist services. Wealthy Calvinist townsmen found that their religious affiliation prevented them from promoting the interests of their sons in the pursuit of royal office because of their religion. The judicial rights of individual Calvinists were whittled away through lawsuits brought against them in courts that favoured Catholics. Calvinist churches were closed down on the grounds that they had been opened in contravention of the Edict of Nantes, even though in some cases they had been built on territory that had not been part of the French monarchy in 1598. Finally, in the 1680s, troops were billeted on Calvinist households in the expectation that acts of violence and harassment would put pressure on them to convert. As a result of these so-called *dragonnades*, between 300 000 and 400 000 Calvinists converted to Catholicism in the 1680s. The size of the Huguenot community had already fallen in the previous two decades because of widespread emigration, on the one hand, and conversions to Catholicism among the young, on the other, who saw this as the only way in which to become fully integrated in French society.

Limitations on the freedom of worship in Catholic France and the southern Netherlands gave rise to a new phenomenon, the presence of Calvinist immigrants in German cities that had been Lutheran for two or three generations. There were no ground rules for dealing with Calvinists. Until the Treaty of Westphalia, Calvinism had no official status in the empire. On the other hand, it was now a political and religious reality in western Europe. Not only had the Calvinists established their confession as the official religion of the newly independent United Provinces of the Netherlands, within Germany itself a whole series of free imperial cities, Emden, Wesel, Aachen and Bremen, had become Calvinist, and they were to be followed by the Elector Palatine and his subjects.

The degree to which Calvinist migrants were accepted in German cities seems to have been in proportion to their contribution to the economy. In seventeenth-century Hamburg, most of the Calvinists were merchants of Dutch origin who were subsequently joined by Huguenot exiles. They were welcomed by members of the city's élite with whom they intermarried and many of whose values they shared, even if they did not subscribe to the same religion. In order not to antagonise pro-Lutheran sentiment, they worshipped in Stade, which lay beyond the city's jurisdiction. A further compromise was reached when the council arranged for Calvinists to be buried in the cathedral, which lay outside the jurisdiction of the city's Lutheran clergy. The clergy had always been suspicious of any move that might endanger the integrity of a social order that was tightly linked to the Lutheran Reformation of 1529, but, as in the case of other religious minorities in Hamburg, their views carried less weight than economic imperatives. Open Calvinist worship in the city itself remained a problem until the exigencies of European politics allowed the Dutch ambassador, and later the representative of the Great Elector, to take them under their protection and offer facilities for services in their houses.

Hamburg was unusual in that it was one of the few imperial free cities to experience economic expansion in the seventeenth century. Most of its neighbours suffered from declining economies and, in consequence, asserted laws against religious minorities with considerable rigour. More favourable conditions were offered by territorial rulers, such as the kings of Denmark and the Electors of Brandenburg Prussia, who recognised the advantages to their plans for economic expansion. The same may be said for the Calvinist Electors Palatine, who built and subsequently rebuilt the prosperity of their capital at Mannheim on economically motivated toleration of religious minorities. Lutherans, Catholics and Calvinists were all encouraged to settle in Mannheim, the only stipulations being that they offered a skill that was in demand or brought capital and commercial connections with them. These criteria did not change when a junior Catholic branch of the ruling family in the Palatinate acceded to the electorate in 1685 and Catholicism became the official state religion. Calvinists and Lutherans continued to worship and work without restrictions.

The circumstances that created a Calvinist minority in England were political rather than religious. The diversity of belief and practice within the Church of England since its re-establishment in 1560 had enabled people with widely differing religious views and practices to remain part of the official Anglican church until at least the 1630s. While fragmentation within the Church of England increasingly polarised extreme Puritans and purist Arminians, there is evidence that every effort was being made by the monarchy to maintain a single Protestant church. If we leave aside the religious turmoil of the civil wars and Interregnum, official discrimination against groups to the left of the church did not take place until the Restoration of Charles II in 1660. The newly elected 'Cavalier' Parliament, which was heavily dominated by High Anglicans, introduced legislation to put two of the more radical religious groups, the Presbyterians and the Independents, beyond the pale of the church. Strong Dissenter minorities manifested themselves in Norwich, Bristol, Taunton, Gloucester and Dover. The legislation of 1661 was not intended primarily to discriminate against the Dissenters, but to exclude men from political office who were known to have strong political and religious links with the Protectorate. The Corporation Act of 1661 obliged all candidates for political office, in towns as elsewhere, to take an oath of loyalty, which included a declaration that they had taken the sacrament according to the rites of the Church of England during the past 12 months.

However, as in the cases of Lutherans in Bavaria and Münster and Calvinists in Hamburg, the force of national discriminatory legislation in England was mitigated by local circumstances. The commissioners appointed by the monarch in Norwich were lenient over candidatures for office from men known to have Dissenting sympathies. It is not absolutely clear why this should be so, but it seems that the size of the urban community in Norwich played a part in this. With a population of around 29 000, Norwich was the second largest city in England, with a long tradition of harbouring foreign exiles and of contacts with the Netherlands. Neighbouring Yarmouth, where the Act was applied much more rigorously, was only a third of its size. The tolerance accorded to Dissenting office-holders in Norwich was extended to religious practice. Conventicles were held in and around the town, numbering sometimes as many as 300 people. Little attempt was made to hinder them, either by the magistrates or by the bishop, who was known to have Dissenting sympathies. It was only in the late 1670s, when a new and enthusiastic Anglican Lord Lieutenant of Norfolk, Lord Yarmouth, began to enforce the law against Dissenters in earnest that toleration came to a temporary end.

The position of Catholic minorities in European urban society was much less clearly defined at the outset than that of either the Lutherans or the Calvinists. This was a reflection of the tentative way in which the Reformation was introduced in many towns. Many urban governments followed a policy of minimal change to meet the demands for evangelical forms of religious expression. They were hesitant to forbid religious practices that had been deeply rooted in urban culture, even if they recognised the need to install new clergy, and took the opportunity to close most religious foundations and put their buildings to other uses. The sensitivity with which many members of cathedral chapters, friars, monks and nuns were treated by the newly Protestant urban authorities underlined the latter's unwillingness to make a complete break with the past.

In Strasbourg, in spite of the Reformation Edict of 1534, the cathedral chapter continued to be recognised in law. The Teutonic Knights, the Knights of St John and the Carthusians, as well as the Dominican nuns of St Margaret and St Nicholas and the Penitents of St Mary Magdalene continued to celebrate mass. Mass was also held in private houses. In Calvinist Emden, the parish church was shared equally between the Catholics and the Calvinists until the 1540s. Masses were celebrated at an altar standing next to a table used for evangelical communion and, even when these practices ended, Catholic services continued for a further decade in a Franciscan priory.

The Reformation settlement of 1560 in Aberdeen was interpreted as conservatively as possible. People drawn from every level of society remained members of the Catholic church, while attending Protestant services. In a solution that combined diplomacy with pragmatism, a chapel outside Aberdeen was put to use as a lighthouse. A former priest was invited to become the lighthouse keeper. The city now had a new lighthouse and a place within convenient walking distance to which Catholics could go for worship.

The enthusiasm with which the Aberdeen élite found an accommodation for its Catholic members in order to avoid open dispute was matched in Colmar in 1575, when the political problems of introducing a Reformation very late by comparison with other German towns were solved by guaranteeing the political position, economic power, status and religious beliefs of Catholic members of the élite. In the Dutch province of Holland, although political pressures obliged a number of Catholic families to resign from town councils, this was on the understanding that their replacements would also be Catholic members of the élite.

The position of the Catholic minority in seventeenth-century Hamburg resembled that of the Calvinists. No substantial rump of Catholics had remained in the city after the Reformation, and the Catholics who lived there in the seventeenth century were immigrant merchants from the Mediterranean who had come to Hamburg to take advantage of its economic expansion. Like the Calvinists, too, the Catholic community gained spiritual solace through the intervention of outside diplomatic representatives. The

Imperial Resident employed a number of Jesuits as his chaplains, and it was under his auspices that a building was constructed in 1682 to provide a chapel for the Catholic community. Once again, the interests of the city's Lutheran clergy were set to one side in favour of economic and political benefits to the secular community.

The numbers of Catholics in English towns after the Reformation remain unknown, for obvious reasons, but there is persistent evidence that, despite the savage anti-Catholic legislation of the 1580s, little was done to persecute urban recusants. On the contrary, much evidence suggests that there continued to be strong sympathies for the ideas and rituals of the old church. Even when vestments, stained glass and statues were removed from churches, members of the local community took them into safe keeping or bought them in case they should ever be needed again. Catholic traditions also persisted in the celebration of the Feasts of St Katharine and St Clement in later sixteenth-century Bristol.

While the ways in which Lutheran, Calvinist, and Catholic minorities were treated by their host communities reveal a great deal about the latter's preoccupations and the reasons why some forms of toleration were socially acceptable, the diversity of responses to members of religious minority groups can be seen even more clearly in the case of resident Jewish communities. Jewish communities were the European urban religious minorities *par excellence*. Many towns chose to exclude Jewish residence altogether. Jews were allowed in during the day to do business but were expected to live elsewhere. Jewish visitors to Lübeck lived under the protection of the Duke of Holstein, the lord of neighbouring Moisling. Many Jewish visitors to Münster, where they were unwelcome residents after 1562, lived in Hamm, which lay within the territory of the Prince-Archbishop but not within the jurisdiction of the city itself.

Jewish settlement was officially prohibited in England until 1656, and in Spain and Portugal from the late fifteenth and early sixteenth centuries. Elsewhere, a minority of towns in Germany, Italy and the Netherlands officially admitted Jews within their walls and consequently developed policies towards them as a religious minority. These policies, for all those characteristics that were specific to the treatment of Jews within a Christian urban society, bore a distinct family resemblance to those that were applied to Christian minorities.

The most important contrast between the treatment of Christian minorities and the Jews lay in the relative precariousness of the position of Jewish communities. Excluded from Christian society, there was always the danger that religious antipathies would outweigh the usefulness of their economic role and that they would have to either flee in the wake of an anti-Semitic riot or move on because the authorities had chosen to expel them. Nor was permission to settle in a town necessarily definitive. In 1535, Jews were invited by the Bishop of Münster to take up temporary residence permits subject to annual renewal, but they were immediately expelled by the city council upon his death in 1562. In 1572, Emmanuel Filibert, the Duke of Savoy, attracted Sephardi Jews to settle in Nice in order to develop its Levant trade by promising to protect them from any proceedings taken against them by the church for having once lived in the guise of Christians. Only 13 months later, he had to bow to pressure from Spain and the Papacy and give the Jewish community six months' notice to quit.

Three groups responded to the presence of the Jews as an urban minority, the city or territorial authorities, the clergy, and the population in general. While these reactions were frequently contradictory, the interplay between them shaped the conditions in which Jews were able to settle. The ultimate decision whether to admit or expel Jews lay in the hands of the political authorities, but they were both subject to considerable pressures from the church and had to take into account the potential dangers to public order of economic and religious anti-Semitism from the mass of the population. These factors were as valid whether the urban authorities chose to enclose the Jewish community in a ghetto in order to achieve the greatest possible separation between Jews and Christians or allowed them to settle in the town according to more limited restrictions.

Restrictions on the areas to be inhabited by Jews and on the kind of clothing they were permitted to wear were commonplace during the Middle Ages, but it was not until 1516 that a ghetto in the classic sense was first established in Venice. The Venetian ghetto went on to become both an enduring symbol of the determination of a Catholic state to separate the Jews from its Christian subjects and a model enthusiastically taken up by urban authorities elsewhere, primarily in Italy and the German-speaking territories. The ghetto may be seen as part of a practice by the urban authorities of enclosing those, such as lepers, beggars and prostitutes, whose presence threatened the order of urban society. The principle was the same everywhere. A small area of land was set aside for exclusive Jewish residence. In Venice, it lay in the parish of S Geremia on the edge of the city. Venetian Jews were given freedom to work outside the ghetto in order to carry out activities that the state believed complemented those offered by Christians. In Venice, these included a pawnbroking service, which was restricted to such low rates of interest that it was run at a loss, a heavy involvement in the second-hand trade, as well as small numbers of musicians, physicians and long-distance merchants. In early seventeenth-century Frankfurt am Main, legislation known as the *Stättigkeit* limited interest charged by Jewish money-lenders to a rate of 8 per cent. As in Venice, they were prevented from engaging in productive activities that might compete with the guilds, and the rule that only burghers could open retail shops obliged them to peddle second-hand goods in the streets.

At nightfall and during Christian religious festivals, Jews were obliged to remain within the confines of the ghetto, which were guarded by men employed by the state but paid for by the Jewish community. Within the confines of the ghetto, the Jewish community was allowed to run its own affairs. A board of elders acted as intermediaries between the state and the community, but there was general acquiescence in the open practice of ritual and of Jewish life in general, as long as it was carried out within the *cordon sanitaire*. As a result, Jewish cultural activities developed on a scale larger than anything known since the 'Golden Age' in medieval Spain. It is something of an irony that, in religious matters, greater toleration was accorded to the Jews in ghettos than to any community living in conditions of relative freedom or, for that matter, to any Christian minority. The obligation to live in ghettos also accentuated a strong desire on the part of Jewish communities themselves to remain apart from their Christian neighbours. For all the evidence of business, social and cultural contacts between Jews and Christians, centuries of living in dangerous conditions imposed by a Christian society enhanced a very strong cultural identity and, while the Reformation and the Counter-Reformation engendered increased attempts at conversion, these were often counterproductive.

These ghetto restrictions were not entirely effective. While the urban authorities successfully confined religious practice to the ghetto, they were unable to prevent Jews from engaging in economic activities from which they were prohibited or from wearing clothes that enabled them to merge with the local population in the streets.

The increase in the numbers of Jews resident in centres, such as Frankfurt am Main, as the result of migration not only placed strains on the accommodation available to them in the ghettos, it also obliged Jews to take up occupations that were in direct competition with Christians. The obligation to restrict trading to second-hand goods had never been taken particularly seriously in Venice. Levantine Jews had frequent and profitable trading links with their co-religionists in the Ottoman Empire and, therefore, constituted both an important economic link with the eastern Mediterranean and a valuable additional source of Jewish income, which could be taxed by the state. There was a very thin dividing line between this kind of trade and others, and religion does not seem to have been a barrier to the kind of business relationships, such as the partnership in the silk trade set up in 1660 between Salamon Annobuono and the wealthy and high-status Procurator of St Mark's, Almoro Tiepolo di Domenico. In Frankfurt am Main, the competition between Jewish and Christian retailers became the subject of much contention. While working within the rules, which obliged them to sell goods on the streets only, Jewish retailers took the opportunity to undercut the prices that Christian shopkeepers asked of the large numbers of soldiers passing through the city during the Thirty Years War. As in Venice, the advantages to the city council of a prosperous Jewish community capable of carrying a heavier tax burden ran counter to the economic interests of the burghers. The compromises of the later seventeenth century pleased no one, but they did leave the door open for a Jewish economic expansion outside the ghetto.

The case of Frankfurt am Main is an example of how difficult it is to make a clear distinction between towns that imposed ghetto restrictions on their Jewish communities and those that allowed them a limited amount of freedom. Political and economic imperatives above all dictated whether Jews were permitted to stay in a town and, if so, whether they could stay in the long term. The same recognition of the Jews' economic utility affected urban and territorial authorities alike. Like the Calvinists, Jews were encouraged to settle by territorial rulers as part of their plans to develop new trading centres. Successive Popes attracted Jews to Ancona. The Grand Dukes of Tuscany followed the same policy in relation to Livorno (Leghorn). In the late seventeenth century, Frederick William of Prussia invited Jews to settle in Memel as part of his plans to rival the eastern Baltic port of Königsberg. Economic warfare also benefited the Jews of Glückstadt when Christian IV of Denmark gave his support to the Emperor during the Thirty Years War.

Permission to settle in a town and contribute to its economy was necessarily bound by precautionary restrictions. The fundamental principles that identified Jews as outside the pale of the Christian community remained everywhere. They might be given commercial privileges, but there was very little religious toleration in the modern sense. Hamburg and Amsterdam, both of which had benefited from the settlement of Marrano Jews from Spain and Portugal in search of commercial opportunities, did introduce slow and grudging measures of religious toleration. In Hamburg, it was not until 1650 that the city council gave official permission to the Sephardi Jews to hold services in private. In Amsterdam, the authorities also discriminated between the wealthy Sephardi Jewish merchants and the poor Ashkenazi immigrants from the east. The Sephardim were eventually allowed to build a synagogue in 1639. More important than the visible presence of Jewish worship in public were the unofficial accommodations made by many civic authorities, who controlled virulently anti-Semitic preachers, while failing to prosecute Jews for contravening restrictions on their economic activities. In the Netherlands, too, pictorial representations of the Jews lost their stereotyped form and may be seen as part of a series of artistic genres, which spanned sacred and secular subjects.

Philosophical arguments in favour of religious toleration in post-Reformation Europe carried little weight in urban centres. The clergy remained as implacably opposed to Christians of other confessions as before. The Jews continued to have no place in a Christian society, not even in the Netherlands, where the Calvinists regarded themselves as the true Children of the Covenant. The sequel to the religious bitterness and violence of the sixteenth century was often discriminatory pressure, which led to the departure or conversion of many members of minority groups.

This is not to suggest that religious differences ceased to matter when economic or political imperatives were dominant or that religious minority groups were assimilated in urban society to the point that they gave up many of their distinctive practices and attitudes. It would be better to speak of a spectrum of toleration ranging from permission to erect churches and synagogues for public worship, as in the case of Dissenting chapels in late seventeenth-century England and the synagogues in the Italian ghettos, to the tacit acceptance that members of minority groups could settle temporarily in order to trade in an urban centre without privileges or official recognition. The point along the spectrum at which host communities tolerated religious minorities and the limits to that toleration depended on many factors. Members of religious minority groups who were long-term urban residents with strong social and economic links with members of the majority religion were often in a strong position until they were displaced by external ideological forces. The experience of Lutheran and Calvinist minorities in Germany was fairly positive until the Counter-Reformation movement began to gain momentum in the last years of the sixteenth century. Elsewhere, immigrant religious groups were tolerated in those urban centres that were experiencing rapid economic expansion both because they represented little threat to jobs and because they were part of a broader movement of betterment migration, which created a heterodox society. Here, of course, the distinction needs to be made between city states, such as Hamburg and Amsterdam, where opportunist immigration was largely uncontrolled, and centres in territorial states, such as the Grand Duchy of Tuscany or the Palatinate, where a deliberate policy of controlled immigration was introduced. The converse was also the case. Religious toleration was far less common in urban centres experiencing economic stagnation or decline, and there is a close correlation between discriminatory attitudes and time of economic difficulty in those towns in which religious minorities had been tolerated. The growing hostility of local artisans towards the Jews in Frankfurt am Main is a case in point.

The treatment of religious minorities also had implications for the unity of urban communities. In many cases, adherents of the minority religion were members of the élite. As such, they had close links with the urban authorities through marriage, common business interests and a common cultural perspective. There was frequently a contradiction between the severity of discriminatory laws and the unwillingness of the urban authorities to apply them with any enthusiasm. This was as valid in late seventeenth-century Coventry as it was in Münster in the 1560s. Where discriminatory policies were applied as the result of outside pressure, this created considerable strains, with the élite and families belonging to the majority confession often placing social considerations above those of the state. This said, it is necessary to ask whether the persistence of religious diversity within urban society represented the end of communal unity. The answer to this question is dependent on the extent to which the forces leading to social disunity inherent in conditions of religious heterodoxy were over-ridden by economic relationships. It is also necessary to make one final point. Peaceful co-existence between religious minority groups and their host communities was constantly in danger of being brought to an end. The experience of Jewish communities is instructive but was not limited to them alone. There were many cases in which lengthy periods of peaceful co-existence with their hosts could be interrupted if not ended by outbreaks of violence, such as the Bamberg pogrom in 1699. What took place in Bamberg is indicative of the potential speed with which the very conditions that had encouraged economic co-operation with and tacit toleration of religious minorities of all kinds could be overturned.

THE CHALLENGES
OF CHANGE

6

The urban fabric

The environment in which most townspeople lived changed little during the sixteenth and seventeenth centuries. Most towns retained their medieval street plans and the majority of their buildings for very practical reasons. There was no incentive on the part of landlords to build new houses because, in spite of the demographic pressure of increasing numbers of new arrivals, few immigrants had the resources with which to pay for fashionable new accommodation. Besides, the spatial organisation of the town, which had been developed during the Middle Ages, continued to serve the economic, social and spiritual needs of the population. Nor were many urban governments in a position to expend large sums of money to improve conditions. The economic stagnation of most towns and the priority given to military expenditure on new fortifications and additional troops at times when the towns' very existence seemed to be under threat meant that little money was available for extensive civilian town planning.

In the minority of towns in which these conditions did not prevail, a number of important changes to the urban environment took place, which were imitated later by other towns in the eighteenth and early nineteenth centuries. The pace was set initially during the sixteenth century by those centres experiencing major economic expansion through international trade or industrial production, but the most significant changes to the urban fabric were initiated in capital cities and administrative centres and did not take place until much later. There was a marked contrast between Ulm, where urban development was frozen by an economic downturn in the mid-sixteenth century, and Turin, where the capital of Savoy was largely transformed into a baroque city in the last quarter of the seventeenth century and became a model for Vienna, Prague and many German towns during the next hundred years.

Five separate but related changes took place to the urban fabric during the sixteenth and seventeenth centuries:

- New buildings or buildings with remodelled frontages were inserted into the existing urban fabric.
- The existing urban fabric was modified as the result of the construction of new ecclesiastical buildings, town halls, mansions for the wealthy and the remodelling of squares and major thoroughfares.
- Extensive new fortifications were constructed, which protected towns in strategically sensitive areas, while enclosing large tracts of land that could be used for housing.
- Entirely new residential quarters were built beyond the existing urban area to provide homes and facilities for resident nobles, office-holders and lawyers.
- On a very small scale by comparison with the twelfth and thirteenth centuries, a number of new towns were planted by territorial rulers, mostly for military or ceremonial purposes.

This discussion of the early modern European urban fabric and its modification falls into four main sections: the nature of the existing urban fabric and the factors that discouraged urban development in so many centres; modifications to the existing urban fabric; the construction of new fortifications and its implications; and the development of new urban quarters.

The medieval inheritance

At the beginning of the sixteenth century, urban settlement in western Europe had well-established characteristics. Each town had a well-defined street plan, laid out in some cases along a grid plan inherited from the Romans and in others following lines dictated by topography and the patchwork ownership of the land upon which houses had been built. Broader streets linked the gates in the walls with important buildings serving political, economic or ecclesiastical functions. Paved open spaces of variable shape and size provided the setting for commercial activities, religious processions or public gatherings of burghers. It was customary to find a concentration of the largest and most imposing buildings clustered together in the centre of the town. Where the town was located on the coast or on a navigable river, there were well-developed port facilities, once again linked to centres of commercial activity. Fortifications, consisting of a high stone wall or walls bounded by a water-filled ditch, were still very common, although several Italian towns were already endowed with the bastions and earthworks which were to become so common elsewhere later on. While the walls marked the symbolic limits to towns, they had not prevented the evolution of suburbs beyond them nor the establishment of a scattering of more isolated buildings, taverns, convents and mills, which had been constructed to serve the needs of the urban population.

The street plans inherited from previous centuries were not exclusively shaped by topographical conditions. They were also a reflection of landownership patterns and a function of the way in which many towns had expanded to absorb their suburbs. The simplest form of street plan was to be found in small centres, such as the Devon town of Totnes. Totnes, which acted as the export centre for the nearby port of Dartmouth, was constructed along a single main street along a ridge, with a few side streets fanning out at one end where the ridge broadened. Houses were built on narrow strips of land, known as burgages, which ran perpendicular to the line of the street, and this pattern of strips had determined the width of all houses built on the site. Burgages on the side streets were shorter but retained the same general shape in relation to the street.

In other towns, the nucleus of the street plan was provided by the market square, as in Lübeck, by the castle, as in Devizes, or by the cathedral, as in Hildesheim and Bamberg. As in the simple model of urban development, the presence of strips running perpendicular to each street ensured that the main streets were not too close together and that spaces were initially retained behind each house. Over time, these became built up with rear extensions to existing houses, which gradually became a complex of courtyards housing tenants, acceded to by a network of minor alleyways. The existence of these passages, which had an ambiguous semi-public status, created alternative routes for pedestrians, which acted as 'rat runs' parallel to the main streets. A few examples may still be seen in the seventeenth-century streets of Besançon.

Each of the towns referred to so far developed around a planned core, although subsequent changes were to modify the street plan considerably. In contrast, Venice and Genoa developed as a series of clusters of housing, which gradually coalesced to form a whole. In Venice, these clusters were built on areas in the city, effectively little islands, on which powerful families built their palaces, endowed the parish church and encouraged the establishment of a local market-place. Housing for their dependents and craftsmen who were attracted to this node of urban settlement rapidly grew up around the palace according to a pattern determined by the presence of lanes (*calli*) running alongside the palace to the waterfront or the market square. In Genoa, the effect was the same. Long before the pace of urban development joined these nodal points together into a single urban fabric, élite families had established their mark on their own areas. It was only when demographic pressures led to the use of the land lying between each development that a continuous street plan was established. In Genoa, the line of the streets was particularly sinuous as they marked out the frontiers between earlier nodal developments, a function carried out in Venice by the canals, but even in Venice, the individual disposition of key points on each island of development determined that the land routes which came to link them followed a twisted logic of their own.

The incorporation of suburbs into their host towns during the Middle Ages was accomplished by the expedient of constructing a new wall to take in the outlying housing. This was chiefly for military reasons, for suburbs were uniquely exposed to attack, occupation and destruction by besieging armies, but the effect on the street plan of the expanded urban centre was to complicate it almost beyond recognition. The line of the existing walls and their gates had determined the position of markets held in squares close to the point at which the commodities on sale entered the town. The construction of a new wall not only made these spaces redundant but also encouraged the development of new markets further out. As was to be expected, the street plans inherited from these former suburbs lacked the density and uniformity of those that had been enclosed within the walls. Many larger towns had expanded so much by the beginning of the sixteenth century that several generations of suburbs had been caught up by successive walls. Florence was endowed with six successive walls, the most recent of which had been completed in the fourteenth century.

The urban environment was differentiated further by the presence of even more recent suburbs, whose importance may be gauged by the fact that a disproportionate number of the urban population lived there. In early sixteenth-century Leicester and Winchester, nearly half of all the inhabitants lived in the suburbs and, while around one in six people in the small Andalucian town of Carmona already lived in the suburbs in 1466, this proportion was to rise to one in three in 1528. In Strasbourg, nearly 30 per cent of all houses recorded by a census in 1581 were built beyond the city walls.

Travellers' tales of dark, narrow winding streets crowded with people and vehicles have endowed medieval and early modern European towns with a character that is only partly accurate. While an increase in the population did lead to ever more concentrated housing, and economic expansion and changes in forms of personal transport all contributed to this picture, beyond the inner core the urban fabric was frequently interspersed by open spaces in which few people lived. In early sixteenth-century Exeter, nearly a third of all land within the walls remained open. So much land was enclosed by the new wall built around Cologne at the end of the twelfth century that the space was not fully built over for another 700 years. The last Florentine city wall of 1284–1333 enclosed an area six times that of its predecessor. The fourteenth-century wall in Nördlingen equally served the local population without strain until well into the seventeenth century.

As a result of the retention of substantial open spaces, townspeople continued to be familiar with the cultivation of crops close at hand and the presence of animals in the streets. The latter is testified to by frequent references in anti-plague legislation. Ducks, pigs and geese were banned from the main streets of the French town of Châlons-sur-Marne in 1467. More than 200 years later, the magistrates in Lille enforced a similar prohibition, although in their case goats were the prime suspects.

Open spaces remained for a variety of reasons. The terrain may have been too marshy and insalubrious for easy settlement, as was the case of the area to the west of the Bastille in Paris. Known as the Marais (literally 'the marshland'), it was enclosed by the fortifications of Charles V in the late fourteenth century but remained unused until the development of a new aristocratic quarter in the seventeenth century justified the cost of drainage. Elsewhere, spaces were created when housing was abandoned by families leaving to find work in times of economic difficulty as in sixteenth-century Winchester and Coventry. In England, but not generally on the Continent, land and buildings belonging to ecclesiastical institutions dissolved during the Reformation were transformed into orchards and gardens for the recreation of their new lay owners. But the main reason for the presence of open land in the later Middle Ages, as it was to be in the sixteenth and seventeenth centuries, was the absence of any stimuli strong enough to change land use from gardens and pastures to buildings within the area enclosed by the most recent fortifications. The scale of such enclosures may be explained by military considerations. Although the rationale changed over time, the effects were the same. Earlier enclosures on an ambitious scale were predicated by the belief that such lengthy walls would deter potential besieging armies. During the early modern period, much greater space was needed for earthworks. The need to keep the area in front of them free for the line of defensive fire also precluded any possibility of formal housing outside the walls and encouraged the creation of space for planned expansion within the new circuit.

Little concrete evidence remains of urban housing from the sixteenth and seventeenth centuries, and the nature of the buildings that survive has perhaps led to an unnecessary emphasis on large houses and churches clad in stone and designed along classical lines. While they have their place in urban history, they were far from typical of the developments that occurred during the sixteenth and seventeenth centuries. In England, for example, the Italianate liking for columns and porticoes was rarely seen outside London except in country-house architecture. Classical buildings were a characteristic of the eighteenth century in the provincial centres. On the other hand, thanks to the increasing numbers of studies of surviving examples of minor architecture and of analyses of urban inventories, it is possible to make a number of general comments about the external appearance of houses in towns and the internal arrangement of space within them.

Most houses continued to be constructed with timber frames. Timber was the most easily available construction material. It was also relatively light, with the exception of oak, and could therefore be used for rapid construction, demolition and even wholesale transfer to another site. New building techniques kept costs down by developing ways of using less timber to support these structures. Jerry-building practices were widely used. Houses in the east London suburbs, which used timber frames with Flemish wall infill, were not expected to last very long. Even in the more fashionable areas of west London in the sixteenth and early seventeenth centuries, the existence of relatively short-term leases was an incentive to builders to construct houses with built-in obsolescence. Similar motives encouraged builders in the rapidly expanding Spanish capital of Madrid, where even ecclesiastical buildings were in some danger.

The introduction of stone as a major building material was very slow. Even in areas where stone was available at relatively low cost, such as the English Cotswolds, timber frames were retained because they could be carved with greater ease. Timber gable ends conformed to the fashionable appearance of houses in other parts of England. Increasing numbers of stone houses were built in Paris after the introduction of a Royal Edict in 1604 banning the use of timber frames because they were believed to be a fire risk, but there was a delay before this practice was taken up elsewhere in France. In Rouen, the only houses to be built of stone in the seventeenth century were 150 mansions for the very rich. Stone houses were introduced in Cambrai in the second half of the century as a direct result of the rising cost of oak. Timber-framed houses were also being superseded in the Netherlands. Although the authorities in Amsterdam ordered stone facades to be built from 1521 in order to avoid fires, it was brick, rather than stone, which became the major building material in the United Provinces. Brick-making became one of the area's major industries.

Of all the physical changes to the urban environment between 1500 and 1700, the most striking was the abandonment of thatched roofs in favour of tiles or slate. Already commonplace in the Baltic and the Mediterranean, such roofs became the norm elsewhere. When the seven-year-old Thomas Platter first came down from the Swiss mountains to accompany a cousin to Germany in the early sixteenth century, he was overwhelmed by the sight of red-tiled roofs in Lucerne. As he wrote later in his journal, 'At Lucerne, I saw my first tiled roofs; I stood dumbfounded before them.' [Thomas Platter, *Autobiographie*, translated and edited by Marie Helmer. Paris: Armand Colin, 1964: 31. (Author's translation)] There were obvious benefits in reducing a fire hazard, and the expense of making the change increasingly came within the means of most landlords.

When Philip II of Spain chose Madrid to be his permanent capital, he ordered its inhabitants to give up the upper storeys of their houses to accommodate an army of royal officials. It is said that the inhabitants of Madrid then chose to build single-storey houses in order to avoid this requirement. Whatever the reason for this decision, it reflected a pattern of house design that was to be found all over Europe. In general, houses in towns were designed to be occupied by one family only. They were one or two storeys in height, except in the largest cities where the pressure of population encouraged the construction of taller buildings to take advantage of sites with limited dimensions. Their narrow street frontages, limited to one or two rooms only, obliged them to build out to the rear to accommodate goods, additional sleeping facilities and stables.

There was considerable unanimity in the use of space inside houses. In general, there was a movement away from the urban equivalent to the medieval lord's great hall, a single room stretching up to the ceiling with a fireplace but no chimney. A hole in the roof served to let out all smoke. This large space served as a shop or workshop, storage room, living room, kitchen, eating space and bedroom. It was still to be found in York in the early sixteenth century and in the German towns of Osnabrück, Münster and Lemgo, although this pattern had been given up in Lübeck and Brunswick long since. Upper floors were put in to enable a single multifunctional space to be replaced by a multiroomed house in which specialised activities could be carried out in some privacy. At the same time, chimneys were installed, permitting fireplaces in several rooms, and there was an increasing use of the internal staircase. Until then, upper storeys were reached by an outside staircase rising from the courtyard to the rear of the house. Kitchens, which had been located in cellars or in a separate building to the rear of the house for fear of fire, were incorporated in the main structure and took on multiple functions in the smaller houses. Inventories in Paris frequently listed the kitchen as a child's or servant's bedroom, a living room or a dining room. There was greater use of glass for windows and, in wealthier houses, of wainscot panelling. The timing of internal improvements varied, but most of them appear to have been introduced by the end of the sixteenth century.

One room on the ground floor facing the street did not have a fireplace because it functioned as a shop or artisan's workshop. Although rear rooms on the ground floor were used for living space, it was more common to use the first floor for entertaining, eating and sleeping, with further bedrooms either on the second floor or in an additional structure built around the courtyard.

One detailed example can be found in the inventory of Georges Desquelot, apothecary-spicer in the rue St-Honoré in Paris during the seventeenth century. The ground floor of his house was occupied by his workshop, a hall and the kitchen. On the first floor were two bedrooms and a privy, while the second floor housed two more bedrooms and two specialised workrooms, one for making jams, the other for distilling spirits. Grain was stored on the third floor. Desquelot's house was large enough for himself, his wife, two children, six servants, who must have helped him in his work, and a chamber maid.

Such an internal layout corresponded to the houses of other artisans and merchants. Where merchants continued to live in older housing stock, they had no alternative to living in accommodation in which space had to be set aside for storage, display and accounting, where the dividing lines between business and the domestic household remained undefined. As Hermann von Weinsburg's chronicle reported in 1547, when Maria, the wife of the governor of the Severin's gate in Cologne, died, her house was so full of packets of linen cloth remaining from her export business along the Rhine and the Mosel that no one knew what to do with them.

The poor did not live in houses with street frontages; they occupied shacks in courtyards, cellars and ramshackle dwellings on the edge of the city, and their growing numbers during the period did nothing to improve their living standards (see Chapter 7). Surviving inventories record the presence of a few truckle beds, some boxes and stools, coarse sheets, earthenware and iron cooking pots.

There is little evidence of multi-occupation in urban housing; most was specifically designed to be for single families. Only rooms around the courtyard to the rear of houses were frequently rented out. Multi-occupation was a seventeenth-century phenomenon, which characterised larger houses, particularly in Paris and the western suburbs of London. It is difficult to establish whether houses were built with multioccupation in mind or whether the growing pressure for accommodation led to the subdivision of properties.

What is striking is the way in which multi-occupation was the preserve of the wealthy rather than the poor. Both London and Paris attracted large numbers of people who needed accommodation either because they had to carry out some official function or because they wished to live in the area in the hopes of obtaining personal preferment. Their numbers were swelled by those whose business brought them to the capital and sought lodging in a private house rather than in a tavern. In Paris, the rising demand for rooms led to the creation of the dispersed apartment in which rooms rented by the same tenant could be several floors apart. A lawyer working for the Paris *parlement* in the parish of St-Jean-de-Grève in the 1680s occupied parts of four floors: a living room and kitchen on the ground floor, a study on the first, a bedroom and a cabinet on the second and a granary in the attic.

By implication, the social composition of the beehive house packed with tenants of differing social classes suggests that Sjoberg's centre–periphery model of the social zoning of the preindustrial city was not universally applicable to early modern Europe. Sjoberg argues that there was strict segregation between different urban social groups, where the housing of the élite was located around a central core, which included key political, religious and economic buildings such as the town hall, the cathedral and the market-place. There was considerable diversity in the location and type of housing used by different urban social groups even before the construction of new quarters, which by their very nature were located away from the traditional core. There were indeed towns, such as Strasbourg, Coventry, Toledo, Rouen and Nantes, where the wealthy parishes were at the centre and the poorer parishes on the edge of town, often overlapping into the suburbs. This was partially dictated by the logic of access and the cost of housing. Merchants often found it more convenient to live close to the commercial centre, lawyers to the law-courts and government officials to their offices. Similarly, the poor lived close to their work, which by its very nature was placed on the periphery of the city in order to avoid pollution or the danger of fire and to take advantage of sources of water power. Housing on the periphery was generally cheaper and smaller.

The Sjoberg model was never perfect. In Lübeck, for example, the élite may have lived in the two streets that ran along the ridge upon which the city was built and gave access to the market and the town hall, but they also occupied houses along the streets that ran down to the harbour on the River Trave, which constituted one edge of the city. Some councillors lived in houses in the parish of All Saints. On the other hand, as aerial photographs of the historic town centre amply demonstrate, Lübeck artisans lived in a quarter that ran between the walls and the central market, which was characterised not so much by a peripheral location as by the narrowness of its streets and comparatively cramped housing. (*See* Fig. 4.1, p. 79.)

In London and Paris, the centre–periphery model did not apply at all. This may have been a function of the cities' role as capital or simply one of size, but detailed analyses of the social and fiscal composition of London in the period after 1660 and Paris in 1573 suggest that some alternative housing distribution patterns were in use. While there was an evident concentration of wealth in the houses in the centre of Paris, the wealthiest Parisians of all lived in the Temple on the north-east fringe of the city, next to one of the streets for which tax assessments were the lowest, the rue du Temple. What is more, some groups of artisans were well established in the centre, such as the second-hand clothes dealers in rue de la Friperie. In the City of London, wealthy parishes were to be found scattered from east to west, with a certain concentration of merchants along the streets leading to London Bridge.

The centre–periphery distinction might well be replaced by social distinctions between housing along major thoroughfares and housing in back alleys. This was certainly the case in Paris, Amiens and the City of London, but it does not always work so well for Italy. In Venice, the location of patrician palaces along the Grand Canal conformed to the general European practice of building the houses of the wealthy along major thoroughfares. But those noble families and other wealthy property owners who were not so fortunate as to live on the Grand Canal occupied palaces all over the city. Only the arsenal quarter and the commercial 'ghetto' of S Giacomo di Rialto were free from wealthy residents. In mid-sixteenth-century Rome, men taxed to raise the shared cost of widening their street ranged from a nobleman and the son of a bishop to a baker, a shoemaker and several carpenters, a picture that is not in the least surprising, given the habit of noblemen of building palaces wherever they happened to own land.

One significant element in the social distribution of urban housing was to be seen quite early in French towns. In both Paris and Rouen, merchants, royal officials and lawyers chose to live in different parts of the city, setting up a distinction that was to become all the more important in those cities that expanded into new quarters. In general, wealthy merchants remained in the old cities, not least because they lived close to their economic interests, while the lawyers, office-holders, nobles and entrepreneurs were the chief residents of the new quarters, which were built with them in mind. Multiple élites had multiple locations.

The modification of the existing urban fabric

Demographic pressures alone had little effect on the urban fabric. While one might have expected the building stock to have expanded to take account of the relatively large numbers of immigrants looking for accommodation, the laws of supply and demand did not operate so smoothly. While there were some adjustments to the number and size of buildings in Europe's larger towns to take account of the growing numbers in the population, there was no direct correlation with the construction of new areas of housing, which came to characterise urban development at this time. Instead, additional storeys were added to existing buildings and small open spaces were filled in with extra houses or temporary shacks. In the parish of St-Germain-l'Auxerrois in Paris, the total housing stock was increased by 10 per cent between 1525 and 1553. A sharp increase in rent levels in Marseille, which reflected a population that rose from 45 000 in 1600 to 65 000 in 1660, encouraged landlords to add extra storeys to their houses. In Nîmes, the population density in what was becoming an overcrowded and unhealthy walled city reached a level of 37.6 per hectare. Roman city maps of 1577 and 1593 show pockets of very high-density housing in the inner city around the Palazzo Farnese and near the Ponte S Angelo.

Migration also swelled the older suburbs. Traditionally areas of low-rent housing with opportunities for unskilled industrial jobs beyond the jurisdiction of either the urban authorities or the guilds, they were also the point at which new immigrants first came into contact with the towns and where they first sought accommodation. Giving lodging to migrants also supplemented the incomes of those who were already there. The most prominent area of suburban expansion in response to immigration was the East End of London. The area tended to attract subsistence migrants rather than the betterment migrants who showed a preference for other developments taking place to the west. This expansion was uncontrolled in the sense that there was no overall plan for new housing, but it is significant that it replicated what was taking place in inner cities elsewhere. In spite of the opportunities offered by extensive space for building, immigrants preferred to settle in the well-established and already densely populated suburbs, such as St Katherine's or East Smithfield, than in the more easterly areas of Poplar or Bow. Southwark, London's oldest suburb, which lay on the other bank of the Thames across London Bridge, also took in large numbers of immigrants. In 1678, its population of 31 700 numbered more than Norwich, England's second largest city. The pressures for the construction of illegal housing in London's easterly suburbs were indeed so intense in the early seventeenth century that official attempts were made to pull them down, to the great distress of their inhabitants, as illustrated in the scene in Shakespeare's *Measure for Measure* when Mistress Overdone is thrown out of her lodgings.

Even if the influx of large numbers of people seeking accommodation did not act as an incentive to alter the urban fabric, we are entitled to ask why the authorities did not undertake radical changes to the inner city when they might have done so. One of the major problems of which they were aware was the increasing difficulty of moving about the streets. While this affected pedestrians as much as those in vehicles, it was the latter who were inconvenienced most by the volume of traffic in narrow streets often encumbered by market stalls, piles of raw materials and unofficial extensions to house frontages. The Quai de la Mégisserie in Paris was constantly encroached upon by scrap metal merchants and carriage demolishers. Horse-skinners used the nearby rue de la Blanchette as an open air workshop, leaving piles of skins and intestines. The problems were multiplied elsewhere by the presence of market traders who set up their stalls wherever they could.

In large cities, the problem of moving around was compounded by changes in private transport for the wealthy. In sixteenth-century Antwerp, most of the existing streets were unpaved and were too narrow for two vehicles to pass in opposite directions. The merchant, Frans de Taler, recorded that

> Every day, the streets were so full of people, carts and horses that frequently they remained so entangled for half and hour or more that no one could pass. It was necessary to make a detour of three or four streets to get round.
>
> (H. Soly, L'Urbanisation d'Anvers au xvie siècle, *Revue du Nord*, 63, 1981: 396, Author's translation)

Some 150 years later, a German visitor to Paris in 1718 was impressed by 'innumerable coaches and hackney carriages driving here and there until night has fallen, and those carriages do not go gently but at a gallop.... One has to look out in all directions.' [A. Pardailhé-Galabrun, Les déplacements des Parisiens dans la ville aux xviie et xviiie siècles. Un essai de problématique. *Histoire: Economie et Société* II, 1983: 206. (Author's translation)]

The wealthy residents of the great cities profited from improvements in carriage design to travel longer distances in greater comfort and greater privacy and took the opportunity to use the size of their carriages and the number of their horses as status symbols.

The urban authorities made several unsuccessful attempts to improve the circulation of traffic, but they were frustrated because their abstract plans failed to take account of the dynamics of urban life. The emphasis on streets lined by houses with uniform frontages to be found in so many planning regulations arose in part from the inability of urban authorities to enforce rules restricting householders from building out into the street. Nor were market traders more amenable. The Roman magistracy responsible for the conditions of the streets made arrangements during the pontificate of Alexander VII to move all vendors of fish, meat and vegetables from the Piazza della Rotunda and other streets to a shopping area constructed in a new wing of the Collegium Germanium. Within a few weeks, they were all to be found in their original positions, where it was more convenient to their customers.

Traffic control was no easier, not least because regulating the movement of wheeled vehicles offended members of the élite. A one-way system was introduced in Amsterdam in 1615, but this proved to be only a temporary solution to street blockages. When the radical solution of banning private carriages from the city altogether was introduced in 1634, it had to be modified after protests from the élite that they were inconvenienced when travelling to and from their country estates if forced to make their way on foot to the edges of the city before they could travel in comfort. A compromise was worked out by which coaches were permitted to come into the city to pick them up and take them home but could not be used for journeys within the city. A similar attempt by the English monarchy to license hackney coaches and limit the number of private vehicles in the City of London in the 1630s was equally unsuccessful, as was a French edict passed in 1679, which tried to ban all commercial wheeled traffic in the city.

Alterations to the medieval street plan to accommodate the needs of the élite were piecemeal and infrequent. Pope Alexander VII registered a small triumph when he arranged for a number of buildings to be demolished in the street leading to the church of Sta Maria della Pace in Rome. This permitted a high-ranking congregation, which included many lawyers who liked to travel to mass by coach after the courts closed at noon, to reach the church by travelling down the next street, turning through the gap created in front of the church and later departing along a one-way system.

Many private building initiatives did little to alter the fabric of the area in which they took place. Such private entrepreneurs could have done little without support from the urban authorities because the complex of ownership and feudal rights in the crowded inner core represented an almost insuperable obstacle to change. On occasion, however, derelict buildings left as a result of local economic changes did provide a rare opportunity for a complete change of use. The parish of S Giovanni Grisostomo in Venice contained a characteristic mix of housing for the city, combining noble palaces opening out onto the Grand Canal with a shopping street, a soapworks and many smaller buildings housing artisans. In 1677, one group of these smaller buildings in a state of increasing decay was demolished to make way for the new Teatro Grimani.

In a number of cities, the presence of a new princely court led to the competitive construction of great houses by a newly resident nobility. This was the case in Rome, where the Popes encouraged the leading noble families of the Papal States to establish themselves in order to be close to the prestige and patronage offered by the Papal court, and in Naples, where the Spanish viceroys conducted a similar policy of concentrating potentially dangerous and distant noble opponents around the point of royal patronage. Both groups built on land that they already owned in the cities, but while in Rome there was space for fairly unrestricted construction, in Naples they built where they could, beginning with plots of land in the old city that already belonged to them. No attention was paid to the incongruity of inserting buildings with magnificent facades into streets that were too narrow to permit the proper appreciation of their splendour required by contemporary architectural theory. The same occurred in late seventeenth-century Vienna, where for once the construction of new fortifications confined all new housing for courtiers to the inner city.

The relatively small scale of these developments serves to emphasise the virtual impossibility of making major changes to the existing urban fabric. The effort and cost involved in dealing with multiple householders and landowners with complicated feudal jurisdictions were a major deterrent. Even when opportunities for extensive planned development in the inner city created by the fortuitous large-scale destruction of buildings as a result of fire or warfare presented themselves, the urban authorities were either relatively reticent in their responses or incapable of accommodating existing patterns of economic activity.

Fire was a common hazard in most towns, given the heavy use of timber in their construction and the presence of combustible materials on their roofs. When a disastrous fire broke out in a goldsmith's workshop and destroyed 470 houses in Valladolid in 1561, Philip II took a personal interest in plans for rebuilding the quarter. Although the king had already taken the decision to establish his court permanently in Madrid, rather than Valladolid or Toledo, he and his architect, Francisco di Salamanca, insisted that the city must be rebuilt as an ornament to the kingdom, with standard street widths and house heights and one uniform pattern for doors, windows and balconies. The new quarter was built, at considerable expense, but old ways soon reasserted themselves. Within a short time, the authorities were complaining about the impossibility of stopping pigs from wandering the streets or preventing butchers from throwing out internal organs.

The damage caused by the fire that destroyed much of the City of London in 1666 also aroused considerable government interest. It is said to have destroyed 13 700 houses, including four guildhalls, St Paul's Cathedral and 87 other churches. Although the monarchy tried to take the opportunity offered by the fire to create a modern city along classical lines to rival the new quarters being built in continental capitals, Wren's designs for the cathedral and several churches had to be inserted into the existing street plan. The fire may have effaced large numbers of buildings, but it could not remove the extant patchwork of ownership, and reconstruction had to take place where buildings had stood before. An Act of Parliament for the rebuilding of the city was passed in 1667, obliging all sites to be rebuilt within three years and establishing a precise relationship between the width of streets and the height of the buildings that abutted them. There were no other controls on the appearance of the buildings, and the resulting organic growth of the city recreated a crowded centre, which continued to contrast with the new élite quarters being built to the west. The 12 markets returned to their old positions.

Even where the inner core was spared by fire or warfare, the municipal authorities, the territorial state and the Catholic church were able to insert a number of buildings and spaces, which had a progressive impact on the fabric around them. These may be summarised as the construction of new town halls, administrative buildings and hospitals and poorhouses; the remodelling of old squares and the insertion of new ones; attempts to impose regulated facades on existing street frontages; and the remodelling or construction of new ecclesiastical buildings in more exalted settings. Although these changes were introduced within the framework of the old urban fabric, they were based on the same principles as the new quarters, which were constructed beyond the inner core and should be seen in the same light. Often, where no large-scale development was possible, these modifications were the only evidence of the aspirations of the secular and ecclesiastical authorities.

New town halls and other administrative buildings were constructed in a variety of urban centres. The construction of such buildings combined solutions to the practical problems of overcrowding and inappropriate or dispersed accommodation, but this was equally an opportunity to express the authorities' sense of self-assertion and power, both in the face of their subjects or fellow citizens and in competition with their neighbours. Major new town halls were completed in Paris (1551), in Strasbourg (1566), in Augsburg (1615–26) and in Amsterdam (1660s). The decoration on the facade of the Amsterdam town hall, which illustrated the story of the golden calf from Exodus, conveyed the self-confident message that control of the law was safer in the hands of the secular authorities (Moses) than in those of the Church, which was associated by implication with the idol-worshipping priests of the story. The growth in English urban prosperity was reflected by the refurbishment and construction of new buildings in towns of all sizes, which frequently combined market halls, guild-halls and meeting places of town councils and courtrooms. Even where the authorities were unable to rebuild town halls, they did their best to embellish them in the latest style. A substantial new external staircase along Italian lines was added to the Gothic town hall in Lübeck in the sixteenth century to provide an entirely new entrance at first-floor level suitable to the aspirations of a city state which still saw itself as one of the leading Baltic powers and the home of the Hanseatic League.

In Florence, a populous area was razed on the orders of the early Medici Dukes in the sixteenth century to allow for the concentration of the ducal administration in the new Uffizi palace, while the Venetian authorities employed Sansovino to complete the remodelling of St Mark's Square, in which two sides of the trapezoid accommodated government offices in arcaded buildings with shops on the ground floor.

The extension of government responsibilities was reflected by the construction of new buildings. A new arsenal to store a foundry, munitions and other military materials, such as lead, saltpetre and gunpowder, was constructed in the centre of Augsburg in 1584 on the site of a former granary opposite the Fugger palace. In spite of the dangers of fire and the disadvantages of pollution, the authorities used this opportunity to emphasise the priority that they placed on the city's defensive needs. Poor-houses and hospitals were built in every urban centre of any size to accommodate the increasing numbers of beggars. In design and appearance, they were intended to convey the new power of the state and its wish to underwrite an ordered society (see Chapter 7).

The remodelling of existing squares and the insertion of new spaces represented attempts to regulate the urban fabric at certain key points. Several parallel concerns were in evidence, some of which increased in importance during the later seventeenth century in particular. Squares were used for commercial purposes, enabling people to meet, goods to be bought and sold retail and business to be transacted. They were used to ease the movement of pedestrian and wheeled traffic where main thoroughfares from ports or gates crossed each other. They were also used as public spaces within which collective, civic and ecclesiastical ceremonies could take place involving the mass of the population. In their multifunctional use, they were an integral part of the urban fabric at the beginning of the sixteenth century.

This multifunctionality began to give way to two parallel developments. Squares became more specialised, and the buildings around them were constructed to reflect this use. As this specialisation increased, the divergence between squares intended for trading and squares intended to convey a political or a religious message was matched by their location. While squares for commercial use remained where they were within the old fabric, connected to trade routes and bridges by existing streets, squares constructed to provide a forecourt for important buildings were inserted in relation to those buildings rather than to any ease of access. The ultimate development, modelled on the square surrounding the classical equestrian statue of Marcus Aurelius in Rome, focused on the monument itself as an expression of princely power, to be seen in its most widespread form in the France of Louis XIV, where city councils competed with each other to erect monuments to their monarch. The presence of the monument created its own logic and was inserted in the urban fabric at points that bore no relation to nearby buildings, streets or economic activities. The development of the specialist square also altered the density of use. While market squares remained spaces to work in, the new public spaces, which owed so much in their conception to stage set designs and to classical models, were seen as spaces to cross, spaces to which there was only restricted access, in which all activity was strictly regulated by the state or the church.

According to the French architect, Pierre le Muet, who published his *Manière de bâtir pour toutes sortes de personnes* in 1647, a modern town had to be characterised by uniformity along its streets. Such principles were relatively easy to apply to the construction of new squares and quarters, but some urban and princely authorities took this a stage further and attempted to integrate new buildings with the old by insisting that street frontages matched each other. In Nuremberg, the council published precise building ordinances to ensure consistency in the building of facades, precisely described ornamentation and careful distribution of oriel and bay windows. State regulations in late seventeenth-century Turin compelled owners of older buildings on main thoroughfares to match the facades of the new. Similar actions were taken in Madrid, Paris and Amsterdam. In some places, such as Turin, this was particularly successful. Elsewhere, the old and the new subsisted chaotically alongside each other as evidence that the aesthetic sensibilities of the urban authorities were not always matched by those of their fellow townspeople.

In the Catholic areas of Europe, the resurgence of religious enthusiasm during the Counter-Reformation brought about the construction of new churches and other buildings for the religious orders and the remodelling of many existing churches (see Chapter 5). Rome was a case apart, in which the work of successive Popes created settings for numerous new religious buildings, which accentuated the process of discovery as pilgrims and others walked down carefully designed streets. Elsewhere, the choice of cruciform buildings topped by domes shifted the symbolic external focus of church buildings from the spires, which had helped to shape towns' skylines and therefore their external identity, to a more immediate impact on the area around the church. In Paris, the church of St-Eustache, the parish that held the city's central market, Les Halles, was rebuilt between 1532 and 1637 on lines that octupled the size of the original building and required the demolition of substantial numbers of houses to clear the site and leave space to appreciate its symbolism as an expression of the Counter-Reformation.

Fortifications

For centuries, the town wall had been one of the most important signs of the town. As a physical barrier, it was intended to protect townspeople from all kinds of external dangers, military attack, unwanted visitors, disease, even the unseen dangers of the night. As late as 1523, the French king, Francis I, granted the small town of Montmorillon in the Poitou the right to build walls because 'the said poor inhabitants do not dare to live there nor keep their possessions in security for fear of the soldiers, vagabonds and pilferers who go to live there.' [B. Chevalier, *Les bonnes villes de France du xive au xvie siècle*. Paris: Aubier Montaigne, 1982: 55 (Author's translation)]. In symbolic terms, too, urban fortifications represented the autonomy of the town in relation to local feudal jurisdictions and, rather more ambiguously, in relation to the territorial ruler. Fortifications numbered among the major objects of pride listed in urban encomia and travellers' journals alike. Montaigne gives a chilling and detailed description of the way in which travellers arriving at the city gates in Augsburg after dark were obliged to pass into an isolation room within the walls while their credentials were inspected. The Swiss traveller, Thomas Platter, recorded in the early sixteenth century that he was unable to enter Munich in the morning when the gates opened unless there was someone in the city to vouch for him.

By the end of the seventeenth century, urban fortifications had come to represent a different kind of reality. For many towns, they had no practical purpose at all and had either been allowed to fall into decay or had been demolished. The spread of suburban housing had rendered them useless as a practical physical barrier between town and countryside and, although they continued to function as a jurisdictional frontier, most of the efforts of customs officers at the main gates were rendered impotent because the dilapidated condition of the stonework at various points between town and suburb permitted goods to be brought in through the wall. The stones also made excellent building materials. During the seventeenth century, fortifications in a number of French towns were deliberately destroyed by the monarchy and replaced by continuous tree-lined promenades. This began in Rennes in 1602, but the most striking example took place in Paris in 1670, when the length of wall between the Bastille and Porte Saint-Martin was levelled, and two baroque arches were erected as a joint symbol of the continuing distinction between the city of Paris and its suburbs and of Louis XIV as a conquering hero in the classical mould.

The decline of urban fortifications, primarily in England and the French interior, was brought about by a number of factors. The most important was the way in which changes in military technology had rendered the traditional town wall utterly redundant. Beginning with the Italian campaign conducted by Charles VIII at the end of the fifteenth century, the use of artillery and mines demonstrated that tall, thin, stone walls could no longer resist a besieging army. Stone or metal balls were fired from a distance beyond the range of defending forces and smashed through barriers built to deter an army that had to use ladders to scale them. The height and smoothness of the walls were also a disadvantage when groups of men could move in below them to dig ditches under them in which to place explosives. Shooting down at ninety degrees was an impossibility.

The new fortifications that were developed to combat this bore no resemblance to their predecessors. They were essentially earthworks, thrown up some distance from the town, dressed with stone and interrupted from time to time by bastions, whose semi-circular or pointed shapes permitted soldiers to direct their fire to attack any group approaching the main fortifications. Earthworks absorbed the energy of projectiles and were also much more difficult to mine.

The construction of earthworks and bastions led to major alterations in the suburban landscape. Many houses and religious buildings had to be sacrificed in order to make way for the new fortifications and to keep open land between the earthworks and any external threat. The new walls around Lucca extended for more than four kilometres and took over a century to complete, by which time advances in military technology had made them out of date, and all the suburbs to the east and the south had been demolished. The work involved in constructing new fortifications was heavily labour intensive and, although much of the labour that constructed new urban fortifications was unpaid – the able-bodied urban poor or local peasants who had been pressed into service – modern fortifications often represented a cost that the urban authorities were not prepared to bear.

In both England and France, the decision to build new fortifications was largely taken out of the hands of the urban authorities as this became a matter for national rather than local defence, and the location of new earthworks was determined by major strategic considerations. This is why most English efforts were directed towards the recently acquired town of Berwick-upon-Tweed in the second half of the sixteenth century. The only other building that took place during the period was carried out quite hastily after the outbreak of the Civil War. Berwick lay on a sensitive border with Scotland and was also open to attack by sea from the French. Sir William Brereton described them on a visit in 1634 as 'the strongest fortifications I have met with in England, double-walled and out-works of earth, and the outer walls like unto Chester walls, and without the inner walls a deep and broad moat well watered.' [E. Hawkins (ed.), *Travels in Holland, the United Provinces, England, Scotland and Ireland, 1634–5 by Sir William Brereton, Bart*, Chetham Society: I, 1844: 94–6, reprinted in R.C. Richardson and T.B. James (eds), *The urban experience: a sourcebook. English, Scottish and Welsh towns, 1450–1700*. Manchester: Manchester University Press, 1983: 17–19.]

In 1604, control of all French urban fortifications was transferred to the monarchy, which was then in a position to select which fortifications to renew and which walls to neglect. The Bourbon kings were often tempted to choose a policy of neglect, because urban fortifications were still being used against the monarchy in the 1630s to keep out tax collectors and other unwelcome officials and proved a major problem during the Fronde in the 1640s.

The presence or absence of new urban fortifications was also determined by the political geography of warfare in early modern Europe. After the French Wars of Religion came to an end, there was no more widespread military activity in the French interior. All the more reason why efforts should have been concentrated on a chain of strategically sensitive places around the country's borders. In the 1670s and 1680s, Louis XIV used the services of the great military engineer, Vauban, to construct a series of citadels linked to major fortifications in Marseille, Toulon, Nîmes, Besançon and Lille and to establish new fort-cities at Neufbrisach, Sarrelouis and Longwy, among others.

The reconstruction of urban fortifications was particularly intense where the dangers of attack were at their greatest. Italian fortifications were among the earliest to be renewed but, as much of the internecine warfare and invasions from north of the Alps came to an end with the dissolution of the League of Cambrai in the early sixteenth century, there was little encouragement to build yet more bastions. A citadel, the Fortezza da Basso, was constructed in Florence in 1534 by Duke Alessandro de' Medici, but its primary function was to deter any thoughts of rebellion by Florentine citizens. Similar anxieties led the Spanish viceroy to extend the city walls in Naples. Only to the north of Italy, in the mainland territories of the Republic of Venice, were new fortifications built on any scale. The Venetians feared attack from the French and the Austrians and, latterly, from the Turks. In the second half of the sixteenth century, many of Venice's subject towns had to set aside over half of their income for military expenditure, and the dangers of attack from the north-east led the Venetians to create an entirely new military town at Palmanova in 1593.

The greatest number of modern fortifications were built in Germany. In the collection of German town plans published by Matthaus Merian the Elder in the 1680s, there was scarcely an important urban centre without its due ring of bastions and moats. The circumstances are self-explanatory. The subdivision of the Empire into large numbers of small territorial states, among which the free imperial cities were noteworthy because of their lack of hinterland, both encouraged conflict and concentrated on sieges rather than on pitched battles. Fortifications were an essential item of expenditure, even when their cost stretched urban finances beyond all limits of tolerance. The risks of not being properly defended were too frightening to consider. Magdeburg was attacked and burnt to the ground in 1631 during the Thirty Years War. It was only later transformed into a heavily fortified city when it became part of Brandenburg-Prussia in 1666. In 1689, the French burned Heidelberg, Mannheim, Oppenheim, Speyer and Worms. Towns of particular strategic importance lost any say in how they were fortified. Stade, on the lower Elbe, acquired new bastions and a Dutch-style outer fortification with eight ravelines, earth walls and water-filled ditches in the course of the second half of the seventeenth century when it became the capital of two Swedish provinces in Germany.

The most substantial alterations to the urban landscape took place in the Netherlands, which were rocked by military conflict from the later sixteenth century onwards. In the second half of the seventeenth century, the Spanish improved existing walls at Ypres, Brussels, Namur, Nieuport and Ostend and created a new fortress city at Charleroi in 1666. To the north, the truce between the newly independent United Provinces and the Spanish monarchy gave the Dutch a breathing space to build extensive fortifications around their towns. These were probably the most highly developed in Europe, making effective use of earth, stone and water. Trees were planted on the ramparts to strengthen them. In 1673, the ramparts around Leiden had over 2000 trees.

The new quarters

In the absence of opportunities or incentives to make major changes to the fabric of town centres inherited from the Middle Ages, a number of attempts were made to build outside the existing network of streets and squares and to create entirely new quarters. The impetus for these changes came from a variety of sources, the aristocracy and office-holding élite, urban governments and, increasingly, from territorial rulers. These last frequently linked the expansion of new residential quarters with the construction of new fortifications.

There was no shortage of ideas about how such new quarters should be designed and organised. The urban authorities and territorial rulers were well aware of writings about the ideal city by Alberti, Filarete, Serli, Leonardo da Vinci, Dürer and others. Drawing on the ideas of the Roman writer, Vitruvius, Alberti and Filarete first introduced an Italian humanist audience to the idea of the harmonious city in the fifteenth century. It was to have a harmonious form, with a series of broad regular streets lined by buildings with uniform frontages and interspersed with squares and prominent structures for the use of the church and the state. As Alberti put it in *De rei aedificatoria*, 'the principal monument of the city will arise from the disposition of the streets, squares and public edifices, their being laid out and contrived beautifully and conveniently; for without order, there can be nothing handsome, convenient and pleasing.' [Leon Battista Alberti, *De rei aedificatoria*, Book Seven. Translated as *On the art of building in ten books*, by J. Rykwert, N. Leach and R. Tavernor. Cambridge, MA: MIT Press, 1988: 191]. The ideal city was also planned to facilitate social harmony through careful zoning to separate the poorer classes from the élite and to ensure that every member of society knew their place. To quote Alberti once more, 'the city will be more secure and less disrupted if those in power are separated from the feckless mob of poultry salesmen, butchers, cooks and the like' (Alberti, *De rei aedificatoria*, Book Four, p. 118). Such ideas met with increasing approval among the Italian princely rulers who were the first to remodel their cities, as the concept of an ordered existence was not only an integral part of Renaissance philosophy but corresponded to a practical need to dominate, impress and control their subjects. This was to become the subtext to all town planning carried out by *ancien régime* rulers in Europe.

For the first time, the widespread circulation in print of the aesthetic and theoretical principles behind the planning of new residential quarters led to considerable uniformity throughout western Europe. Each city acted as a model for others and, while the circumstances in which the new quarters were brought into being varied considerably, an international architectural vocabulary came into use, which undermined much of the individuality of which townspeople had been proud in the past. There was indeed a strong family resemblance between seventeenth-century Turin, Vienna and Dresden, a resemblance that spread ever more widely during the eighteenth century.

In this new international architectural vocabulary, form took priority over function. One might even say that, as what appealed to those who initiated these schemes was the overall impression of authority and order given by what was built, form became function. The construction of new quarters gave architects and their patrons ample opportunity to put these new ideas into practice.

The new quarters built in Antwerp and Amsterdam stand out as something of an exception. Unlike the capital cities and administrative centres, their urban expansion was largely shaped by their position as European commercial centres. Even then, the development of new quarters in Antwerp was a delayed response to the almost impossible strains on a merchant community struggling to come to terms with rapid commercial expansion. In the early sixteenth century, only 12 ships could moor in the port at any one time and, although smaller vessels could use four small canals, they were encumbered by overhanging houses and low bridges. Many ships had to wait up to six weeks to dock. The public weigh-house was inadequate, warehousing facilities were not centralised and perishable goods suffered from being stored out of doors. It was not until the 1540s that a single entrepreneur, Gilbert van Schoenbeke, created two new districts in Antwerp around a new public weigh-house and a major new market, each linked to the old centre by new thoroughfares and each offering sites for merchant housing. A third initiative, the so-called New Town, involving three new canals capable of taking ships up to 200 tons into a suburban area, which was also intended to become a centre for the brewing industry, enjoyed only partial success because it coincided with a slump in the city's prosperity.

Until the end of the sixteenth century, Amsterdam was bounded by the Singel, a semi-circular canal, which served jointly as a waterway and as a line of defence. In order to take advantage of the city's growing trading links, the Regents planned an ambitious expansion of the city through three further semi-circular canals running parallel with the Singel, linked by transverse canals and streets. The space thus made available was carefully planned to ensure that different economic activities were separated from each other and that the frontages of the main canals should be reserved for the houses of the wealthy. While a strongly vernacular architectural style was adopted, Amsterdam belonged to the wider tradition of European town planning because of the symmetry with which its canals were planned and the care with which social zoning was administered. In time, as the kings of Denmark and Sweden sought to extend their political power through a policy of maritime expansion, Amsterdam became the model for Copenhagen and Gothenburg.

New quarters elsewhere were largely developed for the use of noblemen, administrators and time-servers as the result of the initiative of a territorial ruler or his representative, for whom these areas were to serve as a reflection of their personal glory. In Naples, Philip II's viceroy, Don Pedro de Toledo, created the Spanish quarter in the 1530s along a new street linking the royal palace near the port to the foot of the hill of Capodimonte. As well as keeping troops close to the city in case of trouble but away from an unfriendly Neapolitan population, the Spanish quarter attracted both noble tenants and an unexpected number of tavern-keepers and prostitutes attracted by the proximity of the barracks. At the end of the sixteenth century, the return of Emmanuel Filibert of Savoy to Turin initiated the development of new quarters on three sides of the city within its new fortifications. As in the case of Naples, the overall plan of each quarter was determined by great axial streets leading to the centre of the city. It took over a century for the plans to be completed.

In Paris, the small-scale residential quarters developed by Henry IV in the first decade of the seventeenth century around the Place Royale (later Place des Vosges) and Place Dauphine, which opened out onto the Ile de la Cité off the new Pont Neuf, were dwarfed by the Quartier Richelieu. In order to build a palace worthy of his position, Louis XIII's chief minister moved part of the city's fortifications outwards to take in the three existing suburbs of St Honoré, Montmartre and La Ville Neuve. This provided him with enough space for a palace and several streets running parallel to its sides where he lodged his dependents.

Only in the later seventeenth century did the French monarchy encourage the construction of new urban quarters outside the capital, and this was substantially influenced by military factors. The new quarters in Marseille, whose overall surface was to be doubled according to plans sent to the city in 1666, and Lille, where Louis intended to add a third to the total area of the city, were a by-product of Louis XIV's new policy of constructing citadels in places of considerable strategic sensitivity. Marseille was France's major Mediterranean port and had recently rebelled against the monarchy. Lille was a recent acquisition from the Spanish, and there were doubts about the loyalty of its subjects. The new fortifications, which linked the citadel to the existing earthworks around the city, gave the king the opportunity to enclose a large area for urban development and to impose his own values on the population.

The case of Rome was symptomatic of the complex processes by which a new urban environment was created. When the Popes returned from Avignon, they found that the city had shrunk in size, that it had no functional centres and that it did not conform with the idea of a concrete expression of a holy city at the centre of the Church. Successive Popes put into train a building programme, which was intended to make Rome the most beautiful city in Europe, in which the chief purpose of architecture was to elicit a deep sense of piety among the thousands of visitors who came to the city each year. It was a slow process. It took 120 years to complete the construction of Bramante's great church of St Peter, first begun in 1506 under the pontificate of Julius II. While the main outlines of the new Rome were established by the mid-sixteenth century, the development of the new quarters took place as an accretion of projects initiated by successive Popes, aided or hindered by the availability of the capital necessary for the embellishment of their city. The loss of fiscal income from those parts of Europe that established Protestant churches was a major setback, only partly compensated for by the income from the newly exploited alum mines at Tolfa.

The original intentions of the planners were not always entirely fulfilled. To a large extent, they could control the built environment, although there are many cases of building regulations being honoured more in the breach than in their application. The difficulty lay in ensuring that new quarters were fully completed and that residents of the desired social composition made their homes there. The process is well illustrated by the experience of Paris and Versailles. Early building in Paris from the mid-fifteenth century to replace houses destroyed during the Hundred Years War gave the nobility the opportunity to construct houses in the open spaces near the city walls. Within a very short time, smaller, cheaper houses were being built close to them to meet a more general demand for housing. The new Place Royale was planned as a centre for bankers and jewellers to serve a wealthy clientele, but Henry IV was obliged to abandon this idea even before the square was built in favour of a general high-class residential quarter. All that remained of his original plan was the use of the large space in the centre of the square for drilling troops.

Versailles was an extreme example of this gap between plan and reality. The planners of Louis XIV's new capital, which was intended to house royal officials and a large number of merchants and artisans, used the three streets that ran into the Piazza del Popolo in Rome as a model to create an outline of ambitious proportions. Following good architectural practice, these three streets not only permitted a view of the palace at the end of each one, but also formed the main outlines of a carefully planned new quarter. Early building was carried out on plots lining the main streets, using the now conventional uniformity of facade and height but, by the time that additional housing plots were sold in the first decade of the eighteenth century, attempts at symmetry had been given up. The plots sold slowly. There were unfortunate gaps reminiscent of older styles of town plan and, as the economy of Versailles expanded to meet the demand for services from its own inhabitants rather than from the court, the social composition of the population also came to be much more heterogeneous.

The social segregation that the construction of the new quarters had been intended to bring about was not entirely successful either. Certainly, residents of the new quarters were able to escape the inconvenience of living in the inner city. On the other hand, even the most exclusive of planners and their patrons had to recognize that it was necessary to install shops to meet the demands of this new population. As the political arithmetician, John Graunt, put it in 1686 when writing about the western suburbs of London, 'where the consumption of a commodity is, viz. among the gentry, the vendors of the same must seat themselves'. [J. Graunt, *Natural and political observations ... upon the bills of mortality*, (London, 1686), reprinted (in part) in P. Clark and P. Morgan, *Towns and townspeople 1500–1780. A document collection*, Milton Keynes: Open University Press, 1977: 33–4.] But the planners omitted to take into account the fact that people went to great expense in order to buy or lease a house in a prestigious new quarter and frequently sought to defray their costs by subletting their accommodation. These conditions conspired to introduce into the new quarters the very people from whom their first residents were trying to escape. This was particularly evident in cases in which the scope of the planners far exceeded the demand for housing among the élite, and it became necessary to sell smaller plots for building or to subdivide buildings in order to recoup the original investment in using land for development.

As time passed, there was also a tendency for families to seek ever more exclusive places of residence to escape the company of those with whom they did not wish to mix and to keep up a reputation for being fashionable. This was an important impetus behind the development of the western suburbs of London. Unlike the other capitals of Europe, London was not subject to the same royal interest in town planning, and expansion proceeded according to the readiness of landowners to release their land for building. While the pattern of development remained the same – the construction of elegant town houses by members of the aristocracy on their own land for their own use and others of high status – the location of these residential quarters moved steadily northwards and westwards as the seventeenth century proceeded.

The Earl of Bedford began the process in the 1630s with the Italianate Piazza at Covent Garden, designed by Inigo Jones. By choosing a site north of the Strand, he broke with the custom of building houses close to the Thames so that their occupants could move easily upstream to the court or downstream to the City. As time passed, once their short-term leases had expired, the residents of Covent Garden left to take up houses in the new developments in Leicester Square and Soho Square. Their place was taken by the less wealthy, for whom such a move was also an expression of their rising sense of status. During the last quarter of the seventeenth century, the noble landlords in the once fashionable Strand district demolished their own great houses and built new structures more appropriate to the new clientele.

New towns

By comparison with the Middle Ages, few new towns were founded in early modern Europe. The reasons for their foundation overlapped considerably with the circumstances in which changes were made to existing towns. The role of princely rulers was overwhelming, if not exclusive. New towns were an undistracted opportunity to put into practice the architectural ideas upon which the construction of the new urban quarters were based. Like the plans for new quarters, many of the new towns were overambitious and often only lasted as long as the original circumstances that had brought them into being. This was particularly true of towns founded for the purposes of personal aggrandisement, which rarely survived the demise of their founders, but was also a feature of towns built for military or naval purposes. For this reason, these two categories will be considered first, before any discussion of the new princely capitals and economic centres.

Two new towns above all were built for the purposes of personal aggrandisement, Pienza in the Republic of Siena, and Richelieu, in the French province of Poitou. Both were founded in their natal villages as a monument to themselves and their families by eminent churchmen who were also major political leaders, Pope Pius II and Cardinal Richelieu. In the case of Pienza, the town was literally planted on the existing village of Corsignano, with a new church and palaces for the Pope and his cardinals. While it remained the fief of the Piccolomini family into the sixteenth century, the town remained a considerable anomaly. In 1552, it was considered to be too unimportant to be defended against possible attack by the Spanish. Richelieu, completed in 1624, has been likened to a formal garden surrounded by buildings rather than a town. It was bounded by a wall measuring some 500 by 700 metres and contained a castle in one corner, a market square and a single axial main street, which bisected the town into two equal halves and was bounded by 28 identical houses. Although the town of Richelieu was given a number of tax exemptions and hosted a range of institutions including an academy to educate young nobles in French and in the sciences, it never really prospered and continues to stand in the French countryside in its original form.

Proof too of disappointed dreams is the town of Brouage close to the west coast of France. Originally founded in the mid-sixteenth century under the name of Jacopolis by a local landowner, it was transformed by Louis XIII in the 1620s as a military stronghold with access to the sea to counter the threat from the English and their allies in La Rochelle. It was endowed with up-to-date earthworks, barracks, a magazine, general living quarters, a forge and a special reservoir for collecting rainwater for drinking. Within two generations, it had been largely abandoned, the victim of the rise of nearby Rochefort and of the disease-ridden marshes that developed as the sea retreated.

The case of Brouage was both typical and exceptional. It was exceptional in that its position was so exposed to the elements, but it was typical in that few, if any, of the many new towns built for military or naval purposes expanded to take on the ordinary attributes of an urban centre. In this sense, the military towns were victims of their own planning. They were conceived as enlarged citadels, and their potential for development was strictly limited by the confines of their fortifications. Nor were they successful in attracting a voluntary civilian population. On the other hand, Philippeville in the Spanish Netherlands, Palmanova in the Veneto, Neufbrisach in the Rhineland and the other star-shaped urban fortresses were the epitome of the ideal city. They all shared a central square with either a grid-plan or roads radiating out to the bastions in order to facilitate the movement outwards of troops and munitions and the movement inwards of wounded soldiers. They were symmetrical and, above all, they served as practical architectural textbooks for town planners.

Naval centres were essentially a phenomenon of the last third of the seventeenth century as the English, the Dutch, the French and the Scandinavian powers competed for naval supremacy in the Atlantic, the North Sea and the Baltic. Unlike the fortress towns, their importance was sustained into the eighteenth century but, in common with them, the naval dockyards rarely took on new economic functions, and some, like Rochefort, suffered from unsatisfactory sites. Lying up the River Charente, Rochefort was unable to act as an effective naval base as well as a naval dockyard, because the river was so poorly navigable that cannons had to be unloaded before they could move upstream to dock. Brest, which was strategically well placed on the Breton coast to control the approaches to the English Channel, suffered from an inhospitable hinterland, which was incapable of supplying the raw materials for shipbuilding. The English town of Portsea, which grew up alongside the naval station at Portsmouth at the turn of the seventeenth century, contrasted oddly with its French counterparts in that no attempt was made to use fashionable planning schemes for its buildings. The regularity of its streets was determined by the distribution of the original strips of land upon which houses were built.

The construction of new towns as princely capitals was a feature of the new territorial states that were developing in the Empire. Frequently, as in the cases of Mannheim and Karlsruhe, the prince planned his town with three functions in mind. The first was as an expression of his military power. Mannheim, founded in 1606 by the Elector Palatine, was dominated by a large star-shaped citadel from which fortifications extended round the new town. The citadel was therefore both an effective form of defence against an external attack and a constant reminder, like its equivalent in older towns, of the prince's capacity to suppress disorder among his subjects. Mannheim's second function was as a capital city, the concrete expression of political power. Lying to one side of the citadel with a fortified park behind it, the prince's residence was a focal point for the streets leading to it. As a capital city, it was also expected to be economically viable and, to this effect, the Elector Palatine invited large numbers of immigrants of all confessions to settle there, on condition that they contributed useful skills or capital and commercial expertise. In this, Mannheim was only the latest of a long series of towns founded by minor German rulers to attract refugees from religious persecution and benefit from their capital and their skills. Otterberg had been founded in the 1550s to shelter Dutch Calvinists. New Hanau, not a completely new foundation, was enlarged in 1597 to attract a similar population, while Friedrichsstadt was founded in 1599.

In the British Isles, several landowners built towns in order to exploit the natural resources of their estates. A charter was granted to the port of Falmouth in Cornwall in 1660. Sir John Lowther developed Whitehaven in Cumberland at the end of the seventeenth century as a port from which to export coal from his land. The population of the town almost doubled in 20 years. In Scotland, 64 new burghs were established in the lowlands between 1600 and 1650, mostly in areas of coal and salt production. A further 150 new burgh markets were established between 1661 and 1707. As Sir Robert Sibbald commented in 1698, 'Not only all the towns that were built in that last age are very much increased in buildings by what they were then, but several were built where there were none in the last age.' [I. H Adams, *The making of urban Scotland*, London: Croom Helm, 1978: 51.]

7

Poverty and poor relief

References to the poor appeared increasingly in the official records of sixteenth- and seventeenth-century Europe. Towards the end of the sixteenth century, the Ipswich Commissioners of the Poor noted that Bartholomew Warner, a 63-year-old labourer living in St Matthew's parish with his wife of the same age, a spinner, and supporting two children of 11 and 12, was in need of firewood, clothing and a spinning wheel. In February 1595, the Roman authorities arrested a 16-year-old named Pompeo from the Trevi district for begging in the streets while pretending to be ill. During the sharp winter of 1693–94, Antoine Romieu, a Genevan journeyman cloth-shearer, was arrested for forging bread coupons. Their cases illustrate the complex phenomenon of urban poverty in the sixteenth and seventeenth centuries and the variety of responses that it elicited. While all three individuals came to official notice because of their poverty, their cases also illustrate three different responses to urban poverty. The arrest of Pompeo emphasised how attitudes to begging were increasingly founded in suspicion and irritation. The care taken to discover the needs of Bartholomew Warner and his family illustrates the way in which official programmes of poor relief were being introduced all over Europe to support the 'deserving poor'. Forging bread coupons during a period of rationing introduced during severe food shortages, on the other hand, was an example of the extent to which a skilled artisan, who would have been able to afford bread under normal circumstances, chose to break the law in order to eat. The contrast between the early attempts to confront the problem of poverty in Ipswich in the later sixteenth century and the bread-rationing schemes in Geneva over 100 years later may also be taken as a paradigm for the way in which official poor relief schemes both developed in complexity during the intervening period and became increasingly associated with harsh legal controls.

The rising numbers of the urban poor during the sixteenth century brought about both a major increase in relief programmes and long debates among theologians, moralists, humanists and other social commentators about the causes of poverty and the best way in which to deal with its manifestations. In the wake of these debates, this chapter will attempt to address a number of issues related to poverty and the responses to it in early modern towns, beginning with a discussion of the causes of urban poverty and of the different categories of the population who, at one time or another, fell into the poverty trap and drew the attention of those to whom they were a source of concern. The range of poor relief schemes that were introduced progressively and concurrently during the sixteenth and seventeenth centuries raises not only the question of the extent to which these responses appear to have overridden geographical and religious differences, but the contribution of different bodies of ideas, both religious and secular, which influenced changing attitudes towards the poor. Any consideration of ideas about poor relief and their application in this period also introduces questions about the relative influence not only of the urban authorities, the Church and the state, but also of private individuals whose willingness to donate money may have aided the poor more consistently than the ambitious plans, which have been the focus of much writing about the subject. Indeed, the most difficult question to answer of all is the extent to which all this activity brought benefits to the people whom it was intended to help.

Causes and types of poverty

Poverty is a relative concept, which many modern commentators choose to see less in terms of an absence of wealth and more in terms of relative or absolute deprivation. In the context of early modern European urban history, we may define poverty as the absence of personal resources to act as a cushion at a time of personal or general difficulty or, alternatively, among those of higher social status, as the inability to keep up the standards expected of a person of one's rank. Unemployment or underemployment, illness, infirmity or the loss of a wage-earner in the family could all contribute to a condition of deprivation in which food, clothing and shelter could no longer be guaranteed by the individual, and it became imperative to seek support from others through loans, begging, theft or organised charity. According to these criteria, the urban poor could be said to comprise most journeymen and some master craftsmen, as well as the traditionally indigent groups of the unskilled, the old, the infirm, the sick, widows and children. Without a cushion of resources to fall back on, these groups were all potentially indigent. In times of employment and good health, artisans had a standard of living superior to the homeless, old and sick but, in times of personal or general economic crisis, they were exposed to the same pressures and dangers. This distinction appears clearly in the data in Richard Gascon's study of standards of living in the Lyon building industry. According to Gascon, if the poverty line may be said to be represented by the point at which the price of bread exceeded 50 per cent of the daily wage rate, then the high inflation of the last quarter of the sixteenth century pushed journeymen builders over this threshold in one year out of 25, *laboureurs* in 17 years out of 25 and piece-workers every year.

Urban fiscal records offer a supplementary, but far from accurate, measure of poverty. While they confirm that a very high proportion of urban income was concentrated in the hands of a small economic élite, tax registers do not offer a very satisfactory record of those on low incomes. Practice varied from one city to another. In some cases, only the heads of households who actually paid taxes were recorded, offering information about those in the lowest tax bands who were in danger of falling into poverty. In others, the authorities did record the names of those residents who were deemed to be too poor to pay taxes, but without setting out the criteria by which the capacity to pay taxes was measured. The floating population of temporary migrants was rarely recorded in this way. Even with these reservations in mind, the proportions of non-taxpayers in urban fiscal records are high enough to underline the large numbers of people on low incomes in towns. Some 76 per cent of the population paid no taxes in mid-sixteenth-century Antwerp, 75 per cent in Lyon, 50 per cent in Norwich and between 50 per cent and 70 per cent in sixteenth-century Verona.

The urban poor have left few traces of their own behind them that could enable us to identify them with ease. The testimony of more privileged witnesses, such as court officials, poor relief administrators, tax officials, the clergy and social commentators, is necessarily highly subjective. Most of the time, the poor who were noted by their contemporaries were anonymous, usually referred to collectively by various disparaging terms such as 'the common people', 'beggars', 'rogues' or 'vagrants'. Pope Sixtus V's Bull of 1587 stated that 'Not only do these vagabonds... fill public places and private houses with their cries and their groans. They distract the attention of the faithful even in the churches themselves.' [J. Delumeau, *Rome au xvie siècle*, Paris: Hachette, 1975: 97–8. (Author's translation)] A century later, Father Andrea Guevarra, also writing about Rome, recorded that

> It is a strange thing to see such an infinite multitude of vagabonds, who move around from morning to evening, entering houses and churches. They are everywhere in the town, importuning first one, then another, almost snatching alms from their hands by force to use them in scandalous and dishonourable ways.
>
> (A. Guevarra, *La mendicità provedutta nella città di Roma*, Rome, 1693, quoted in B. Geremek (ed.), *Truands et misérables dans l'Europe moderne (1350–1600)*, Paris: Gallinard, 1980: 152. Author's translation)

Although there were frequent attempts to categorise the poor, there was little contemporary recognition that a very large proportion of the urban population, perhaps as high as 70–80 per cent, lived in conditions of relative poverty with few resources, if any, to fall back on in times of need. Except in times of crisis, the presence of the non-indigent poor did not impinge on the sensibilities of their more fortunate contemporaries with the same force as the sight of vagrants, children, the old, the sick and the disabled begging on the streets. This may explain why there was sometimes a mismatch between solutions to the symptoms of poverty and the underlying causes of poverty itself.

We may distinguish at least four different types of poverty in early modern urban society: structural poverty, crisis poverty, genteel or 'shamefaced' poverty and voluntary poverty. The structural poor were unable to find enough work to keep them above the poverty line at any time. Many could not work at all because they were old, sick or handicapped or too young to work. Women comprised very high proportions of the recorded poor in urban centres of all sizes. For many of them, the problem of economic survival was compounded by the effects of widowhood. The absence of family support for orphans and foundlings also placed them within this category. Ideally, orphans were cared for by members of their kinship groups or by neighbours, often women living alone. Such adoptions offered some security for the future, in that the child became legally entitled to an inheritance from their adoptive parent or parents. For other orphans, however, or children abandoned when very young, some of whom like the deaf-mute and the hunchback recorded in the baptismal records of the Strasbourg parish of St-Guillaume were disadvantaged from birth, the danger of poverty was a very real one.

Others suffering from structural poverty worked when they could, but the intermittent, unskilled and poorly paid nature of this work obliged them to supplement their income by begging, theft or both. Particularly in the winter months, their numbers were swelled by subsistence migrants who sought food, work and shelter in towns because there was no demand at such times for labour-intensive tasks, such as sowing or harvesting. The structural poor conformed most closely to contemporary images of the poor – unreliable rogues without any sense of morality or place in society. An early draft of an English law against vagrants in 1536 referred to 'men ... which be retayned in no man his wages but lyve idley in Cities and Townes (and namely in the Citie of London), procuring and makying assaultes and affraies, hauntying and frequentying the taverne and vicious places'. [Quoted in G. R. Elton, An early Tudor poor law, *Economic History Review*, VI, 1993: 62.] Sympathetic definitions of the structural poor were few and far between. Writing in 1634, the French Bishop Camus defined the *pauvre mendiant* as

someone who is not only deprived of all income, but is reduced to such a point of misery that he cannot earn his living from working even if he wished to do so, even were he in good health and not prevented through infirmity or illness.

(Quoted in J.P. Gutton, *La société et les pauvres. L'exemple de la géneralité de Lyon, 1534–1789*, Paris: Les Belles Lettres, 1972: 9. Author's translation)

At times of short-term subsistence crises resulting from famine, war or outbreaks of epidemic disease, the structural poor were supplemented by the crisis poor who were thrown into poverty when the high price of food, primarily of grain, made it impossible for them to buy enough for themselves and their families. Pierre Goubert tells of a Beauvais serge-weaver, his wife and three daughters, all employed as spinners, who earned 1296 *deniers* per week in 1693. When the price of bread stood at five *deniers* per pound, their combined weekly consumption was well within their means but, when prices rose sharply during the year, they were obliged to register with the poor office in December. Within five months, the father and two of his daughters had died of starvation.

The problem of survival during subsistence crises was compounded by the arrival of many more from outside, seeking food in the towns where it was known to be stockpiled. The increased pressure on resources from the conjunctural poor was such that existing forms of relief were frequently unable to cope with the demand, and subsistence crises became an important spur to the development of newer forms of relief. While only 740 indigent outsiders were housed in the Strasbourg *Elendherberge* in 1574, the figure for the famine year of 1575 soared to 24 303.

The records of relief institutions offer a more detailed picture of those who sought help. Contrary to the contemporary image of vagrants as lazy, unskilled and unemployed, many practised skilled occupations, the identity of which reflected the nature of the local urban economy. According to the census of the poor carried out in Norwich in 1570, most of those recorded were natives of the city or had lived there for over 20 years. The majority claimed to be working in occupations ranging from labourers and textile workers to cobblers, tailors and cordwainers. Most of them were aged between 30 and 50. Around 40 per cent of those entering the Hôtel-Dieu in Lyon in the sixteenth century also claimed to have occupational skills, chiefly artisans, followed by silk-workers. Similarly, the tax rolls from the smaller centre of Chateaudûn at the end of the seventeenth century listed 142 non-taxpayers, of whom over a third were wine-growers, gardeners or agricultural labourers.

While structural poverty remained a constant aspect of urban society throughout the sixteenth and seventeenth centuries, the levels of conjunctural poverty varied according to local economic conditions. In later seventeenth-century England, for example, the level of provision for the poor was reduced because increases in agricultural productivity lessened urban poverty levels as more food was available to meet demand and increased rural employment levels reduced the flow of rural–urban migration.

The genteel or 'shamefaced' poor suffered from a different level of deprivation. Like the structural and conjunctural poor, they were the victims of circumstances over which they had no control. Unlike them, their material misfortunes had brought about a much more rapid descent from high status, contravening the social norm, which demanded that an individual of a certain status should have the material means to support it. Such a change in circumstances ate away at their sense of honour and placed them in a social condition of considerable ambiguity, which required great circumspection and secrecy in treatment. Both the men and women who had experienced this rapid descent into poverty and their contemporaries who were in a position to help them recognised that the genteel poor were a distinct group with distinctive needs. They were often given priority by relief organisations. In 1564, they were exempted from an edict at Aix-en-Provence, which otherwise prohibited alms-giving to individuals. The Lyon hospital of La Charité deliberately kept the anonymity of the *pauvres honteux* to whom they distributed bread. The Scuola Grande di S Rocco in Venice, one of several important confraternities in the city, devoted considerable charitable effort to helping those of its members who had fallen on difficult times. In addition to providing grants so that such members could be buried without cost alongside their confraternal brothers in the church of S Rocco, the *scuola* placed considerable emphasis on the provision of dowries to ensure that their daughters could make appropriate marriages.

The concept of voluntary poverty had been at the centre of early thinking about the giving of alms during the Middle Ages. The tradition of itinerant clergy asking the faithful for alms so that they might go about their spiritual business without the need to assure their material well-being remained strong in all Catholic towns and was particularly evident in major centres of pilgrimage, such as Rome or Santiago di Compostela. Although the Council of Trent took measures to reduce the numbers of poor clergy by preventing men from taking holy orders unless they had benefices with which to support themselves, itinerant clergy continued to look for alms. Even at the turn of the seventeenth century, the Parisian authorities were still complaining of strangers begging in the streets who claimed to have taken holy orders and were, in some cases, dressed as priests.

The example of the itinerant clergy was imitated by students, pilgrims and those beggars who believed that an air of sanctity about them would elicit more generosity from alms-givers. The *Liber Vagatorum*, the classic early sixteenth-century German guide to beggars and their ruses, described how certain family groups travelled across the country with their hats and coats covered with holy signs. 'When they arrive in a town or village, they beg before one house in the name of the Lord, before another in the name of St Valentine, before a third in the name of St Querin.' [Quoted in Geremek, op. cit.: 192–97. (Author's translation)] Such beggars were judged by the *Liber* to be 'half bad and half good', and donors were recommended to give them alms if they wished to do so.

Contemporary explanations for the increase in urban poverty ranged from economic factors to a belief in a lack of moral fibre among the poor. Hans Guldenmund's *Zwölf Vagranten*, published in Nuremberg in 1524, made a firm connection between poverty and individual responsibility. His typology of vagrants included moral failures, takers of foolish actions and men who had paid dearly for mistakes while at work. The large numbers of children begging on the streets of Amiens in 1573 led one commentator to develop the theory that beggars married early in order to raise numerous children who could subsequently beg on their behalf. William Lambarde, writing in England in the crisis years of the 1590s, suggested that there was a causal link between the rise in the population and the increase in poverty. Others linked poverty to changes in the local economy, to shortages of small coins or to changes in agricultural practices, which created greater rural unemployment and increased migration to the towns.

Modern explanations for the rise in urban poverty have not progressed much further. No single explanation, such as the effects of the demographic increases of the sixteenth century or the associated rise in prices, is entirely valid. Nor is the Lis and Soly thesis that urban poverty was sustained by employers in order to ensure a regular supply of cheap labour entirely tenable. Several contributory factors can be identified with some certainty. The numbers of the urban poor were swelled by subsistence migrants, whose lack of skills or capital left them exposed to poverty, either upon arrival in a town or as soon as they were hit by subsistence crises.

While the possibilities for employment and improved material conditions offered by urban economic growth may have acted as a major pull factor for migrants, the inherent instability and unevenness of the job market generated even more poverty. Poverty levels for workers paid by the day or the hour were sharpened by uneven employment during the year. They were not paid for two days at Christmas, the very time when they needed to pay more for heating and often had to find money to pay the rent. The Easter break also coincided with the regular seasonal rise in wheat prices. Without a contract, employers of unskilled men were under no obligation to their employees, and the unceasing flow of new arrivals allowed unsatisfactory workers to be replaced by others at a moment's notice. Employment levels were also affected by outside factors. In Milan, a decline in exports following the revaluation of the currency in 1630 was followed by a refusal on the part of employers to maintain production, and employment levels fell briefly as a result. Elsewhere, unemployment rose because of a long-term decline in a town's major industry, as in the case of the Genevan silk industry, which collapsed during the second half of the seventeenth century in response to a sharp fall in demand from Lyon. The general switch in expenditure patterns away from commodities to food during subsistence crises also had an effect on the demand for other goods, which in turn had a knock-on effect on employment levels.

There was also a close link between crisis poverty and both natural and man-made subsistence crises. While famine and drought rarely affected every part of western Europe at the same time, the frequency and intensity of such constraints on food supplies rose sharply from the 1540s, as did plague epidemics. Large parts of Mediterranean Europe suffered major economic disruption, personal distress and high demographic losses during the 1570s and 1630s. As a result, food prices were not only driven to levels that were inaccessible to most of the urban population but, by causing exceptionally high levels of in-migration from the surrounding countryside, subsistence crises placed an extra strain on the demand for food, work and shelter. In crisis years, not even the provisioning policies followed by most larger centres to minimise the effects of bad harvests could compensate for food shortages (see Chapter 8). Similar pressures arose in times of warfare, when the movement of armies not only disrupted communications to the detriment of many urban economies but also displaced large numbers of peasants in search of food and safety to towns already under pressure.

The 'new philanthropy' and the old

Responses to urban poverty during the sixteenth and seventeenth centuries were a complex combination of the persistence of later medieval practices and attitudes and attempts by the urban authorities to find new large-scale solutions. In spite of some differences in emphasis between practices in Protestant and Catholic towns because of the formal dissolution of ecclesiastical charitable foundations and of confraternities during the Reformation, there was considerable uniformity in the poor relief schemes introduced all over western Europe. Only in Spain did a particularly strong network of urban confraternities obviate the need for alternative measures.

The state of urban poor relief at the beginning of the sixteenth century was a reflection of the diversity of ways in which individuals and institutions had attempted to come to terms with the problem of human indigence. While gifts of money, food and clothing in the street or at the doors of private houses were still the most widespread responses to need, the Church had long encouraged more organised distributions of alms to the parish poor financed by the gifts of the living and bequests from the dead. Confraternities took on the responsibility for caring for pilgrims, looking after the sick or providing for other categories of the poor on a scale commensurate with their own limited numbers of members. Occupational confraternities associated with guilds directed resources to help the families of members who had fallen ill or died.

The needs of children, the sick and the elderly were also catered for by hospitals established by private bequests or by the Church. These hospitals were very small in scale and often offered shelter rather than medical treatment. At this stage, the secular authorities played a limited role in poor relief. With the exception of Lyon, which was the first to take over and rationalise the administration of a number of hospitals for the poor in 1478, and Nîmes, where the Hôtel-Dieu was established in 1483, the urban authorities preferred to concentrate their efforts on the control of vagrancy, in so far as it represented a threat to public order and health.

At the turn of the fifteenth century, the provision of poor relief represented widespread but unco-ordinated attempts by the church and lay people to ease the indigence of the poor. They were motivated above all by the sanctity of the act of giving, which they believed to be central to their ultimate salvation. The identity of those who received help varied from all who asked for alms to those selected as deserving cases according to the criteria of need, local residence and a reputation for high moral behaviour. Although the distinction between the idle poor and the deserving poor had been well established from the second half of the fourteenth century, the argument that all people were equal in the face of poverty continued to be influential well into the early modern period.

The evolution of newer forms of relief from the early sixteenth century was uneven and, in many cases, tentative. These changes to poor relief represented the combination of two major approaches to poverty – the development of co-ordinated institutions to help those in need and the creation of mechanisms to distance the impact of poverty in general, and begging in particular, from the rest of urban society. In their fullest form, personified by the French *Hôpitaux Généraux* of the later seventeenth century, these institutions succeeded in creating an enclosed and disciplined environment within which the poor were housed, clothed, fed, cared for and subjected to a regime dedicated to punish them and reform their morals before restoring them to society. On the other hand, while the French model owed much to earlier initiatives taken elsewhere in Europe, many poor relief schemes undertaken in England, Germany and Italy were far less single-minded.

One of the first new steps taken by the urban authorities was to collect detailed information about the poor in their locality. Registers of the poor collected by parish priests in order to identify need were a long-standing practice. Lists embracing entire urban areas were drawn up in Paris in 1525, where the authorities ordered a list of the poor to be drawn up to enable alms to be distributed parish by parish, in Toledo in 1543, following a famine, in Grenoble in 1545, where the census distinguished between the needy poor, the genteel poor and those liable for expulsion, and in Norwich in 1570, where it was a key element in the scheme introduced to replace public begging. Such lists increasingly enabled the authorities to establish the scale of the problem of indigence and to put into practice the principle of selectivity between those who should be helped and those who should not.

The distinctions between the able-bodied poor and the deserving poor remained central to early modern attitudes towards poor relief. As Juan-Luis Vives' influential early sixteenth-century treatise on poverty and its relief, *De subventione pauperum*, stated, the first task of municipal officers was to take an annual census of the sick beggars and vagabonds in order to identify foreign beggars, who were to be sent home, and local beggars, who should receive help.

The Calvinist *Almosenordnung* issued in the Palatinate in 1574 made the more rigorous distinction between 'the indispensable alms due to the really poor members of Christ' and 'the shameful abuse of alms by the lazy'. [Quoted in B. Vogler, *La politique d'assistance dans les pays protestants Rhénaus (1555–1619)*. In *Assistance et assistés jusqu'à 1610*, Paris: Bibliothèque Nationale, 1979: 177. (Author's translation)]

Although alms-giving continued throughout the period, there was a growing belief among the authorities that public begging was undesirable. It led to indiscriminate charity at a time when most commentators agreed that not everyone was an equally deserving case. Alms-giving in the streets not only diverted valuable funds from more precisely directed aid to the poor, it was also an encouragement to the poor to beg in preference to working and to resort to subterfuge to cheat the well-meaning alms-giver of their money. Begging was morally wrong because it encouraged laziness among beggars, who would otherwise engage in productive activities, and equally wrong because it encouraged those in receipt of alms to spend the money on a way of life that was far from the spirit of Christian piety in which alms were to be given and received.

Initial attempts to control begging through a careful system of licensing crumbled in the face of increasing numbers of beggars on the streets, particularly in times of subsistence crises. The Strasbourg *Bettelbruderschaft* or beggars' corporation, established in 1411, lasted until 1523, the same year as the dissolution of the beggar's guild in Freiburg. The Basle brotherhood of foreign poor was closed down in 1491. Although beggars' organisations became rare, special licences continued to be issued to deserving individuals. Both the Spanish Poor Law of 1540 and its successor in 1565 provided for licences to be given to identifiable deserving poor and mendicant friars. In 1610, the Bavarian authorities granted extraordinary licences to beg to victims of fires and former prisoners of the Turks, a dispensation also extended in 1655 to veterans of the Imperial and Bavarian armies.

Beggars were also believed to create additional threats to public order through disturbances in the streets and to public health by spreading epidemic diseases. As was to be the case so often, the identification of the poor to whom help would be given was influenced as much by pragmatic reasoning as by the need to find scapegoats. The strongest expressions of this kind tended to coincide with a realisation that there was not enough money available to help everyone begging in the streets. Given the principle of selectivity, it is not surprising that serious attempts were made to remove beggars from the streets by prohibiting all private alms-giving and displacing beggars from the churches, inns and markets where they were accustomed to find the largest concentrations of donors. Many were expelled or used on enforced labour projects. Over time, the emphasis shifted from expulsions of vagrants, whose lack of status and marginal lifestyle made them suspect, to the more general removal of individuals who could not be dealt with otherwise.

Beggars were under constant risk of expulsion, but the behaviour of the urban authorities proved to be both intermittent and inconsistent. They responded to the numbers of beggars in their streets by expelling them in some years and not in others. The criteria for expulsion and the severity with which it was carried out varied from one town to another. Enforced departures at short notice under pain of corporal punishment were common, but there were also many instances of bread being donated to beggars about to be expelled in times of famine. In April 1539, the council of the Spanish city of Zamora ordered all foreign beggars to assemble on the bridge of S Zulian between 7 and 10 the following morning to receive a loaf of bread and some money before leaving. Healthy beggars were also sent on their way with money from Strasbourg in 1523.

Distinctions were not always drawn between local and 'foreign' beggars. Expulsion edicts passed in Amiens in 1545 and in Rennes in 1563 evicted all 'foreign' poor from the city on pain of being whipped. In contrast, the Venetian authorities chose to expel all the able-bodied poor during the famine of 1528; so did the council of Aix-en-Provence in 1564. In 1590, the Valladolid authorities expelled only foreign beggars but chose, in 1599, to include all the able-bodied poor.

An alternative to the expulsion of beggars was their employment on unpleasant but civically useful tasks under strict supervision in the towns or, when manpower needs required it, as naval oarsmen. Public works were not necessarily regarded as an equivalent to expulsion. They were used variously as punishments for able-bodied beggars and sources of income to relieve the poor in times of crisis. Contrast the practice in sixteenth-century Paris of taking 'incorrigible vagrants' in chains under guard to the city's fortifications to work from 6 in the morning to 5 in the evening with the use of large numbers of the poor on the fortifications in Rouen in 1586, a year in which around 20 per cent of the population of 14 000 were in receipt of relief during the summer months. Those deemed to deserve help in Grenoble in 1545 were set to work on roads and rivers and in workshops. The poorest inhabitants of Aix-en-Provence were required to clean the streets and sewers in 1564 and, in 1591, over 3000 of the poor were used to construct fortifications in Perugia. This represented a new development in the treatment of the poor, which was to become incorporated in many programmes in the seventeenth century. By requiring the poor to work, the costs of providing them with relief could be balanced by the savings arising from using them on civic works.

At the same time that the secular authorities were attempting to control begging by the able-bodied poor, several interest groups were addressing themselves to the equally important problem of providing relief to those who were perceived to be really in need. It had become abundantly clear in the early years of the sixteenth century that existing provision for the old, the young, single women, the sick and the disabled was not only insufficient to meet the demand for care, but was also badly managed. In addition to the very small and scattered provision offered by hospitals with 10 beds or fewer, the terms of many bequests created circumstances which, in the long term, benefited their administrators or employees rather than those in need. The picture for the early modern period is patchy. Although concerted efforts were made in many cities to amalgamate small hospitals into larger units during the sixteenth century, the Hospital of S Bartolomé in Valladolid in the early seventeenth century still had a ratio of three administrators to each of the five inmates, while enjoying a very large income. Indeed, there was considerable resistance in Spain to any proposals for amalgamation. In Zamora, plans sponsored by Philip II came to nothing in the face of hostility from local confraternities, who argued that there was no reason to amalgamate hospitals on the basis that centralising funds would lead to more efficient poor relief, as centralisation would lead to the dissolution of the confraternities and the consequent loss of the money that they provided to run their own small hospitals. A compromise approach evolved in Rome, which had its own unusual problems arising out of the large number of pilgrims visiting the city. Ten new hospitals administered by confraternities or religious orders, often with financial support from the Pope, were established by private initiatives during the course of the sixteenth century.

In many French cities, successful amalgamations of hospitals took place under the aegis of the municipal authorities. This represented a transfer of responsibility for this aspect of poor relief from groups of lay or ecclesiastical administrators to bodies set up by the urban authorities. In the early stages, the Hôtel-Dieu, an organisation run by the church, was used as the new focus for relief. The *Consulat* in Lyon took over the local Hôtel-Dieu in 1478, while the Parisian government appointed eight lay administrators to replace the chapter of Notre-Dame in 1505. In Protestant cities in Germany, hospitals run by the Church before the Reformation were transferred to lay control. Similar transfers took place under royal patronage in London, where Edward VI took over the responsibility for St Thomas' and St Bartholomew's Hospitals.

Later, hospital administration was transferred to special magistracies established to deal with the poor, such as the *Chambre des Pauvres* in Dijon, the *Grand Bureau des Pauvres* in Paris, the *Ufficio dei Poveri* in Genoa and the *Provveditori alla Sanità* in Venice (in the last case, supervision of the poor was added to the responsibilities of a magistracy set up to deal with matters of public health). When famine brought extra pressures on poor relief provision, it was official bodies such as these that organised large-scale relief. After the famine of 1527, the Venetian authorities established four hospitals by mid-April 1528, capable of feeding and lodging 1000 at a time. On an even larger scale, the authorities in Strasbourg opened the empty

Barfusskloster and *Elendherberge* in 1529 to accommodate famine victims. During the 12 months from June 1530, the latter provided for 23 548 outsiders, a figure only exceeded during the famine of 1575.

More formal long-term aid to the poor was established in Germany, the Netherlands and France through the mechanism of the *Aumône Générale*. Following the precedent set by Nuremberg in 1523, *Aumônes Généraux* were set up in Ypres (1525), Lille (1527), Paris (1530), Lyon (1531) and Rouen (1534). They continued to offer customary forms of help to the poor, while combining this with a new emphasis on training for the young and controls on begging in the streets. In Lyon, the *Aumône Générale* distributed bread to the poor, offered children the opportunity to become apprentices in the silk industry and appointed beadles to patrol the streets and city gates to prevent begging. Unlike earlier attempts to maximise the income from existing foundations, the *Aumônes Généraux* were funded by a combination of donations, taxes and municipal income. In Lyon, collecting boxes were placed in churches, shops and inns. Some police fines and fees charged for permission to sell meat during Lent were diverted to the new institution, and a voluntary tax was raised, which could become obligatory in times of crisis. Most other poor relief schemes adopted similar sources of income. House-to-house collections supplemented alms boxes in Grenoble, Ypres, Lille and Lyon. Direct taxes to aid the poor were introduced in Venice, Amiens and Norwich. In most Protestant areas, these sources of income were heavily supplemented by income from pre-Reformation pious foundations or monastic lands, the responsibility for which had passed to the secular authorities, by direct donations to the poor boxes and by income from poor rates. The latter had been established following the precedent of the regulations for the poor at Leisnig drawn up by Martin Luther. If the detailed figures for the funding of poor relief in Lille during the sixteenth century matched the pattern elsewhere, then the gradual assumption of responsibility for poor relief by the urban authorities was accompanied by a decline in the proportion of the total income contributed by personal donations and an increase in the proportion provided by taxation.

During the late sixteenth and seventeenth centuries, there was a change in emphasis in the thinking about poor relief, first in northern and central Italy, then in France. Rather than concentrating on institutionalised alms-giving and the provision of shelter in times of crisis and medical aid to the sick, it was proposed that the poor should be rounded up and enclosed in permanent buildings. The principles were enunciated by Cardinal Richelieu in 1625 in a note entitled *Pauvres renfermez*.

> Since divers vagabonds and good-for-nothings instead of working as they should to earn a living have turned to begging, lifting the bread from the invalid and deserving poor to whom it is due, incommoding the inhabitants of the towns and depriving the public of the service which they should receive from their work, we desire that in every

town in our kingdom rules and regulations for the poor should be established, so that not only all those of the said town but also of the neighbouring areas should be enclosed and fed, and those who are able to do so should be employed on public works.

(Quoted in J.P. Gutton, *La société et les pauvres en Europe (xvie–xviie siècles)*, Paris: Presses Universitaires de France, 1974: 124–5. Author's translation)

Programmes to enclose the poor were pursued with the greatest enthusiasm in French towns. Over 1000 beggars of both sexes were enclosed in the Hôpital St-Germain in Paris during the second half of the sixteenth century. Although this initiative failed during the regency of Louis XIII, the momentum was taken up by the authorities in Lyon, where the poor were enclosed from 1614.

A whole stream of other large provincial towns followed: Reims (1629), Aix-en-Provence (1640), Marseille and Dijon (1643), Montpellier (1647), Toulouse and Béziers (1650) and Tours (1656). An *Hôpital Générale* was also established in Paris in 1656, bringing together several existing institutions for the poor under a single administration. A second wave of foundations to enclose the poor followed a French royal edict of 1662, which required all other major towns to enclose their poor using the Parisian model. Unlike the earlier institutions, however, these hospitals were only intended to house the deserving poor.

Similar schemes to enclose the poor were introduced elsewhere, but on a much smaller scale than in France and with far less success. Hospitals were established in Italy in Bologna (1560), Turin (1583), Modena (1592), Venice (1594), Florence (1621) and Naples (1667). There was a constant tension between lack of money to run the hospitals and the growing numbers of beggars who should have been enclosed in them. In Rome, the high numbers of beggars inspired more than one Pope to arrange for them to be enclosed, but to little effect. At the end of February 1581, Pope Gregory XIII led a procession of 850 of Rome's 'deserving poor' to the former monastery of S Sisto, where they were to lodge under the care of a confraternity.

Notwithstanding the failure of this scheme within two years, Pope Sixtus V opened a new structure in 1587 to accommodate 2000 poor at a cost of around 33 000 écus. It was organised in ways that were to become familiar in France. Those who were incapable of working were kept in a hospice, dressed in grey with their hair cut off. Girls were taught how to sew and boys how to read, write and practise a trade. Like the first scheme, this attempt at enclosure was short-lived because the Papal authorities lacked the means to keep the poor enclosed, and the outbreak of a famine swelled the number of poor in the streets. By 1601, only 150 inmates remained. Even when beggars remained in the hospitals, economic considerations made it impossible to sustain the amount of support that they were given. Entries to the *Conservatore di San Salvatore* in Florence were strictly limited in the middle of the seventeenth century in order to save money. When the drain on resources continued, the hospital's administrators took the radical step in 1672 of expelling all male inmates. Similar failures were recorded in the Spanish Netherlands during the seventeenth century when hospitals were unable to accrue sufficient revenue from sales of goods produced by inmates.

Many more hospitals were established in France and Italy than in parts of Europe where some form of Protestantism was the dominant confession. The level of enthusiasm for enclosure may have been determined in part along confessional lines, but this was not the only consideration. The strongest movement in favour of enclosure took place in the Calvinist Netherlands. Twenty-six *Tuchthuiser* were established, following the model of the Amsterdam hospital of 1589. In Germany, hospitals were only established in Bremen, Lübeck, Hamburg and Danzig during the same period, all Hanseatic ports, although there was a later move to set up hospitals in the 1670s in a range of free imperial cities (Nuremberg, Frankfurt am Main and Königsberg) and capitals and major provincial centres in the larger territorial states (Breslau, Vienna, Leipzig, Magdeburg and Berlin).

In contrast, enclosure was never fully implemented in England or in Spain. The houses of correction established in London and elsewhere in the mid-sixteenth century may have been an inspiration to those on the continent searching for solutions to begging, because they were among the first to discipline sturdy beggars and to set them to work, but neither they nor their short-lived successor, the London Workhouse, set up in 1647, were ever residential. In contrast to the United Provinces, where power was largely devolved to the major towns, which then determined their own social policy, the Elizabethan Poor Law and its successors were dedicated to returning the poor to receive relief in their parishes of origin rather than enclosing large numbers in a limited number of urban centres. In London, the large scale of poverty and the absence of a single unitary authority to make decisions about the poor and raise money to pay for them created a confused situation, which was only temporarily resolved in times of major crisis through executive action taken to protect the court by the Privy Council.

The proposals to enclose the poor united many of the practices, such as the provision of hospitals for old women or children, which had already emerged during the sixteenth century, but they also added a new and punitive dimension to the treatment of the poor. It was a logical extension of the desire of the urban authorities to remove begging from the streets, to deter the able-bodied poor from sinful behaviour and to punish the poor for immoral behaviour, which was seen as a threat to both public order and high standards of morality. There was unanimity among contemporary commentators that setting the poor to work was the only way to their redemption. As the English Puritan, William Perkins, wrote in 1601, the only hope of the poor was to be set on work 'so that by diligence in a calling, they may be once again restored to a disciplined … community, to a settled congregation, and to the promises of salvation offered to believers through the church'. [A treatise of the vocations or callings of men. Quoted in C. Hill. The Puritans and the Poor, *Past and Present*, II, 1952: 43–4.]

Perkins' comment was a good example of the way in which contemporaries of both confessions associated the relief of poverty with a responsibility to offer salvation to the poor. There was general agreement that a life of poverty encouraged the sins of laziness, blasphemy, drunkenness and fornication, and that relief schemes would only enhance this unless they were properly regulated and linked to conditions in which the poor received proper religious instruction. In both Protestant and Catholic towns, the young were carefully instructed in the catechism, for it was believed that they were the most likely to give up a life of sin, but adults were also obliged to attend religious services and listen *en masse* to improving sermons. Many of the men and women who played a leading part in encouraging programmes to control and employ the poor while exposing them to prayer and religious enlightenment were primarily motivated for religious reasons. At the same time that the control of poor relief was moving away from the Church to the secular authorities, the main impetus for change came from men and women imbued with the need to express their religious beliefs, even if the theological reasons for helping the poor differed sharply between Protestants and Catholics. In England, Puritan magistrates, such as John Ivie, the mayor of Salisbury, took a leading part in introducing change. In France, the clandestine Company of the Holy Sacrament, whose members were drawn from the highest levels of society and which had branches in all the country's major cities, infiltrated the administration of hospitals in order to fulfil their mission. Similar activities took place in Italy, where the *Compagnia del Divino Amore* effectively controlled the *Uffizio de' Poveri* in Genoa.

Personal salvation was not, of course, the only reason for attempts to control the poor. Often, religious belief merged into the general secular concern to create an organised society from which all potential threats of disorder had been excluded. The growing body of mercantilist literature in the second half of the seventeenth century placed more emphasis on the need to set the poor to work to avoid a drain on the economy and contribute to the strength of the state. In every case, however, officially inspired relief schemes were the product of considerations that had little to do with indigence directly.

In spite of the energy expended in controlling the poor, the 'New Philanthropy' did not replace older forms of relief in their entirety. Private alms-giving remained common all over Europe. It was particularly effective in times of crisis when more formal kinds of relief were overwhelmed by the numbers in need of food and shelter. Nor can it be argued that the 'New Philanthropy' represented either the substitution of lay for ecclesiastical control of poor relief or the replacement of a multiplicity of initiatives by unified schemes organised by the urban authorities. The medieval Church had presented charity as the expression of piety through seven acts of mercy:

ensuring that the hungry were fed; the thirsty were given drink; the naked were clothed; the sick were visited; captives ransomed; the homeless lodged; and the dead were buried. Private alms-giving by individuals in the street and from their houses continued to be a major form of relief in both Catholic and Protestant urban centres throughout the sixteenth and seventeenth centuries. In Catholic centres, it was encouraged by many Church writers, who remained faithful to the older tradition of charity as a major route to individual salvation. As Domingo de Soto, the prior of a Salamanca convent, wrote in 1545, alms-giving should be permitted to enable the rich to accomplish good works. During the crisis of 1556–59, Cardinal Siliceo of Toledo wrote that no one should close the door to the stranger. Helping the poor brought spiritual gain. Proposals to introduce formal relief schemes to eliminate begging also brought strong ecclesiastical arguments in favour of the efficacy of alms-giving, such as Friar Laurent de Villaricencio's opposition to the new poor relief scheme in Bruges on the grounds that begging was still legitimate if caused by necessity, and the well-known critique of the Ypres plans by the local mendicant clergy, who appealed to the theology faculty at the Sorbonne for a ruling. Indeed, the Ypres ordinances were modified in 1531 to permit voluntary alms-giving by the citizenry.

Readiness to give alms was particularly prevalent during subsistence crises when the combined pressure of the indigent and subsistence poor overwhelmed what could be offered by organised relief schemes. Such crises also heightened the charitable impulses of those who were better off because they came face to face with people in immediate and urgent need. As Jean de Vauzelles wrote of Lyon during the crisis of 1531, the poor were 'like bodies dug up from their graves'. Lyon was 'so thickly sown with poverty that it resembled rather a hospital of the famished'. Nor were the authorities loath to take advantage of these charitable impulses. Whether they liked it or not, more prosperous citizens could be required to give food, money and shelter to the poor in extreme circumstances. In the face of an imminent outbreak of the plague in 1520, the Bishop of Grenoble distributed alms to the poor on behalf of the town. During the crisis of 1580, house-to-house collections on behalf of the poor were made in Aix-en-Provence. In Toledo, beggars had to be taken into people's houses in 1546 unless the householders were willing to pay towards their upkeep elsewhere. Lists of the poor to be fed were attached to the doors of the wealthy in Lyon during the plague of 1628, and householders were warned that their houses would be opened up by force in the face of any refusals.

While the continuation of alms-giving into the eighteenth century reflected, and indeed encouraged, opportunistic begging, it was also given tacit recognition by the authorities when they organised strictly controlled begging under licence. The origins of such controls lay in the growing discrimination between foreign and local beggars, and the able poor and the deserving poor during the later Middle Ages. The tradition of granting begging licences to members of strictly controlled brotherhoods or corporations of the poor had largely died out by the early sixteenth century.

The spiritual regeneration associated with the Counter-Reformation also led to opportunities for individual acts of charity through membership of confraternities. In France, following the example of St Vincent de Paul and the Capucin, Yves de Paris, parish activity groups were set up by laymen in increasing numbers during the seventeenth century to help the poor with food, medicine and clothing while giving them spiritual consolation. Members of Spanish and Italian confraternities were engaged in similar acts of piety.

While the persistence of alms-giving among Catholic townsmen may be explained by the long tradition to which Christian charity belonged, the evidence for the continuation of similar practices by Protestant townsmen is more surprising. While both Luther and Calvin emphasised the Christian responsibility to succour the poor, their deliberate rejection of the link between spiritual grace and good works should have reinforced the secular criticisms of the efficacy of indiscriminate aid to the poor. According to Paul Slack, however, indiscriminate alms-giving through direct aid and testamentary bequests in England almost certainly equalled official poor relief in value during the sixteenth and seventeenth centuries. There is also abundant evidence that a strong tradition of alms-giving remained throughout the sixteenth century and, as on the continent, played an important role in times of crisis. In Norwich, the well-organised civic poor relief scheme of 1570 was unable to take the strain of a plague outbreak nine years later, and local citizens were asked for direct help. In 1596, after the third successive bad harvest, the Privy Council ordered Londoners to give up their supper on Wednesdays and Fridays and to give what they had saved to the poor. The livery companies were also asked to collect alms for the poor after the sermons in Holy Week and on Easter Sunday, so that bread and money could be distributed to the poor.

Other older kinds of charitable help in the form of bequests also remained widespread but experienced some modification during the period, as their efficacy was put into doubt or the ends to which the money was used were modified to take account of more organised forms of larger-scale relief. Food and money were distributed to the poor by parish clergy fulfilling charitable bequests. Such donations ranged from requests to distribute food and money on the day of an individual's funeral to more regular distributions and bequests directed to addressing more specific problems. The progression from indiscriminate to directed bequests over time may well be interpreted as a response to both the growing numbers of the urban poor and the presence of more institutional routes to relief, which depended in part on private charity for their income. Hence, we find a contrast between the York alderman, Percival Cornforth's, request in 1571 that 1000 halfpenny loaves be distributed to the poor on the day he was buried and a bequest by Alderman Agar to the city corporation in 1631 'to set the poor on work'.

The effectiveness of poor relief

In spite of all efforts, urban poverty was never eradicated. People continued to live in insalubrious and unsafe buildings. Their diets continued to lack vitamins and, as a result, there was a high incidence of anaemia, rickets, pellagra and scurvy. When food ran short during subsistence crises, the poor continued to suffer disproportionately. Nor can the case be made that the objectives of those who set carefully regulated poor relief schemes were fulfilled. There was sustained hostility from the poor themselves, who resented having to give up begging and submit themselves to a rigorous discipline, which controlled the conditions under which they could receive help. In Rouen, groups of the poor working on the fortifications in 1586 openly criticised government policy and behaved with an insolence that scandalised a contemporary witness. Even the children's hospital of the Trinity in Paris openly admitted that earlier efforts to place children as apprentices had failed. Many of the children had left their master's service and needed to be placed elsewhere. Others had returned to begging and stealing, often with the encouragement of their parents.

There are numerous reports of members of the public, who disapproved of regulations to enclose the poor, using force to prevent beggars from being taken away. Officials in Dijon leading beggars off to be sent to the galleys in the 1530s were stoned by a hostile crowd, even though the town was under great pressure during a subsistence crisis. Even the deserving poor objected to the atmosphere of suspicion with which their claims were treated and to the strings that were tied to the alms they were given, such as the prohibition in Lyon on using alms for gambling or in the ale-houses. If a Somerset Justice of the Peace is to be believed, the vagrants whom he visited in a local house of correction in 1596 were willing to confess to imaginary crimes or do anything to avoid the harsh conditions there.

More serious than the negative responses of the poor themselves was the inability of many formal schemes to raise the funds necessary to make a long-term impact. The history of plans to deal with the poor tells us more about the intentions of those whose primary purpose was to cleanse society of sin and to inculcate a new sense of responsibility among the poor than it does about the projects' effectiveness. The frequency with which the same measures were put forward in individual towns tells the sad story of their inability to solve the problem of indigence. The continued presence of beggars on the streets was inevitable when the buildings destined to accommodate them were either too small or the cost of their upkeep was too high. Sources of funding, which had seemed generous during the initial bout of enthusiasm during which hospitals for the poor were established, were eroded by inflation. It is not surprising that the movement to enclose the poor never spread fully within northern Europe, nor that, even in France, where it had enjoyed support at the highest levels, there was a movement towards alternative forms of relief at the turn of the seventeenth century.

Even when dragnet operations to round up beggars in order to expel or enclose them were successful, neither they nor the measures taken by the urban authorities to patrol the streets or guard the gates were any match for the continuing pressure of inward migration by those in search of food and shelter. Potential beggars were not always easy to distinguish, as the gate-keepers of Strasbourg discovered during the winter of 1530–31. In their defence, they explained that they had allowed in many fairly well-dressed men, women, boys and girls, whom no one could have taken for beggars. Like so many others who had to deal with the poor, they had been misled by the stereotype of the vagabond. Nor could controls on the gates ever be effective when, as in the case of Lyon, beggars who had been expelled from the city's main gates made their way back in along the banks of the Rhône and the Saône or, as in the case of increasing numbers of urban centres, fortifications were either removed completely or allowed to crumble (see Chapter 6).

In contrast to this general picture of gloom, the immense efforts devoted to urban poor relief during the sixteenth and seventeenth centuries deserve some recognition. Without the distributions of bread and offers of accommodation at times of subsistence cries, it is probable that many more would have died of starvation. In spite of the limited numbers who could be accommodated in buildings devoted to the care or 'correction' of the poor at any one time, the evidence that most inmates only stayed a relatively short time indicates that, over the years, these institutions touched a substantial number of the poor at one time or another. The resources devoted to those groups, such as the sick, orphans and widows, who were targeted for long-term help, also bore fruit.

The success of poor relief schemes should perhaps be measured less in terms of the proportion of the poor given food and shelter at any one time than in terms of the way in which their activities supplemented the incomes of the poor at one time or another. Although this was contrary to much of the rhetoric that motivated urban poor relief, such help may have made the difference between total indigence and survival. Nor should we ignore the growing body of evidence that both the soliciting and giving of alms in the streets and private schemes dedicated to supporting the needy persisted in spite of repeated attempts in both Catholic and Protestant societies to condemn it, which leads to the conclusion that the 'new philanthropy' may not always have contributed as much as the old.

In the end, however, urban poor relief could only ever have had a limited success because, with the exception of the national schemes established in England and the Netherlands, it was unable to confront the macroeconomic causes of poverty. All too often the success of one urban poor relief scheme only displaced the problem elsewhere.

8

Social order and disorder

The concept of a harmonious and ordered society runs through the writings of the later Middle Ages and early modern period as a constant theme. Nowhere was this ordered society more eagerly portrayed than in the towns. In his *Panegyric to the city of Florence*, the fifteenth-century Italian humanist, Leonardo Bruni, wrote that his native city had

> outstanding civil institutions and laws. Nowhere else do you find such internal order, such neatness, and such harmonious cooperation. There is a proportion in strings of a harp so that when they are tightened, a harmony results from the different tones; nothing could be sweeter or more pleasing to the ear than this. In the same way, this very prudent city is harmonized in all its parts, so that there results a single, great, harmonious constitution, whose harmony pleases both the eyes and the minds of men.
>
> (B. G. Kohl *et al.* (eds), *The earthly republic, Italian humanists on government and society*, Manchester: Manchester University Press, 1978: 168–9)

Bruni's ideals were shared by everyone in authority and by many others who strove to reach them during the sixteenth and seventeenth centuries. Many of the physical changes made to urban centres during the period were governed by such considerations. On the other hand, just as the best laid plans for impressive palaces constructed along well-organised streets intersecting in geometrically perfect squares were disturbed by the persistence of older, disordered street patterns nearby, those who believed in an ordered urban society were constantly aware of the threats to their vision and of the need to keep them under control.

This chapter is concerned with the relationship between the fear of disorder in towns, the extent to which such fears were justified and the measures that were taken by the urban authorities to forestall or control outbreaks of disorder. As threats and potential threats to order are both relative and highly subjective concepts, it is not easy to define what contemporaries meant by them. On the one hand, they defined disorder in negative terms as the contrary to an ordered society. On the other, when they did refer to disorderly behaviour, they preferred to use imprecise terms, such as 'the great discontent and murmuring of the people … specially of the poorer sort', a phrase used by the Lord Mayor of London in a letter to Sir Robert Cecil in 1597, the 'riot and popular sedition' of June 1635, which was reported to the French government by the councillors of Agen, or the rising of the Strasbourg market gardeners in 1585, which was characterised by the city council as a 'tumult'.

An alternative to these value-loaded terms would be to list a range of actions that were generally recognised as being disorderly, such as the erection of barricades in the streets, the organised theft of bread from bakers' shops, armed attacks on official buildings, churches or the residences of the wealthy or even abnormally large gatherings of individuals in the open air expressing sentiments that were highly critical of the established political order. To do so would be to miss the point that actions were only perceived as disorderly once they crossed the line between what was acceptable and what was unacceptable behaviour and, while armed attacks on individuals and property may have represented a constant and unambiguous threat to order, many other actions did not. They remained within the norms of acceptable behaviour unless they were carried out in an unusual way or unless the authorities' attitude towards them had been altered by circumstances.

While the authorities' perception of threats to urban social order was also shared by those who had a vested interest in retaining their property and privileges, a discussion of such perceptions and the actions that resulted from them represents a limited view of the nature and causes of urban order and disorder in early modern Europe and one that places too much emphasis on the attitudes of those in power. By concentrating on the search for an absolute – a completely ordered society – we are in danger of assuming, on the one hand, that the criteria for such a society remained unchanged throughout the sixteenth and seventeenth centuries, when it is clear that these criteria were profoundly modified by the territorial state, and on the other, that certain forms of behaviour were constantly disruptive when they were not. The role of carnival as a major threat to order is well known, both in the context of the German Reformation and during the French Wars of Religion. On the other hand, it was not carnival itself but the potentially explosive circumstances of the time, which turned carnival into a vehicle of protest and disorder. Carnival is a good example of a cultural phenomenon that ran counter to the ordinary norms of social behaviour but was accepted by the population in general as part of an annual cycle of activity.

Most discussions of urban order and disorder make a number of assumptions about the nature of urban society in early modern Europe. One approach subscribes to the belief, widely shared by contemporaries, that social order was in constant danger from disruptive forces and only survived through ceaseless vigilance. A second view is that the various forces in urban society largely operated in an equilibrium achieved through the common recognition of each other's role in society and a range of shared cultural values. Exceptions to this pattern were the small number of urban centres that were caught up in major crises representing a temporary breakdown in authority and social order. The events in Toledo in 1520, in Paris in 1588 and 1648 and the Masaniello uprising in Naples in 1647 were all cases in which the forces of government power were temporarily overthrown and attempts were made to create alternative power structures. A third approach portrays urban violence as a symptom of a society at war with itself. There are difficulties with all three approaches. In the case of the first two, they suffer from an underlying assumption that there was a single static model of urban society throughout the period, when there is abundant evidence that sixteenth- and seventeenth-century society was undergoing substantial change. While the view that urban violence was a symptom of such changes offers a way forward to a more dynamic model of urban society, it too has its limitations. The difficulty with this approach is that, while it appears to deal with all acts of disorder, by emphasising violence it ignores a much broader range of behaviour, which had the potential to become disorderly under certain circumstances.

In the spirit of this broader definition of behaviour capable of crossing social norms, this chapter therefore attempts to address the difficult question of whether or not early modern urban societies were becoming more volatile during the period. It considers in turn the range of ways in which the social order was disrupted, those whose behaviour was deemed to be disruptive, including particularly volatile elements in society, such as the young and the poor, the causes of disorder and the multiple ways in which order was restored, enforced and reinforced.

Disorderly behaviour

A broad range of disorderly behaviour was recorded by scandalised contemporaries and in the minutiae of judicial proceedings. At one end of the spectrum lay minor acts of violence between husbands and wives, neighbours and drinking companions. They may be typified as minor because of the small numbers of people involved, usually from a very restricted circle. In themselves, they were far from minor acts. At a time when all men wore knives as a matter of course and much domestic violence took place in a space that served as a kitchen where sharp implements were easily available, it is not surprising that disputes could end in stabbings or murder. Ignace Chavatte recorded a fight in his diary on 7 July 1687 between a Lille innkeeper and a man named Dussey, who was stabbed in the arm. A vinegar-maker in Dijon slapped a man in the face and snatched his hat off in a double affront to his honour. Natalie Zemon Davis' study of pardon tales in sixteenth-century France is full of cases of husbands who murdered unfaithful wives, wives who arranged to poison their husbands and drunken butchers who stabbed each other after disagreements over gambling debts. There is no evidence that interpersonal violence was any less common outside France or that it was particularly associated with any one social group. It need scarcely come into discussion in this context were it not that such actions created an atmosphere in which the expression of more general grievances was also violent or could become violent.

Emmanuel Le Roy Ladurie has done more than any other historian to draw attention to the way in which the very nature of carnival carried within it the seeds of violence and disorder. His study of the interconfessional conflict in the French city of Romans in February 1580 is an excellent exposition of how both the organisation of carnival and the spirit of the celebrations themselves came to focus communal antagonisms to the extent that, in his words, 'the night [before Mardi Gras] began with a huge spread, with sausages and lard. It ended in blood and tears.' [Le Roy Ladurie, 1980: 207]. The traditionally playful competition between the Partridge King and the Candlemas Bear became the deadly rivalry between the ropemaker Laroche, a leader of the Catholic League, and Paumier, a master draper with Huguenot support, ending in the latter's murder.

Carnival was the traditional period of midwinter celebration culminating on Shrove Tuesday immediately before the beginning of Lent. It was characterised by a desire to create a structured world, which was a mirror of everyday life. Much has been made of the deliberate contrasts between carnival and Lent portrayed so effectively in Breughel's painting of *The Battle between Carnival and Lent*, in which a mock tournament takes place between a corpulent carnival king, crowned with a meat pie, sitting astride a barrel and armed with a spit, facing the lean figure of Lent, wearing a beehive, seated on a chair from the church, opposing him with a wooden shovel upon which repose two pickled Lenten herrings. But these contrasts, powerful as they were, played less of a role in carnival than the desire to portray an alternative world. The world of work was replaced by a world of play, in which ordinary economic activity gave way to a holiday atmosphere, working clothes were replaced by costumes with masks that not only disguised their wearers and gave them freedom to alter their behaviour without embarrassment, but also enabled them to satirise the social order without danger of offence. Indeed, offensive behaviour was positively encouraged. Large amounts of food and alcohol were consumed, both as a counterpoint to the restricted portions available during the rest of the year and in celebration of the material world. Towns became crowded with participants and spectators from both inside and outside the walls.

The withering of carnival in face of the twin disapproval of Church and state has left a false impression of unbridled licence. As a mirror of the conventional world, it was an intensely stratified and organised experience. The key moments of the season were set pieces of public entertainment, whose organisation was conferred to occupational or social groups under the leadership of a carnival king or abbot, bear or partridge.

The fighting in Romans in 1580 was an extreme example of an activity that always had the potential to go further than was intended. There was nothing subversive in carnival itself until this construction was placed upon it by the authorities in the later sixteenth and seventeenth centuries. On the other hand, the structures of carnival offered a perfect opportunity to make critical statements that were both within the spirit of the celebration and politically threatening to the authorities. Bob Scribner has identified 22 different incidents in Germany between 1520 and 1543 in which carnival was used to make pro-Reformation statements. In February 1521, following a mock autumn carnival procession in Wittenberg the previous year, during which Luther's students had followed a float representing a giant version of a Papal Bull around the town before burning it to the sound of a solemn *Te Deum*, the students carried around a giant effigy of the Pope and set it up in the market-place to be pelted. Processions with floats and effigies of well-known people presented as subjects of derision were commonplace carnival customs even after the Reformation. In Nuremberg, the 1539 carnival procession or *Schembartlauf* featured an effigy of the Lutheran pastor, Osiander, who was well known for his attacks on popular excess. After the procession ended, his house was attacked.

Disturbances related to carnival also took place in the seventeenth century. The Shrove Tuesday riots in the form of ritualised attacks on brothels, which took place almost every two years out of three in London between the accession of James I and the outbreak of the Civil War, may have been a way of using carnival as a safety valve for emotions pent up during the rest of the year, but they were also a source of concern to the authorities. In France, carnival ritual, which was an integral part of the identity of each town, became a means of expressing opposition to taxation by the monarchy. In 1635, the innkeepers of Rochechouart assembled in masks and beat drums to drive away tax collectors before ritually burning the bales of straw that were their symbol. In the following year, some of the sons of wealthy families disguised themselves and took part in a noisy carnival procession to drive two royal officials from their lodgings. In 1651, during the Fronde, the people of Bordeaux carried out symbolic executions of Cardinal Mazarin on three separate occasions during carnival.

Ritualised celebrations also provided the framework for trouble in Naples. A traditional mock battle was held in the Piazza del Mercato every year during the Feast of the Virgin Mary in July, when a castle built out of wood and painted paper was attacked and defended by large groups of young men armed with sticks and fruit. In 1647, a version of the battle coincided with a demonstration against the unpopular fruit tax, and the mock battle became a riot, during which the tax office and its records were destroyed, the first stage of a far more serious rebellion.

If public disturbances at the time of carnival represented both an extension of behaviour characteristic of the season and the coming together of powerful grievances at this sensitive time of the year, they also shared a number of common features with the collective expression of grievances at other times of the year. These included the physical destruction of buildings and other items associated with the objects of the grievance, the erection of barricades in the streets to indicate that control of the area had been transferred away from the authorities to the protesters and mass demonstrations intended to convey grievances and to place pressure on the authorities to meet deputations. The question arises whether these actions were premeditated or the violent or semi-violent expression of a frustrated mass of the population without other recourse. The responses of the authorities show that they were as uncertain about this matter as we are. On the one hand, they were constantly afraid of 'the common people', with the implication that rioting was uncontrolled collective violence. On the other, their search for ringleaders after the event and their readiness to request rioters to choose a deputation from among themselves would suggest that they needed some kind of conspiracy theory to explain collective protests. They argued that the people had been led astray by evil men who were somehow outside the community, vagabonds, members of minority religious groups or agents of foreign powers; the three categories were often seen as one.

Detailed analysis of collective protests suggests that they were structured in a number of ways. The frequency with which the same patterns of behaviour manifested themselves in different urban centres over a long period of time suggests that there was a common vocabulary of protest, as well as a common tradition of making protests, one which was shared and understood across society. These provided a framework within which different groups and individuals could influence protests, either before they had started or once a protest movement had evolved.

One of the most common elements of collective protests was the deliberate destruction of buildings, property and artefacts. While the circumstances in which each act took place varied, all such actions shared two important characteristics. They were highly structured, and their symbolism was as important as the fact of material destruction.

In April 1675, riots broke out in the Breton capital of Rennes. According to the diary of Maître Duchemin,

> Around two o'clock in the afternoon, some unknown scum, and some others who were not from our town gathered together, and in a state of excitement, went to the office which sells tobacco..., and having forced in the doors and the windows, pillaged and took away all the tobacco, even the furniture which was there. They searched all the cellars, took all the wine and cider which was there, threw stones and broke all the windows of the house, and then went to the office where all legal agreements were kept (the *bureau de contrôle et d'affirmations*)

in the same square .... They threw the registers and notebooks into a
fire which they had lit in the square.

(Quoted in Y. Garlan and C. Nières (eds), *Les révoltes bretonnes de 1675*,
Paris: Editions Sociales, 1975: 38. Author's translation)

For this member of the élite, these events confirmed the view that the purpose
of this destruction was looting and an expression of anger against the rich.
He went on to describe how the crowd refused to bow to the authority of
the two militia commanders who then appeared on the scene. His description
can also be read in a different way. The removal of the tobacco, the furniture
of the tax office and the burning of legal agreements in public were all
structured acts of destruction. The tobacco was removed as a sign of
discontent with the way it was being sold as a monopoly from a single point
in order to ensure the collection of tax. It was not destroyed but distributed
to those who normally bought it. The destruction of furniture in the tobacco
office and of records in the *bureau de contrôle* was symbolic. Once eradicated,
it was believed that they ceased to have any force.

The events in Rennes followed a familiar pattern. Furniture and records
in the flour tax offices were destroyed in Marseille in 1603. The tax office
on the Piazza del Mercato in Naples was attacked during the disturbances
of 1647. Often, the focus of attacks was not the offices of tax collectors or
other individuals identified with the subject of the protest, but their private
houses. Once again, these attacks were structured, and the destruction and
theft that took place had clear symbolic significance.

Such is the construction to be placed on the treatment of the house of
Giovan Vincenzo Storace, the Neapolitan chief *eletto*, who was killed during
the disturbances of 1585. After dragging his body through the streets as if
he were a common criminal who had been executed, the rioters attacked his
house and removed all the furnishings as a gift to local monasteries. In the
later Neapolitan uprising in 1647, the houses of 60 men who worked with
the unpopular Spanish administration or were known to be leading financiers
were also attacked and their contents given to the poor, as were goods taken
by the crowd in the market-place. In Dijon, luxuries belonging to Nicholas
Gagne, *trésorier générale de France* for Burgundy, were taken from his house
during the revolt of 1630 and burnt in a public bonfire as a sign of moral
disapproval.

Destruction of property was often also closely linked to economic
grievances. Anti-clerical demonstrations in Osnabrück in 1525 were followed
by attacks on church buildings by weavers who removed the looms, which
they believed to have been the tools of unfair competition by the local bishop.
In the short-lived revolt in Bayeux in 1639, the only two houses to be
plundered were those of the farmer of the new leather tax and his deputy. A
significant part had been taken by local tanners. Direct economic action
was also taken by the master craftsmen in Lille in 1665 as part of their

dispute with competitors who were using new methods to produce longer pieces of cloth in a new style. They made the traditional responses of lobbying the authorities and taking legal action against men whom they believed to be threatening their livelihood, but they also entered their workshops and removed the offending material. Silk-workers in Amiens, thrown out of work after merchants had boycotted their masters in protest against a new tax on silk cloth, attacked their masters' workshops in 1637, cutting down yarn already in the looms and molesting customers.

Movements in favour of Protestantism were punctuated by acts of iconoclasm, although not always with the approval of church leaders. All statues and paintings were removed from each of the 15 churches in Zürich, after Zwingli's sermons against images in 1523. Herbs brought to the church for benediction in Magdeburg were scattered and deconsecrated by evangelical crowds in 1524. During the early Lutheran movement in Meaux in 1525, prayers to the Virgin and the saints on the cathedral walls were defaced. In the southern Netherlands, the summer of 1566 was marked by a wave of church occupations by Calvinists, who removed everything associated with Catholic ritual in order to use the buildings for their own forms of worship. In 1633, a stained glass window in St Edmund's Church in Salisbury was attacked by Henry Sherfield, the Recorder of the city and a leading Puritan.

The origins and purposes of such iconoclastic acts are well known. From the beginning of the Reformation, Protestant preachers emphasised the need to break away from religious beliefs and rituals based on superstition and the intercessory roles of the priest, the Virgin and the saints. Nothing should interpose itself between Christ and a Christian's faith. Any image, painting, sculpture or ecclesiastical furniture, which was associated with such practices, was therefore unnecessary and should be removed. Image-breaking by Protestants therefore fulfilled this requirement, both in a negative sense and as a precursor to the rededication of church buildings for use by adherents of the Reformed religion. Acts of this kind, which scandalised the Catholic laity and the urban authorities for their violence and blasphemy, were consistently limited in their objectives and took place in a structured and organised way.

The crowd disturbances that affected many urban centres at one time or another during the sixteenth and seventeenth centuries were a sign that the complex structures of social control upon which orderly behaviour was based were under such strong pressures that collective grievances could not be contained and came to be expressed in the traditional way. Once again, although there were notable cases in which violence got out of hand during major revolts, pogroms and interconfessional battles during the French Wars of Religion, this 'disorderly' behaviour had its own structures.

Demonstrations had several functions. They were intended to convey certain grievances or ideas to those whom it was believed had the power to remedy them. Only occasionally did they express a clearly formulated political programme, which predicated the complete removal of those in political power. They enabled large groups of people to express their feelings in an atmosphere of excitement, anger, fear and, to a certain extent, one of release. Participation in a large group of people can be empowering. Collective acts of this kind also enabled people to participate in a structured alternative to traditional authority. Demonstrations were frequently organised as processions, symbolising for participants and onlookers alike the formal nature of the protest. In Dijon, for instance, the demonstrators against the royal tax collector in February 1630 were led by four drummers. So too were demonstrators in Osnabrück in 1525, who attacked houses of the clergy before marching to assemble outside the town to the beat of the drum. In La Rochelle, the man responsible for collecting a tax on dried and salt fish was paraded through the streets in 1656 'to show him to the people'. The crowd that had lynched Storace in Naples in 1585 carried his body through the streets in an imitation of the treatment of convicted criminals.

Crowd disturbances were focused on a place, usually the principal square in the city. There were good practical reasons for this. Not only were such squares the only spaces large enough for crowds to gather, they were frequently places where there was already a concentration of people gathered to do business, take part in ritual activities such as carnival or as spectators at some form of entertainment or spectacle, both secular and religious. Open spaces were also frequently the focus of demonstrations, because they faced the buildings housing the individuals or groups against whom the protests were directed.

The next stage was the invasion of key buildings to bring pressure on their inhabitants to listen to their grievances. During the Reformation, burghers in the Baltic city of Stralsund broke into the *Rathaus* at Whitsun 1524 to force the council to make political changes. The Habsburg palace in Vienna was stormed in 1619 by an armed crowd demanding religious liberty and an alliance with the Bohemian rebels. Two to three hundred men – merchants, sailors and members of an anti-debt élite faction – invaded the town hall in Marseille during a meeting of the council on three separate occasions in December 1606 to urge them to set aside a new tax to pay for the port to be dredged. Pressure on the town hall by demonstrators could also lead to the successful admission of a deputation to put their case. Forty men were invited into a council meeting in Hamburg in 1526 after a large-scale protest at a council ban on the Lutheran preacher, Zegenhagen. Two hundred men assembled outside the town hall in Schwäbisch Hall in 1602 to protest against the suspension of a popular clergyman and succeeded in sending in a deputation of nine to put their case.

The identity of those who took part in demonstrations varied. The testimony of reports by the authorities is far from reliable for this purpose, as is the identity of those who were arrested and punished afterwards. Often, a distinction has to be drawn between those with specific grievances, such as members of an occupational group concerned that their livelihood was under threat or representatives of a political faction seeking to put pressure on the authorities, and those who took to the streets for more general reasons, probably the majority.

Several groups, however, do seem to have played a more prominent role in collective action. Sailors were a volatile group in any port, easily recruited by men with more clearly defined objectives, as in Marseille at the beginning of the seventeenth century. The Bishop of St Malo wrote to Colbert in 1675 that he was pleased to have contained trouble in the streets so quickly, 'since in two to three days our fleet is due to leave for the New World and there are more than two thousand sailors here ready to go on board, all heated up with wine'. [Garlan and Nières (eds), 1975: 43. Author's translation.]

Adolescents, and above all apprentices, seem to have taken a leading role in many disturbances. In an intermediate position between childhood and adult respectability, still dependent on parents or masters, they were a constantly volatile element in urban life. Some would argue that, because they were a little detached from urban society, they took on the particular role of articulating the feelings of a much broader sector of the population. Known for their cheekiness, it was appropriate that they should have taken a leading role in satirising the rich and powerful during carnival, in taunting the representatives of law and order when trouble was brewing and the latter were in danger of being outnumbered and in attacking unpopular minority groups, such as prostitutes and Quakers (in Bristol). Many of their actions were only extensions of their semi-formal role as controllers of morals. In June 1595, London apprentices forced the sale of fish and butter being transported out of the city when they believed their prices to be too high. The moral imperatives that lay behind such actions were relatively close to the charivaris, in which adolescents and young men indicated their disapproval of husbands who allowed themselves to be nagged by their wives, widows who remarried and women of dubious morals, summed up by Edward Thompson's classic phrase, the 'moral economy'.

Women were also frequently prominent in collective protests. They were at the forefront in a series of incidents in Montpellier in 1645, which developed into a major revolt. Official reports usually explained their presence in terms of their husbands' influence. By placing women in the forefront of a riot, it was argued, men hoped to gain an advantage over the authorities who would be unlikely to shoot at members of the opposite sex. This may indeed have been one of the reasons why many rioters dressed up as women, but it does not explain such a strong female presence. It is far more likely that two of the most common reasons for collective protests, increases in taxation and rises in the price of basic foodstuffs, affected women directly more than men, and they protested as a consequence.

Responses by the authorities

Many accounts of major disturbances make it clear that their violence caught the authorities by surprise and that the latter lacked the means to handle them. The order of events in Dijon in 1630 is instructive. After the looting and burning of luxuries on a bonfire, the syndic and the municipal guard went to the scene to restore order but were forced to retreat. The mayor and several other notables then went to address the crowd on their responsibilities but had to leave in their turn. When armed men were sent in, the rebels retreated behind barricades in the parish of St Philibert, where they were safe. Even troops brought in from outside on the following day were unable to dislodge them.

It is clear that the Dijon authorities believed that the force of their presence and the impact of their appearance dressed in their official robes of scarlet fabric decorated with golden fringes and velvet facings would be enough to command respect. Under ordinary circumstances, it would have done so. At the height of the Cascaveoux revolt in Aix-en-Provence in 1630, the Baron de Bras, who had taken refuge from an angry crowd, was rescued from the bell-tower of a Dominican church by five members of the *parlement* dressed in their red robes and a group of Dominican friars carrying the sacrament. The authority of the law was complemented by that of the clergy, supported by the power of images and relics.

Once disturbances had been brought under control, the authorities took action to ensure that they did not flare up again by establishing an armed presence on the streets. Spanish soldiers were brought into Naples by sea in 1585 to hunt down the rebels. In London, the Privy Council appointed provost marshals to patrol the streets in 1595 and doubled the strength of the watch. Troops under the command of the governor of Picardy supported by a retinue of gentlemen entered Amiens in 1630. Armed men were posted in key places in Rennes in 1675.

A determined attempt was made to bring the ringleaders to justice and to ensure that their punishment was a deterrent to further trouble. Five Londoners were arraigned for treason in 1595. They were hung, drawn and quartered. After the riots in Aix, one man was sentenced to be hanged, and two of his accomplices were sent to the galleys. Four rioters were condemned to death in Bologna in 1677, 10 were sent to the galleys and a further 23 were exiled. In February 1586, the Neapolitan pharmacist, Giovan Leonardo Pisano, was indicted in his absence for his part in the riots of the previous year. His house was demolished and a monument raised on the spot, exhibiting the heads and hands of those who had been executed.

Causes of disorder

Contemporary explanations of urban disorder were a mixture of the philosophical and the pragmatic. The steps taken by the authorities to ward off potential disturbances when war, famine or disease threatened to upset the economy, to attract large numbers of outsiders within the walls and to increase the numbers of the poor suggest that they recognised the kind of conditions that could give rise to collective protest. On the other hand, the link between demonstrations and protests, which involved groups with a recognisable role in society, such as master craftsmen or merchants, did not conform with their view of urban society as a self-regulating organism, within which burgher status bore the responsibility to contribute to the peace and well-being of the community as a whole. The body social was a concept that was frequently reinforced by both secular and religious rituals, such as Corpus Christi Day processions, mayor making or taking an annual oath in public to maintain the city's good order. It was at the centre of speeches and rituals undertaken to maintain urban unity when under threat.

This emphasis on civic unity led to a public unwillingness to admit that the chief instigators of disorder could be members of the community. It was far more convenient to blame outsiders, usually vagrants, who could not be expected to share communal values, who were often suspected of being former soldiers with a propensity towards violence and whose very existence was disorderly. Lord Burghley, commenting on the disturbances in London in 1597, laid the blame on 'loose persons', in spite of all the evidence that they had been instigated by apprentices. Outbreaks of arson in the north German Protestant town of Einbeck in 1540 were blamed on vagrants acting on the orders of local Catholic rulers.

Few outbreaks of urban unrest during the sixteenth and seventeenth centuries had only one cause. Evidence for undifferentiated class antagonism between the rich and the poor is not easy to find. Attacks on the houses of the rich and violence to their persons and property were rarely indiscriminate. Actions by the crowd were frequently focused on buildings and individuals who were the subject of grievances or who represented the forces of order standing in the way of the crowd. On the other hand, economic conditions, such as competition for employment and the level of prices, played an important part in the case of most protests, even when they could be defined as political. The riots in protest at increases in royal taxation that took place in many seventeenth-century French towns owed a great deal of their support to people who were worried about the potential economic impact of tax rises.

While there are strong underlying arguments for the economic causes of urban disorder, they do not go far enough to explain why the number of disturbances increased during the early modern period. Most urban economies experienced difficulties from time to time during the sixteenth and seventeenth centuries. On the other hand, most urban economies were characterised by stagnation rather than growth or recession, a situation that maintained conditions of hardship for many in urban society without increasing them to the point of collective protest. Something else was necessary to trigger such protests. It can be summarised as a growing gulf between the expectations of those outside the élite and the readiness or capacity of urban governments to satisfy such expectations. In the broadest sense of the term, these expectations were 'political'.

The chief reasons for the growth in such a gap in expectations were threefold: discontent with the religious *status quo*, greater concentration of power by urban élites and the impact of growing fiscal demands by the territorial state. They did not affect every part of Europe to the same extent, of course. In Italy and the Iberian peninsula and, in many ways, in England too, religious differences contributed little to the instability of urban society, in the one case because sympathy for Protestant ideas was limited to a very small minority, in the other because religious change in England was managed very effectively from the top. Only the urban participants in the Lincolnshire Rebellion of 1536 and the Pilgrimage of Grace, both reactions to the Reformation rather than demonstrations in favour of it, could be said to have been motivated by religion.

Elsewhere in Europe, however, the pressure for religious reform and the responses to it were a strong influence on movements for collective action. In the towns of Germany and Switzerland, demonstrations in favour of religious reform took place for a relatively short period of time, affecting different centres at different times from the 1520s to the 1570s. They came to an end either because the movement for reform lost its momentum or because it was fulfilled, even if this did not always conform to the aspirations of the demonstrators. In France and the Netherlands, urban disorder was caught up in broader political conflicts and lasted for at least the final third of the sixteenth century. In every case, these demonstrations may be characterised as part of a political movement. The objectives of those who took part were religious. However, whether they were calls to place the old religion and the new on a level of equality or requests to allow an evangelical preacher to remain in the city or more clearly articulated calls for the general introduction of Protestantism, the impact was political. Change in the church in German towns, for example, could only be achieved through the city council. Even when individual members of city councils were secretly or openly in favour of religious change, it was recognised by citizens who were not usually in a position to influence the urban authorities by conventional means that direct action was their only weapon. The same lesson was borne in upon the Calvinists in France, who, having failed to capture the monarch, took direct political action to take over certain towns to further their objectives. The temporary capture of Lyon by the Huguenots in 1562–63 is a case in point.

Popular pressure in favour of the Reformation was the most successful of all communal protests in the early modern period. Most other protests did not lead to long-term change but were a response to political changes over which the majority of the urban population had no control. The effect of the gradual tightening of élite control over urban government and their inability to rule effectively because of a heavy debt burden was not to create substantial political tensions between those who were disenfranchised and those who were in power but to create a sense of frustration among the common people when they perceived that economic conditions were getting rapidly worse and that nothing seemed to be done to protect them.

There had always been a strong sense that urban governments were paternalist, that their function was to protect the interests of all the citizens. With a largely rentier élite in control, there was a growing divergence between their interests and those of the majority of the population. In times of crisis, this was particularly evident. The response of the latter was still expressed in terms of the kind of contract implied by paternalist government. Most protests can be seen in terms of identifying a social or economic problem and putting pressure on the authorities to find a solution. During the subsistence crisis of 1692 in Lille, the quality of the bread was so bad that the poor carried it in procession to the town hall to show the authorities. In other cases, if the authorities were believed to have failed in their duty, the crowd responded by taking direct action in their place. The classic example of this was the widespread practice during times of sharply rising bread prices of breaking into bakers' shops in order to remove their stock and sell it outside to the crowd at what was believed to be a fair price. The money paid was then given to the bakers in payment.

The heavy burden of debt that many urban authorities had to face during the period not only made social and economic policies very difficult to finance, they also led to increased tax levels and to the growing conviction that a town's problems were the result of corruption and financial mismanagement. These attitudes informed those taxpayers who were wealthy enough to make a substantial contribution, but who were not part of the ruling élite, and played an important part in many German disturbances at the turn of the sixteenth century, such as the *Reiserische Unruhen* in Lübeck in 1598–1605, the Fettmilch uprising in Frankfurt am Main in 1612, which was entangled with a pogrom against the local Jewish community, and the disturbances in Aachen between 1598 and 1612.

The link between urban disorder and the growing role of outside authority was rarely quite so straightforward. When French towns closed the gates on royal tax collectors in the 1630s, the monarchy took this as an affront to its authority and acted accordingly, but most popular disturbances, which were a response to external change, were a combination of criticisms of the authorities in their own towns and of the representatives of royal power. On a number of occasions, the authorities in French towns found it prudent not to intervene when royal officials' houses were attacked, both because they feared that violence would be directed towards them and because they sympathised with the views, if not the methods, of the protesters. Increases in royal taxation at a time of indebtedness meant that taxpayers' capacity to pay local taxes was substantially reduced. When the unrest became too widespread, however, they began to fear for their own lives and property and took steps to suppress the disturbances, even if this meant calling upon the monarchy for aid. In many cases in France, too, popular discontent was caught up in factional fighting among the élite, such as the tensions within the *parlement* at Aix-en-Provence in 1630, 1649 and 1659.

It is something of a paradox that the general level of disorder in European towns did not warrant the extent to which it was discussed by the authorities. Few of the large European urban centres of the time experienced more than two or three extended periods of rioting in 200 years. There were riots in London in 1597 and on the eve of the English Civil War in 1642. The Parisian authorities lost control in 1573 during the Massacre of St Bartholomew, for several months in 1588 when the city was ruled by the Catholic League through the Sixteen and on several occasions during the Fronde between 1648 and 1651. Naples is famous for its two great revolts in 1585 and 1647. Lyon was touched by the Grand Rebeyne in 1529 and by its capture by the Huguenots in 1562, but experienced no major disorder at all in the seventeenth century. Many smaller centres never experienced anything at all on this scale.

The answer to this paradox lies in the fact that, for the majority of the urban population, as well as the secular and ecclesiastical authorities, order was a social norm. This norm, or rather this complex of norms, was the product of long-term conditioning reinforced by a series of measures introduced from above as a conscious attempt to counteract potential disturbances.

Keeping order by force was an option open only to a few urban governments. They could not usually rely on regular soldiers. In any case, the urban authorities had an equivocal attitude towards the presence of troops representing an external authority. Their presence in the town may have helped to deter potential troublemakers but they also intimidated the entire urban body. The newly powerful Medici Dukes of Florence built a fortress overlooking the city. Spanish soldiers were placed in barracks outside Naples as a deterrent to the local population. Troops were installed in a chain of citadels in eastern France towards the end of the seventeenth century as part of the military strategy of Vauban, Louis XIV's Minister of War. It comes as no surprise that there was very little trouble in citadel cities. On the other hand, the urban authorities recognised that the close proximity of troops was capable of causing trouble as well as preventing it. Clashes between soldiers and the local population were common.

The readiness with which the local armed gentry were called upon by the authorities to patrol the streets in times of potential trouble suggests that they were a much more reliable deterrent. When dissent threatened to spread to Nantes from Rennes in 1675, the king's lieutenant toured the streets, accompanied by the mayor, armed gentry and 30 musketeers, with their drums beating and matches burning. According to the autobiography of John Ivie, mayor of Salisbury in the 1620s, when he found himself deserted by all who should have stood by him during an outbreak of the plague, he sent word to all 'gentlemen' in the town to make ready their weapons and to come to his aid upon a prearranged signal.

Armed men were also usually posted at the city gates during the day. In times of crisis, these measures were strengthened. In London, men seconded by the drapers' and vintners' livery companies were ordered to search everyone passing through Cripplegate for weapons in 1580. In Reims, the guard on the city's five gates was doubled at times of plague to prevent outsiders from entering without due cause.

Most measures taken by urban governments to maintain order were preventative rather than deterrent. The most extensive policies put into place to contain potential disorder were generated by the fear of the twin scourges of famine and plague. Neither were exclusively concerned with disorder (provisioning and public health were both matters that related far more widely to the government of urban centres), but public order issues were an important element in their formulation.

The urban authorities understood from experience how famine in the surrounding countryside could create an additional influx of the poor, and this became an integral part of their policies towards beggars and poor relief, but the role of rapidly rising bread prices in fomenting unrest was a separate issue, which affected a much larger proportion of the resident population. Controlling prices in a field as complex as the production, sale and consumption of food in general, and of bread in particular, was not a straightforward matter, and urban governments had a number of strategies in widespread use available to them.

The case of Cologne is a good illustration of the effective operation of provisioning policy in ensuring that food prices remained within reach of the majority of the population and did not become a focus for popular discontent. During the second half of the sixteenth century, the city suffered from a number of serious subsistence crises. During the winter of 1556–57, grain prices rose to over double their normal level. By November 1556, it was clear that the city's customary sources of grain were not going to meet demand. The city subsidised its bakers to enable them to continue selling standard loaves of bread at a standard price and ordered local monasteries to transfer their own winter reserves to city granaries. Supplies were also protected through a ban on exports to the neighbouring territories of Jülich and Berg. More subsidies were given in February as prices began to rise again and, although fresh supplies of grain began to arrive along the Rhine, this only fuelled speculation and panic buying. The council then put a ceiling on all grain prices and banned all speculative purchasers. When this ceiling was reached, a higher one was established. By mid-May, so much grain was being exported from Cologne that it became necessary to limit all sales to those for immediate consumption. At the beginning of June, the council opened its own grain reserves. These controls remained in place until mid-July 1557 when news of a good harvest was reported.

The case of Cologne highlights the fact that supplies of grain for consumption in cities were not usually distinguished from either grain for re-export or grain for use in industrial processes, such as brewing, and that part of the problem of operating a provisioning policy arose from the tensions between these three areas of demand. Cologne was an important trading centre, and the authorities were unable to prohibit exports for long, as this threatened to damage the interests of the export merchants who used it as an exchange commodity. Similarly, maltsters and brewers, who had a degree of political influence in the city, were rarely content to see their supplies of grain diverted to the flour market. This was one of the reasons why the English *Book of Orders* sent to Justices of the Peace in the 1570s to regulate food supplies created a great deal of bad feeling. The subterfuges adopted by maltsters to assure their supplies of grain were far from popular and remained a source of discontent.

Bad harvests were difficult to predict with any certainty, and the capacity of the Cologne city council to supplement the meagre grain supplies available locally with supplies from official granaries suggests a considerable degree of forward planning, which was indeed the case across Europe. Cities increasingly created special magistracies to act in cases of food shortages and to collect supplies of grain in advance. The most organised of all was the Venetian Grain Office, which was primarily concerned with controlling the supply and price of grain in ordinary circumstances to avoid speculation that could create artificial shortages. The Venetians ensured that grain was sold in two public places where conditions could be controlled easily. The magistracy was able to maintain the level of supplies from outside, because they followed a constant policy of releasing grain from official reserves to supplement stocks on the open market and of bringing in supplies from private reserves and from the city's territories in northern Italy once the official holdings fell below eight to 12 months' supply.

Other Italian city states with strong controls over their *contadi* developed similar policies. In the Farnese Po Valley territories, all rural inhabitants were required to report details of their cereal and vegetable holdings within eight days after the harvest. The peasants were further required to supply two-thirds of their surplus grain for sale on the urban market and for storage in the granaries of the *deputati sopra l'abbondanza*.

Plague was a frequent threat to urban order. Between 1582 and 1669, it struck Amiens 19 times, often for several years in succession. Even when it did not take on the dimensions of a major epidemic, relatively minor outbreaks always had the potential to explode. The concerns of the authorities when plague threatened their city were threefold. The disease had to be prevented from spreading, even though this meant interfering with the economy. Men with official responsibilities had to be constrained to remain behind, when it was in the interests of personal safety to escape. Order had to be maintained when the traditional structures for feeding, employing and controlling the population were under severe strain. As a Portuguese priest, Francesco de Santa-Maria, wrote at the end of the seventeenth century,

> The plague is without doubt of all the calamities of this life, the most cruel and truly the worst. ... When it catches alight in a kingdom or a republic, this violent and impetuous fire, we see magistrates lose their sense, populations overwhelmed and a loss of organised government. Law is no longer obeyed, industry comes to a halt, families lose their coherence and streets their bustle. Everything is reduced to great confusion.
>
> (Quoted in J. Delumeau, *La peur en Occident XIVᵉ–XVIIᵉ siècles*, Paris: Fayard, 1978: 112. Author's translation)

There was almost universal agreement about the controls to be introduced to prevent the spread of plague. First developed in fifteenth-century Italy, they were applied increasingly north of the Alps. In real terms, they were only of limited effect in maintaining order. Strict controls were imposed on outsiders suspected as plague carriers, particularly those known to come from areas affected by the epidemic. They were required to state where they had come from and, in certain cases, to produce certificates to prove that they had come from an area free of the plague. Their certificates were disinfected before examination. In Reims, the guard was doubled. In Segovia in 1596, several gates were walled up to force all traffic through one or two control points. Ships arriving in Norwich from Yarmouth were stopped outside the town, and their cargoes were left out in the open to dispel infection. Such measures only had a limited preventative effect. In 1664, although the Belgian towns turned away all people or goods from Amsterdam, Haarlem, Leiden and Utrecht, the disease spread throughout the area for the next four years. Careful watch in Exeter averted major epidemics in 1583–84 and in 1603, but negligent guards allowed infected goods into the city in 1625.

The sick were put into quarantine in their own houses or transported to special plague hospitals outside the city to avoid contact with those who had not been infected. The movements of those who had been in contact with them and might carry the plague were also restricted. All houses where there was sickness in Brussels in 1668 were to be marked with an image of the Saviour as a sign of warning to passers-by. When plague broke out in 1667, the authorities in Lille required all houses where someone had died of the disease to be closed up and marked with white bars. Those in contact with the sick were to identify themselves by carrying a white wand in their hands. They were forbidden to buy meat or to go to the fish market. At the height of the plague in June 1656, the Neapolitan authorities prevented all sick people from leaving their houses on pain of death for them and their households.

Reactions to controls such as these, restrictions on trade, keeping livestock and attending assemblies in the open air and the measures taken to carry away the dead suggest that the severity of the actions taken by the urban authorities did not always have the desired effect of keeping order. Bearers of the dead were unpopular. They were suspected of murder and theft and were objects of fear because of their close contact with the disease. In Salisbury, during the outbreak of 1627, a clothier organised a crowd to attack the house in which they lodged.

Many of the restrictions that were introduced conflicted with customs at the heart of popular culture. There was widespread resentment at the practice of placing the dead in common graves and of interfering with customary funeral rites, which fulfilled such an important psychological role at times of loss and mourning. In England, all attempts to prevent people from following the dead to their graves failed. In Amiens, the sick, who had been segregated in a plague hospital beyond the city walls, broke out of their confines in 1667 and returned home. Such behaviour was understandable. Few people taken to the *lazzaretto* were known to have survived. The sick preferred to be in the company and care of their families. Many Londoners defied quarantine regulations, because they had an intense belief in their responsibility to visit and comfort the sick. Others broke out of quarantine because they needed food.

The problems of maintaining social control at times of plague were worsened by a partial vacuum in government. Although it was the responsibility of the urban authorities to stay where they were when plague broke out, they sometimes put personal safety first and fled or isolated themselves for protection, with obvious consequences. In Santander, the senior official, the *alcalde major*, fled to safety in 1596, leaving the city councillors in control. By February 1597, the position was so bad that several councillors refused to attend meetings for fear of contagion. The authorities in Naples in 1656, on the other hand, having first denied the existence of plague in the city in order to prevent panic and disorder, locked themselves away in the Viceroy's palace for protection. Problems such as these were only resolved when individuals, such as John Ivie, the mayor of Salisbury, came forward and improvised a system of social discipline and public health or when there was a temporary widening of participation in government. In Santander, an assembly of citizens met to take key decisions, such as whether or not to burn the Flemish ship believed to be responsible for the plague outbreak and to impose of a forced loan on absentees to finance food and support for those who stayed behind.

One aspect of government behaviour during plague outbreaks mirrored a much broader concern about the relationship between social order and strict levels of individual morality. When plague threatened, one of the first steps taken by the urban authorities to avoid trouble was the expulsion of all beggars. Beggars were suspected of carrying disease and of fomenting trouble. They were a potential drain on a town's financial resources, which were likely to come under considerable strain if plague broke out. They were also an appropriate scapegoat for a society, which believed that plague was a divine punishment on the community for the sins of the few. Beggars and vagrants were frequently accused of laziness, blasphemy and debauchery.

Plague was considered to be 'the sin of the suburbs' by clergy and secular authorities alike. There was plenty of evidence to support both sides of this view. Plague tended to break out in the poorer quarters of towns. Minor outbreaks were frequently limited to these areas. Even when medical opinion identified natural causes for plague outbreaks, the argument that they were the result of God's displeasure at sinful behaviour still held sway. Sinful behaviour among the poor, swearing, gambling, drunkenness, sexual promiscuity, property theft and work-shyness represented a general threat to the ideal of an ordered urban society. They were the symptoms of a general malaise, which it was the duty of both secular and ecclesiastical authorities to eradicate.

This concern to eradicate immoral behaviour may be seen as the product of both the greater religious awareness of the laity arising from the Reformation and the Counter-Reformation and the increase in authoritarian government at both a local and a territorial level. It is not easy to disentangle the religious from the secular in the growing attempts to control the 'sinfulness' of the poor. Sermons encouraging orderly behaviour arose out of the close identification of the church with the state, and secular groups, such as the confraternities in Catholic towns and groups like the Societies for the Reformation of Manners in seventeenth-century English towns, were strongly imbued with religious feeling.

While the locus of the movement to control morals varied from one area to another, its inspiration remained the same. In northern Europe, for example, social discipline was the joint responsibility of secular and ecclesiastical courts in the Calvinist Netherlands, the secular authorities in Calvinist cities in the Holy Roman Empire and Scotland and in Anglican England and of consistories with both lay and ecclesiastical members in Lutheran Germany. In the south, judging infractions of social discipline was the joint concern of both urban government and the Inquisition.

The enforcement of social discipline was a mixture of deterrence, control and education. Laws enacted to forbid blasphemy, heresy, gambling and begging all contained a strong punitive element, in terms of both the material penalties faced by those who broke them and the well-publicised spiritual punishment for sinners. These were reinforced in some areas by the rules established by the Calvinist church, which threatened persistent transgressors with expulsion, and by many confraternities, which were encouraged to police the morals of their members.

Government controls were directed primarily at public gatherings during festivals and at taverns. The celebration of festivals had always constituted a potential flashpoint for trouble. With the shift in moral attitudes among the clergy and the élite, any public celebration that was outside their control became suspect and was subject to modification or suppression. *Goede Moendag*, celebrated in Münster on the Monday after Trinity Sunday, became notorious for its loud music, fights between drunken journeymen from rival guilds and dangerous horse-riding in narrow streets. By the beginning of the seventeenth century, the church had succeeded in redefining this festival as a student pilgrimage to a nearby shrine. In Lille, the festival of the *Epinette* was suppressed by Philip II in 1556. Dances and games on Sundays and holy days all over the southern Netherlands were banned by the Spanish authorities in the early seventeenth century.

Public spectacles controlled by the lay and ecclesiastical authorities, in contrast, became ever more ornate. The procession of the Vow of Louis XIII, which took place on the 15 August 1638 in Paris was one of the most magnificent. The streets of the Ile de la Cité were hung with tapestries. At the centre of the procession, the statue of the Virgin was carried by two chaplains in white, escorted by two clerks in surplices holding a torch with the royal arms, followed by the casket of the Virgin, carried on the shoulders of *tonsurés*. The city of Paris was represented by the *parlement* and the city council. In late seventeenth-century Lille, the festival of the Holy Sacrament was marked by a procession led by the four militia companies, followed by the corporations of artisans, carrying long staves with torches to which their guild insignia was attached, and then the councillors and the clergy. Strict rules were applied to ensure that no one under the influence of alcohol took part and that attempts to slow down or break up the procession were severely punished. Formal occasions of this kind came to have the twin functions of emphasising the dominance of the church and the secular authorities, on the one hand, and of diverting the urban population from their everyday concerns, on the other.

Some entertainments were deliberately organised in accordance with the traditional Roman policy of bread and circuses. The Duke of Valanzuela, new favourite of Charles II of Spain, announced in 1674 that his policy was *pan, toros y trabajo* (bread, bulls and work). Others, such as the increasing number of public celebrations of royal births and marriages, treaties, military victories, not to mention formal royal progresses, involved the populace as passive spectators and frequently transmitted the message that urban authority was subordinate to the monarch. When Queen Elizabeth I was received outside the gates of Bristol in 1574 by the mayor and his councillors, she was presented with the city's mace as a sign of submission and returned it to them as a sign that their authority was dependent on her favour.

In Catholic towns, the increasing role of the Jesuits as educators of boys and young men and initiators of confraternities led to careful social conditioning in favour of decorous behaviour and the establishment of self-regulating organisations. Members of the Marian Congregation in Toulouse were taught to keep away from taverns, forbidden games and masquerades. All members who transgressed these prohibitions or who bathed immodestly were warned that they would be expelled.

Examples such as these raise the question whether or not the growth in social discipline should be considered as something that was imposed from above through 'acculturation', to use Robert Muchembled's term, and might be characterised as an attack on popular culture. It could be argued with equal force that the early modern period saw the birth, rather than the suppression, of popular culture, because it marked the withdrawal of the élite and the literate from activities that the whole community had traditionally shared and the identification of the latter by the élite as potential threats to order, which were in need of supervision and regulation.

The influence of social conditioning from above through sermons, civic rituals and the like was reinforced by the long-term acceptance by the majority of the community that it was in their own interests to live an ordered life. One example of this is the way in which the common law in England, which differed from the continental legal codes established by territorial and city states, was used widely by people from the middling levels of urban society to settle their differences. There was general acquiescence in and celebration of the law throughout society, because it was seen to be a just way of resolving differences. Oddly enough, too, in spite of the shift in ideology from a consensual to a hierarchical view of authority in urban society, the concepts of communal responsibility and brotherhood remained powerful elements of guild culture and of post-Tridentine confraternities, whose membership stretched far down into society. The work of groups, such as the *Scuole Grandi* in Venice, enabled their members to feel part of an urban community over whose administration they had no control.

Conclusion

This book set out to explore the nature of the urban dimension in sixteenth- and seventeenth-century Europe. The general conclusion to be drawn from an analysis of the experiences of large numbers of towns during the period is that, in spite of the evidence for widespread urban diversity, a number of common patterns do emerge. Several themes and questions run through the chapters:

- How far did the changes of the sixteenth and seventeenth centuries affect the internal and external functions of the urban economy?
- What was the impact on urban centres of the growth of centralised political authority?
- How and why did members of urban élites respond to economic, political and social change during the period?
- How did urban societies and governments respond to the changes brought about by the Reformation and the Counter-Reformation?
- Was the increasing social distance between members of urban élites and other townspeople responsible for more or less social stability in the course of the period?
- How far was the common urban experience mediated by diversity according to size, function, geographical location or choice of confession?

Urban economies

If the distinguishing characteristic of an urban centre as opposed to a rural settlement was the way in which it fulfilled a range of functions exclusive to towns, then these functions remained an urban prerogative throughout the period. The five economic functions that distinguished towns from the countryside: their location as centres for exchange; the presence of artisans;

occupational diversity; regular links with other centres of exchange; and influence over a hinterland, remained at the centre of all urban activity. Even in the cases in which lower costs, fewer corporate controls and easier access to raw materials to supply the demands of export industries encouraged the expansion of industrial by-employment in some rural areas, these developments did not invalidate the key function of urban centres as centres of production. Nor did they weaken towns' economic influence on their hinterlands. On the contrary, the expansion of cheap industrial employment into the countryside, while it may have reduced rural–urban migration by providing alternative sources of income to agriculture, increased the financial hold that townsmen possessed over their rural neighbours.

Rural inhabitants had begun the sixteenth century in a position of economic dependence on their local towns. They were obliged to turn to them to purchase commodities and to sell their own goods, usually at a financial disadvantage, and, while the density of the urban network in some regions enabled farmers and peasants to choose where to do business, the underlying economic conditions remained the same. The expansion of the European economy during the sixteenth and seventeenth centuries reinforced the role of towns as centres of exchange because they offered an unequalled range of goods, many of which had been produced at a considerable distance. The expanded luxury market also brought a significant income flow from wealthier landowners.

The rural influence of urban centres was enhanced by an expansion in landownership by individual townspeople, by institutions and by the urban authorities. At times of economic uncertainty and commercial stagnation, investment in land provided greater financial security, sources of money from rents and service, sources of food and drink, opportunities for a minority to make the transition to the rural élite and, perhaps most important of all, opportunities to make money out of lending credit to country people.

The expansion of rural industrial employment needs to be seen in this context of the broad economic front on which towns influenced their hinterlands. Proto-industrialisation did not lead at this stage to any great concentrations of industrial production, which might, in turn, have fuelled urbanisation. Production was dispersed through existing villages. It did not lead to significant demographic increases fuelled by migration. Nor did it represent the complete transfer of the production process to any single site. Two essential elements remained in the towns, the finishing processes and the sources of capital. The latter was fundamental. It ensured that industrial profits remained in the town. Production control remained in the town and, above all, the dispersal of industrial employment brought about an intensification of the other urban economic controls exercised over rural hinterlands, dependence on the town for both employment and credit.

While the five economic functions that defined urban centres remained unchanged in form if not in degree, the factors that influenced the general state of urban economies experienced an important shift, particularly in the 'long seventeenth century'. De Vries' data on urban demographic change indicate that substantial growth arising out of commercial or industrial expansion was far from a common experience. While many urban centres kept pace with or exceeded overall demographic expansion during the sixteenth century, they did not continue to do so during the next 100 years. The standard of living of most of the population fell, and the gap between the wealthy and the rest of the population grew larger. The success of London, Amsterdam and some of the ports engaged in the Atlantic trade should not mask the fact that their experience was exceptional. On the other hand, many other towns continued to show external signs of prosperity, such as the reconstruction of wooden buildings in brick or stone, the remodelling and decoration of ecclesiastical buildings and the development of a thriving market for luxuries, in spite of the absence of marked commercial or industrial success. The injection of capital that made this possible owed a great deal to the growth in office-holding brought about by the expansion of the territorial state, a process that in turn attracted people and resources from the rural aristocracy, who gradually came to see the benefits of sending at least some of their members to attend courts in capital cities, and others to compete for office and influence in towns elsewhere.

Centralised political authority

The development of territorial states had a far wider impact on most west European urban centres than the partial transfer of political authority from individual towns to the centre. The creation of an élite of office-holders who owed their status to their relationship with the territorial ruler rather than their place of residence transformed urban élites in several different ways. In some cases, a group of office-holders worked in parallel with the traditional élite. In others, after a period of transition, the two élites merged in function and status, a process that was underwritten by marriage. Elsewhere, primarily in commercial centres where there was no concentration of office-holders, members of traditional urban élites attempted to reach out to the newly defined status of élites in the territorial state by adopting a more aristocratic lifestyle as a precursor to the acquisition of titles by purchase.

The state was also responsible for changes to the external appearance of urban centres, either through the creation of extensive new earthworks, complicated geometrical fortifications and citadels or by the decision to demolish older walls and replace them with tree-lined boulevards. In either case, the edge of the existing urban core was redefined as a result of external decisions, on the one hand, by the appropriation of a broad band of land, which effectively isolated the town from its hinterland except at a small number of predetermined points, and on the other by the creation of managed green belt, which combined the attractions of nature with the exclusion of anything associated with productive activity.

The growth of the territorial state encroached more directly on the political autonomy of many urban centres. The fiscal needs of the state, which grew in proportion to the latter's military expenditure and the cost of conspicuous consumption by the court, were bound to have an impact on the relative independence of urban governments sooner or later, and the unwillingness of many councils to offer increased financial support coupled with a mounting debt crisis laid them open to accusations of financial mismanagement and to the introduction of external controls. Patterns varied. In some states, parallel authorities were appointed by the centre to oversee tax collection, defence, the courts and the general implementation of policy decisions. Elsewhere, rulers made increasing use of their powers to nominate members of urban ruling bodies in order to ensure that, while they were not directly instructed which policies to follow, such men tended to adopt those that they believed would not arouse opposition from the centre.

However, there are two important caveats to this scheme of things. Relationships between urban centres and their territorial states had always been reciprocal. Far from becoming exclusively the instruments of centralised authority, urban governments used their new position to lobby for economic and political advantage *vis-à-vis* their neighbours. For a long time, too, state-building was a process of negotiation, procrastination and covert resistance.

The second qualification concerns the position of the city states, far fewer in number than the urban centres in territorial states, but including among them some of the largest, wealthiest and most complex urban societies in western Europe. They did not escape the state-building process. Indeed, several of them might be said to have initiated it during the fifteenth century. Cities, such as Venice, ruled over territories larger than some of the dynastic territorial states north of the Alps and extended political, economic, judicial and fiscal controls in other urban centres under their jurisdiction. Unlike the dynastic states, however, while they enhanced the social position of the ruling élites in their subject cities, they resolutely excluded them from participating in any kind of 'national' office-holding élite.

On the other hand, city states were becoming fewer in number. Venice was exceptional for the size of its power, wealth and territories. Smaller cities were at a disadvantage, particularly in Germany, where the expansion of neighbouring territorial states and the increasing cost and scale of warfare placed the governments of cities, such as Lübeck or Nuremberg, in a very difficult political and financial position. They may have retained their political independence, but only at the cost of expensive fortifications and substantial sweeteners to deter potential military threats. Expenditure on this scale took place while their fiscal base was shrinking because of changes in trading patterns. Some city states, such as Strasbourg and Besançon on France's eastern borders, could not afford to remain independent and were incorporated into their more powerful territorial neighbours. Others, such as Augsburg, while retaining their ostensible status as free imperial cities, had their constitutions modified by the Emperor as a penalty for supporting the losing side in the religious wars.

Élites and problems

One of the recurrent themes of this book has been the response of urban élites to social and economic change. As defined for our purposes, members of urban élites included far more than the small number of men holding positions on governing bodies, embracing all high-status families, including those whose members were office-holders in territorial states. In spite of the changes in the balance of political power in the territorial states, urban élites still exercised a great deal of both formal and informal authority over their own societies. Indeed, the loss of autonomous political power was compensated for by greater external recognition of their distinct position at the head of a hierarchical urban society. The intervention of territorial rulers only accentuated a trend towards greater social exclusiveness, which had been developing for some time.

Members of urban élites remained the opinion formers and the controllers of a substantial proportion of urban incomes. They had an interest in protecting the *status quo* but, when faced with change, they took steps to maintain an ordered society at whatever cost. Even if they showed an initial reluctance to embrace change, particularly religious change, they quickly recognised the need to control changes that they judged to be impossible to prevent. Declining opportunities for the acquisition of wealth as so many urban economies experienced economic stagnation and adversity also encouraged more social rigidity among the élite. More conservative marriage strategies protected social status in succeeding generations.

An entirely functionalist explanation of élite behaviour is unsatisfactory, however. Ideological solutions to social problems, whether they responded to the need to clear the indigent and the sick off the streets, the need to create entirely new residential quarters for the rich and powerful away from the confusion and high demographic densities of the old urban core or to develop strategies to avoid or control social conflict, were discussed in print and communicated from one urban centre to another along the international trading network.

On the other hand, many of these concerns and ideas were shared by circles beyond the edges of urban élites. It is almost paradoxical that, at the same time that the élites attempted to distance themselves from the remainder of the urban population, their concerns and aspirations were being embraced by many other urban inhabitants. These included not only the professionals and wealthy merchants, master craftsmen and minor royal officials with aspirations to join the élite, but everyone else who belonged to the 'stable core' of urban society.

The élite, with the aid of the higher clergy and political, social and architectural theorists, may have articulated the problems and suggested the solutions, but the feelings of unease brought about by the changes of the period were shared by many others leading an existence, which they profoundly wished to be stable. At a time when the rhetoric of shared community that lay behind the transmission of burgher status was being undermined by the greater concentration of social and political power at the sharp end of the social hierarchy, another form of shared concern was being articulated by actions rather than by words. Relieving poverty engaged far more people than the élite and the upper clergy. Indeed, the new spiritual awareness of the Reformation and Counter-Reformation was probably the most important influence on the awareness of social problems and the concept of shared responsibility.

Sharing a sense of community was also the product of the multiple links that brought townspeople together into official and unofficial subunits of the urban population – families and kinship networks, neighbourhoods, parishes and guilds, confraternities and companies of the urban militia – the existence of all of which provided the social stability with which to confront the impact of change.

Membership of the stable core of urban society did not always promote conditions of social stability. The period was marked by outbreaks of social disruption. On the other hand, the over-riding characteristics of urban protests, strikes and revolts were their formality. Rather than being part of the social problems of their time, as the urban authorities tried to argue, they were responses to change and were as much part of the urge to protect the stable parameters of their participants' lives as the exodus of the wealthy to spacious new quarters where they could shelter behind the anonymity of neo-classical facades.

Religious change

The changes embodied in the Reformation and the Counter-Reformation were an odd mixture. Historians have long debated whether or not they were expressions of individual religious belief or institutional changes by religious organisations that were willing to become the tools for the extension of secular authority. The answer seems to be related to different stages in the process of religious reform. Much of the dissatisfaction with the religious *status quo* came initially from below but was shared by some members of the élite, who helped to give this movement intellectual and political weight. On the other hand, there is little doubt that once the deliberations of the Council of Trent had been completed and once decisions had been taken either locally or nationally to support the introduction of Protestantism, the religious authorities, governments, élites and members of the stable core of society worked together to further each other's ends. There was an uneasy tension between fanaticism and pragmatism, which often bore practical fruit in confronting the problems of poverty and social disorder, but equally mirrored some of the competition for jurisdiction between church and urban authorities, and between the élite and the 'stable core'.

The nature of such tensions may be appreciated from the variety of responses to the presence of religious minorities in many urban centres as a result of religious changes at home and abroad. The clergy and members of the 'stable core' all too often found themselves in conflict with the élite over such questions. The latter were far more favourable to the limited toleration of certain religious minorities if this was seen to be beneficial either to the urban economy, as in the case of Jewish communities (sometimes), or to social harmony, where the dissenters belonged to élite families themselves.

Social stability

The threats to urban social stability were fourfold – economic change, greater social exclusiveness and concentration of power among the élite, feelings of uncertainty among the 'stable core' and increases in in-migration. The capacity of urban societies to handle periods of crisis was linked to the extent to which individual townspeople belonged to networks. In the face of a slow pincer movement between the growing exclusiveness of élite groups, whose own composition reflected the political and economic changes of the period, and an increase in the numbers of the poor and the unskilled, it is surprising that the middling groups in society, predominantly the families of artisans, shopkeepers and minor officials, continued to live in a network of self-sustaining social relationships. Only the very largest cities manifested much evidence of great volatility and, once again, as in so many other aspects of the urban history of the sixteenth and seventeenth centuries, the latter were far from typical.

In some ways, it is surprising that there was relatively little social upheaval in individual urban centres, although, when taken together, they do leave a sense of slow social change whose effects were exacerbated by unexpected events, such as new rises in taxation, food shortages, epidemic disease or sharp rises in the numbers of temporary immigrants. In the face of such tensions, the urban authorities were able to deploy their power relatively effectively. Their success depended on the élite's capacity to admit a limited number of outsiders in order to leave the door open to the possibility of social advancement and deprive other groups of their leadership, and to find ways to satisfy the needs of the bulk of the population through provisioning policies and effective programmes of poor relief. Outbreaks of disorder were as much a testimony to their lack of success in these areas as they were to the social frustrations of the lower classes.

Too much emphasis on the politics of protest, however, diverts attention from the capacity of urban societies to absorb many of the migrants who settled from elsewhere. Marriage was a strong integrative mechanism at all levels of society, as were training and apprenticeship. The process of integration was aided by the presence of migrants who had settled successfully themselves and were therefore able to act as a bridge in practical terms for the newcomers to help them to find work, accommodation and to ease them into the pre-existing networks of local residents. For immigrants with these advantages, the cultural gap between their rural conditioning and an urban environment, which was still mitigated by a strong flow of contacts with the countryside and with agriculture, was relatively small. There were limits to this integration. Immigrant merchants, in particular, seem to have kept themselves to themselves, and the role of their ambiguous situation as mediators between their places of origin and their host communities needs further exploration, but their small numbers did little to undermine the cohesiveness of urban society.

Similarities and contrasts

For all that one might write about a common urban experience in early modern western Europe, there were also significant differences in size, in region and in function and, from the middle of the sixteenth century, in religion. How far should this lead us to modify the conclusions that have already been outlined? In many ways, the first three variables need to be taken together. The largest urban centres also exercised the most complex functions, often, but not always, combining manufacturing and commerce with administration, the church and the court. Each function contributed to the demographic expansion of the city and to an infusion of capital and manpower, which compensated for occasional downturns in exports. Paris, London and Amsterdam were not entirely representative of the urban experience but, by their very size and wealth, they amplified many urban developments in the period rather than undergoing experiences that contrasted with smaller urban centres. The construction of new quarters, such as the Marais, the West End and the area around the Singel canal, resulted from the same wish on the part of the élite to live apart from the old urban core, but they were carried out on a larger and grander scale than was possible elsewhere.

The sharpest contrasts in urban experience lay between those centres that experienced substantial growth at some stage during the period and those whose economies stagnated. In visual terms, the latter were frozen in time. There were few new buildings, and most of the luxury trade was concentrated on interior rather than exterior decoration. Migration continued at similar levels and did not constitute either a threat or an opportunity. Their experience was the most common, and this has been reflected in the detailed discussions throughout the book. The minority, which experienced sharp demographic and economic growth, fell into two categories, centres of trade and administrative centres. With the exception of Paris, London and Amsterdam, whose multiple functions have already been noted, the numbers of commercial centres that expanded in the seventeenth century were far outstripped by administrative centres in which social and political change were at their greatest. For the lesser trading centres of England, France and Spain, the impact of the territorial state, while important, was far less significant.

Regional contrasts reflected both urbanisation levels and the disparate economic experiences of the period. Northern and central Italy, the Netherlands and southern Germany remained the most heavily urbanised regions of Europe, as they had been in the later Middle Ages. The shift in emphasis within this framework from the southern to the northern Netherlands provinces was part of the more general shift in the economic centre of gravity to the Atlantic and the North Sea. This shift was not translated into new regions of heavy urbanisation. It was concentrated on a small number of urban centres. The consequence was that the well-developed urban networks and economies of the medieval belts of urbanisation remained, albeit with fewer resources as time went by, which permitted the authorities in the Mediterranean to confront the same social problems as their northern neighbours with similar success and sophistication.

Even the religious divide did not throw up as many contrasts as might have been expected. Many of the cultural contrasts between Mediterranean towns and those in northern and western Europe, such as the importance of extended families among Mediterranean urban élites and the predominance of nuclear families elsewhere or the extent to which the warmer southern climate encouraged different patterns of outdoor activity, predate the religious changes of the sixteenth century, although the contrasts that they engendered became part of the anti-Catholic rhetoric of northern visitors.

Other contrasts, of course, were directly related to the religious changes. The urban landscape was altered. Many buildings used for religious purposes before the Reformation were either demolished or took on new functions in Protestant towns, although the fundamental skyline of the spires and towers of parish churches remained largely untouched. In areas under Catholic control, on the other hand, new churches were built, others were remodelled and additional buildings, such as the new Jesuit schools, were inserted into the urban fabric in such a way as to alter the daily environment.

The contrasts engendered by theological and ritual changes go without saying. And yet, until well into the seventeenth century, it is possible to discern a range of parallel behaviour in which differing religious doctrines were confronted by the same urban conditions and came to very similar practical solutions. The growth of piety and its encouragement in the home as well as in church led to an increased sensitivity to welfare problems and to issues, such as the organisation of married life. At the point at which older corporate collectivities were on the decline, the state and the church, which developed an even closer relationship in both Protestant and Catholic areas, were able to use this piety and enthusiasm to their own ends.

Perhaps the sharpest religious contrasts lay less in the distinction between Protestantism and Catholicism than between those urban centres in which there was religious diversity and those in which the population shared the same religion. The presence of religious minority groups created tensions and opportunities, which forced townspeople to confront their identities and assess their priorities in a way in which religious reform did not. The variety of responses to religious diversity, on the other hand, which ranged from public violence to peaceful co-existence, is a reminder of the complicated range of religious minority groups that had come together at different times and in very different circumstances.

Extra muros

It is impossible to study the urban history of early modern Europe without being constantly reminded of the interaction between towns and their hinterlands, towns and their territorial rulers and towns and the wider population. This study began by arguing that it would be useful to undertake an examination of the urban dimension of European history between 1500 and 1700. Where did urban centres fit into the changes of the period? The answer is contradictory. From an economic point of view, towns retained their roles as centres of exchange, production and consumption, even where urban-financed production took place elsewhere, but the stagnation of the seventeenth century did little to energise the wider economy. Attention has to be focused on the very small minority of towns successfully engaged in an international trading network, which was increasingly linked to a world rather than a European economy. The impact of these centres was disproportionate and reached far and wide. Politically, with the exception of a shrinking number of city states, the decline in urban autonomy and the linked rise in power of territorial states of all sizes also signalled the demotion of towns as local political forces.

On the other hand, the capacity of towns to attract migrants of all kinds, from destitute peasants to the younger sons of noble families hoping to improve their fortunes, was only one dimension of their growing role as centres of information, ideas and services. In cultural terms, the external influence of urban centres was much stronger at the end of the seventeenth century than it had been at the beginning of the sixteenth. It is almost as if, in losing some of their medieval functions, the urban centres of early modern Europe had found the beginnings of a new role, which was to flower in the years that followed.

Further reading

The books and articles in this list are only a small selection of the available reading on the urban history of early modern Europe. This reading list for further study has been organised thematically, chapter by chapter, but many of the issues discussed in this book are also to be found in the monographs devoted to individual urban centres with which this bibliography begins.

General urban histories of early modern Europe

Abrams, P. and Wrigley, E.A. (eds) 1978: *Towns in societies: essays in economic history and historical sociology*. Cambridge: Cambridge University Press.

Clark, P. (ed.) 1976: *The early modern town*. London: Longman.

Friedrichs, C.R. 1995: *The early modern city*. London: Longman.

Hohenberg, P. and Lees, L.H. 1985: *The making of urban Europe, 1000–1950*. Cambridge, MA: Harvard University Press.

MacKenney, R. 1989: *The city-state, 1500–1700: republican liberty in an age of princely power*. London: Macmillan.

de Vries, J. 1984: *European urbanisation 1500–1800*. London: Methuen.

Urban histories of individual countries

Barry, J. (ed.) 1990: *The Tudor and Stuart town, 1530–1688*. London: Longman.

Benedict, P. (ed.) 1989: *Cities and social change in early modern France*. London: Routledge.

Clark, P. (ed.) 1984: *The transformation of English provincial towns*. London: Hutchinson.

Clark, P. and Slack, P. (eds) 1972: *Crisis and order in English towns 1500–1700*. London: Routledge.

Clark, P. and Slack, P. 1976: *English towns in transition, 1500–1700*. Oxford: Clarendon Press.

Le Roy Ladurie, E. (ed.) 1981: *Histoire urbaine de la France III. La ville classique*. Paris: Presses Universitaires Françaises.

Patten, J. 1978: *English towns 1500–1700*. Folkestone: Dawson.

Studies of individual towns

Beier, A.L. and Finlay, R. (eds) 1986: *London 1500–1700. The making of the metropolis*. London: Longman.

Benedict, P. 1980: *Rouen during the Wars of Religion*. Cambridge: Cambridge University Press.

Bennassar, B. 1967: *Valladollid an siècle d'or*. Paris: Mouton.

Dyer, A.D. 1973: *The city of Worcester in the sixteenth century*. Leicester: Leicester University Press.

Friedrichs, C.R. 1979: *Urban society in an age of war, Nördlingen, 1580–1700*. Princeton: Princeton University Press.

Howell, R., Jr. 1967: *Newcastle upon Tyne and the Puritan revolution*. Oxford: Clarendon Press.

Kintz, J-P. 1984: *La société strasbourgeoise du milieu du XVIᵉ siècle à la fin de la Guerre de Trente Ans*. Paris: Ophrys.

Krautheimer, R. 1985: *The Rome of Alexander VII, 1655–1677*. Princeton: Princeton University Press.

MacCaffrey, W. 1975: *Exeter 1540–1640*. Cambridge, MA: Harvard University Press.

Palliser, D. 1979: *Tudor York*. Oxford: Oxford University Press.

Phythian-Adams, C. 1979: *Desolation of a city. Coventry and the urban crisis of the late Middle Ages*. Cambridge: Cambridge University Press.

Pike, R. 1972: *Aristocrats and traders. Sevillian society in the sixteenth century*. London: Ithaca.

Soliday, G.L. 1974: *A community in conflict. Frankfurt society in the 17th and 18th centuries*. Hanover, NH: Brandeis University Press.

Strauss, G. 1976: *Nuremberg in the sixteenth century*. Bloomington, IN: Wiley.

The economy

Bairoch, P. 1988: *Cities and economic development*. Chicago: Mansell.

Belfanti, C.M. 1993: Rural manufactures and rural proto-industries in the 'Italy of the cities' from the sixteenth through the eighteenth century. *Continuity and Change* 8, 253–80.

Brown, J. 1986: A woman's place was in the home: women's work in Renaissance Tuscany. In Ferguson, M., Quilligan, M. and Vickers, N.J. (eds), *Rewriting the Renaissance. The discourses of sexual difference in early modern Europe*. Chicago: University of Chicago Press, 206–24.

Brown, J. and Goodman, J. 1980. Women and industry in Florence. *Journal of Economic History* 40, 73–86.

Davis, N.Z. 1986: Women and the crafts in sixteenth-century Lyon. In Hanawalt, B.A. (ed.), *Women and work in pre-industrial Europe*. Bloomington, IN: Indiana University Press, 167–97.

Farr, J.R. 1988: *Hands of honor: artisans and their world in early modern France. Dijon 1550–1650*. Ithaca: Cornell University Press.

Favier, R. 1993: *Les villes du Dauphiné aux XVIIe et XVIIIe siècles, la pierre et l'écrit*. Grenoble: Presses Universitaires de Grenoble.

Goose, N. 1990: In search of the urban variable: towns and the English economy, 1500–1650. In Barry, J. (ed.), *The Tudor and Stuart town, 1530–1688*. London: Longman, 165–85.

Mackenney, R. 1987: *Tradesmen and traders. The world of the guilds in Venice and in Europe, c. 1250–c. 1650*. London and Sydney: Croom Helm.

Poni, C. 1991: Local market roles and practice. Three guilds in the same line of production in early modern Bologna. In Woolf, S.J. (ed.), *Domestic strategies: work and family in France and Italy 1600–1800*. Cambridge and Paris: Cambridge University Press/Editions de la Maison des Science de l'Homme, 69–101.

Rapp, R.T. 1976: *Industry and economic decline in seventeenth-century Venice*. Cambridge, MA: Harvard University Press.

Thompson, I.A.A. and Casalla, B.Y. (eds) 1994: *The Castilian crisis of the seventeenth century*. Cambridge: Cambridge University Press.

Thomson, J.K.J. 1982: *Clermont-de-Lodève, 1633–1789: fluctuations in the prosperity of a Languedocian cloth-making town*. Cambridge: Cambridge University Press.

Van der Wee, H. (ed.) 1988: *The rise and decline of urban industries in Italy and the Low Countries*. Leuven: Leuven University Press.

Weisser, M. 1973. The decline of Castile revisited: the case of Toledo. *Journal of European Economic History* 2, 614–40.

Wiesner M.E. 1986: *Working women in Renaissance Germany*. New Brunswick: Rutgers University Press.

Government

Bond, S. and Evans, N. 1976. The process of granting charters to English boroughs, 1547–1649. *English Historical Review* **91**, 102–20.

Bonney, R. 1978: *Political change in France under Richelieu and Mazarin 1624–1661*. Oxford: Oxford University Press.

Brady, T., Jr. 1978: *Ruling class, regime and reformation at Strasbourg, 1520–1555*. Leiden: E.J. Brill.

Clark, P. 1984: The civic leaders of Gloucester, 1580–1800. In Clark, P. (ed.), *The transformation of English provincial towns*. London: Hutchinson, 311–45.

Forster, G.C.F. 1983: Government in provincial England under the later Stuarts. *Transactions of the Royal Historical Society* **33**, 29–48.

Foster, F.F. 1977: *The politics of stability: a portrait of the rulers of Elizabethan London*. London: Royal Historical Society.

Hammer, C.I. 1978: Anatomy of an oligarchy: the Oxford Town Council in the 15th and 16th centuries. *Journal of British Studies* **18**, 1–27.

Howell, R. 1990: Newcastle and the nation: the seventeenth-century experience. In Barry, J. (ed.), *The Tudor and Stuart Town, 1530–1688*. London: Longman, 274–96.

Hsia, R.P. 1984: *Society and religion in Münster (1535–1618)*. Newhaven, CT: Yale University Press.

Irvine, F.M. 1989: From Renaissance city to ancien regime capital: Montpellier c. 1500–c. 1600. In Benedict, P. (ed.), *Cities and social change in early modern France*. London: Routledge, 105–33.

Isaacs, A.K. and Prak, M. 1996: Cities, bourgeoisies and the state. In Reinhard, W. (ed.), *Power Elites and State Building*. Oxford: Clarendon Press, 207–34.

Knecht, R. 1981. Francis I and Paris. *History* **66**, 18–33.

Livet, G. and Vogler, B. (eds) 1983: *Pouvoir, ville et société en Europe, 1600–1750*. Paris: Ophrys.

Lunenfeld, M. 1982. Governing the cities of Isabella the Catholic; the *Corregidores*, governors and assistants of Castile, 1476–1504. *Journal of Urban History* **9**, 31–55.

Lynch, M. 1987: The crown and the burghs, 1500–1625. In Lynch, M. (ed.), *The early modern town in Scotland*. London: Croom Helm, 55–80.

Miller, J. 1985. The crown and the borough charters in the reign of Charles II. *English Historical Review* **100**, 53–84.

Rappaport, S. 1989: *Worlds within worlds: structures of life in sixteenth-century London*. Cambridge: Cambridge University Press.

Riis, T. 1981: Towns and central government in northern Europe from the fifteenth century to the Industrial Revolution. *Scandinavian Economic History Review* **29**, 33–52.

Schneider, R.A. 1989: *Public life in Toulouse, 1463–1789: from municipal republic to cosmopolitan city*. Ithaca: Cornell University Press.

Temple, N. 1975: The control and exploitation of French towns during the ancien regime. In Kierstead, R.F. (ed.), *State and society in seventeenth century France*. New York: New Viewpoints, 67–93.

Tittler, R. 1977: The incorporation of boroughs 1540–1558. *History* 62, 24–42.

Verschuur, M. 1987: Merchants and craftsmen in sixteenth-century Perth. In Lynch, M. (ed.), *The early modern town in Scotland*. London: Croom Helm, pp. 36–54.

Élites

Amelang, J.S. 1987: *Honored citizens of Barcelona: patrician culture and class relations, 1490–1714*. Princeton: Princeton University Press.

Berner, S. 1972: The Florentine patriciate in the transition from Republic to *principato*. *1530–1609*. *Studies in Medieval and Renaissance History* 9, 3–17.

Brady, T., Jr. 1978: Patricians, nobles, merchants: internal tensions and solidarities in south German urban ruling classes at the close of the middle ages. In Chrisman, M.U. and Gründler, O. (eds), *Social groups and religious ideas in the sixteenth century*. Kalamazoo: Western Michigan University Press, 38–45.

Burke, P. 1974: *Venice and Amsterdam. A study of seventeenth-century élites*. London: Temple Smith. (Second edn, Cambridge: Polity Press, 1994.)

Clark, P. 1984: The civic leaders of Gloucester, 1580–1800. In Clark, P. (ed.), *The transformation of English provincial towns*. London: Hutchinson, 311–45.

Cowan, A. 1991: Urban élites in early modern Europe: an endangered species? *Historical Research* 64, 123–37.

Cowan, A.F. 1986: *The urban patriciate: Lübeck and Venice, 1580–1700*. Cologne and Vienna: Böhlau.

Evans, J.R. 1979: *17th century Norwich. Politics, religion and government, 1620–1690*. Oxford: Oxford University Press.

Ferraro, J. 1993: *Family and public life in Brescia, 1580–1650*. Cambridge: Cambridge University Press.

Hsia, R.P. 1984: *Society and religion in Münster (1535–1618)*. Newhaven, CT: Yale University Press.

Irvine, F.M. 1989: From Renaissance city to ancien regime capital: Montpellier c. 1500–c. 1600. In Benedict, P. (ed.), *Cities and social change in early modern France*. London: Routledge, 105–33.

Isaacs, A.K. and Prak, M. 1996: Cities, bourgeoisies and the state. In Reinhard, W. (ed.), *Power Elites and State Building*. Oxford: Clarendon Press, 207–34.

Litchfield, R.B. 1986: *Emergence of a bureaucracy. The Florentine patricians, 1530–1790*. Princeton: Princeton University Press.

Roorda, D.J. 1964: The ruling class in Holland in the seventeenth century. In Bromlcy, J.S. and Kossmann, E.H. (eds), *Britain and The Netherlands*, vol. II. Groningen: J.B. Wolters, 109–32.

Zanetti, D.F. 197: The patriziato of Milan from the domination of Spain to the unification of Italy: an outline of the social and demographic history. *Social History*, 6, 745–60.

Social horizons

Archer, I. 1991: *The pursuit of stability. Social relations in Elizabethan London*. Cambridge: Cambridge University Press.

Berner, S.J. 1971: Florentine society in the late sixteenth and early seventeenth centuries. *Studies in the Renaissance* 18, 203–46.

Boulton, J. 1987: *Neighbourhood and community. A London suburb in the seventeenth century*. Cambridge: Cambridge University Press.

Cerutti, S. 1991: Group strategies and trade strategies: the Turin tailor's guild in the late seventeenth and early eighteenth centuries. In Woolf, S.J. (ed.), *Domestic strategies: work and family in France and Italy 1600–1800*. Cambridge and Paris: Cambridge University Press/Editions de la Maison des Science de l'Homme, 69–101.

Clark, P. 1972: The migrant in Kentish towns 1580–1640. In Clark, P. and Slack, P. (eds), *Crisis and order in English towns 1500–1700*. London: Routledge, 117–63.

Clark, P. 1979: Migration in England during the late seventeenth and early eighteenth centuries. *Past and Present* 83, 57–90.

Cowan, A.F. 1986: *The urban patriciate: Lübeck and Venice, 1580–1700*. Cologne and Vienna: Böhlau.

Descimon, R. 1989: Paris on the eve of Saint Bartholomew: taxation, privilege and social geography. In Benedict, P. (ed.), *Cities and social change in early modern France*. London: Routledge, 69–104.

Diefendorf, B. 1987: Widowhood and remarriage in sixteenth-century Paris. *Journal of Family History* 7, 379–95.

Dolan, C. 1989: The artisans of Aix-en-Provence in the sixteenth century: a micro analysis of social relationships. In Benedict, P. (ed.), *Cities and social change in early modern France*. London: Routledge, 174–94.

Elliot, V.B. 1981: Single women in the London marriage market: age, status and mobility, 1598–1619. In Outhwaite, R.B. (ed.), *Marriage and society: studies in the social history of marriage*. London: Europa, 81–116.

Farr, J. 1989: Consumers, commerce and the craftsmen of Dijon. In Benedict, P. (ed.), *Cities and social change in early modern France*. London: Routledge, 134–73.

Farr, J.R. 1988: *Hands of honor: artisans and their world in early modern France. Dijon 1550–1650*. Ithaca: Cornell University Press.

Finlay, R. and Shearer, B. 1986: Population growth and suburban expansion. In Beier, A.L. and Finlay, R. (eds), *London 1500–1700. The making of the metropolis*. London: Longman, 37–59.

Friedrichs, C.R. 1975: Capitalism, mobility and class formation in the early modern German city. *Past and Present* 59, 24–49.

Glass, D.V. 1976: Socio-economic status and occupations in the city of London at the end of the 17th century. In Clark, P. (ed.), *The early modern town*. London: Longman, 216–32.

Goose, N. 1990: Household size and structure in early Stuart Cambridge. In Barry, J. (ed.), *The Tudor and Stuart town*. London: Longman, 74–120.

Jacobsen, G. 1983: Women's work and women's role: ideology and reality in Danish urban society, 1300–1550. *Scandinavian Economic History Review* 31, 3–20.

Kitch, M.J. 1986: Capital and kingdom: migration to early Stuart London. In Beier, A.L. and Finlay, R. (eds), *London 1500–1700. The making of the metropolis*. London: Longman, 224–51.

Knox, E.L. 1988: The lower orders in early modern Augsburg. In Bebb, P.N. and Marshall, S.C. (eds), *The process of change in early modern Europe*. Athens, OH: Ohio University Press, 165–77.

Langton, J. 1990: Residential patterns in pre-industrial cities: some case studies from seventeenth-century Britain. In Barry, J. (ed.), *The Tudor and Stuart town*. London: Longman, 166–205.

Mackenney, R. 1987: *Tradesmen and traders. The world of the guilds in Venice and in Europe, c. 1250–c. 1650*. London and Sydney: Croom Helm.

Pardailhé-Galabrun, A. 1991: *The birth of intimacy: privacy and domestic life in early modern Paris*. Philadelphia: University of Pennsylvania Press.

Roper, L. 1987: 'The common man', 'the common good', 'common women': gender and meaning in the German Reformation commune. *Social History* 12, 1–21.

Rosenthal, E.G. 1988: The position of women in Renaissance Florence: neither autonomy nor subjection. In Denley, P. and Elam, C. (eds), *Florence and Italy*. London: Westfield College, 369–81.

Verschuur, M. 1987: Merchants and craftsmen in sixteenth-century Perth. In Lynch, M. (ed.), *The early modern town in Scotland*. London: Croom Helm, pp. 36–54.

Weissmann, R.F.E. 1989: The importance of being ambiguous. Social relations, individualism and identity in Renaissance Florence. In Zimmermann, S. and Weissmann, R.F.E. (eds), *Urban life in the Renaissance*. Cranbury, NJ: University of Delaware Press, 269–80.

Wiesner M.E. 1986: *Working women in Renaissance Germany*. New Brunswick: Rutgers University Press.

Wiesner, M.E. 1988: Paternalism in practice: the control of servants and prostitutes in early modern German cities. In Bebb, P.N. and Marshall, S.C. (eds), *The process of change in early modern Europe*. Athens, OH: Ohio University Press, 179–200.

Religion

Abray, L.J. 1985: *The peoples' Reformation: magistrates, clergy and commons in Strasbourg 1500–1598*. Oxford: Basil Blackwell.

Barnes, A.E. 1988: Religious anxiety and devotional change in sixteenth-century French penitential confraternities. *Sixteenth Century Journal* 19, 389–405.

Benedict, P. 1979: The Catholic response to Protestantism. Church activity and popular piety in Rouen, 1560–1600. In Obelkovich, J. (ed.), *Religion and the people, 800–1700*. Chapel Hill: University of North Carolina Press, 148–90.

Black, C. 1989: *Italian confraternities in the sixteenth century*. Cambridge: Cambridge University Press.

Brady, T., Jr. 1978: *Ruling class, regime and reformation at Strasbourg, 1520–1555*. Leiden: E.J. Brill.

Broadhead, P. 1980: Politics and expediency in the Augsburg Reformation. In Brooks, P.N. (ed.), *Reformation principle and practice*. London: Scolar Press, 53–70.

Chatellier, L. 1989: *The Europe of the devout: the Catholic Reformation and the formation of a new society*. Cambridge: Cambridge University Press.

Chrisman, M.U. 1980: Lay response to the Protestant reformation in Germany. In Brooks, P.N. (ed.), *Reformation principle and practice*. London: Scolar Press, 33–52.

Collinson, P. 1982: *The religion of Protestants. The church in English society 1558–1625*. Oxford: Clarendon Press.

Davidson, N.S. 1987: The inquisition and the Italian Jews. In Haliczer, S. (ed.), *Inquisition and society in early modern Europe*. London: Croom Helm, 19–45.

Davis, N.Z. 1981: The sacred and the body social in sixteenth-century Lyon. *Past and Present* 90, 40–70.

Farr, J.R. 1985: Popular religious solidarity in sixteenth-century Dijon. *French Historical Studies* 14, 192–214.

Flynn, M. 1989: *Sacred charity: confraternities and social welfare in Spain, 1400–1800*. London: Macmillan.

François, E. 1993: *Protestants et catholiques en Allemagne. Identités et pluralisme, Augsburg 1648–1806.* Paris: Albin Michel.

Guggisberg, H.R. 1987: The problem of 'failure' in the Swiss Reformation: some preliminary reflections. In Kouri, E. and Scott, T. (eds), *Politics and society in Reformation Europe.* London: Macmillan, 188–209.

Haigh, C. 1984: The Church of England, the Catholics and the people. In Haigh, C. (ed.), *The reign of Elizabeth I.* London: Macmillan, 195–219.

Hoffmann, P.F. 1984: *Church and community in the diocese of Lyon, 1500–1789.* Yale: Yale University Press.

Hsia, R.P. 1984: *Society and religion in Münster (1535–1618).* Newhaven, CT: Yale University Press.

Hsia, R.P. 1989: *Social discipline in the Reformation: central Europe 1550–1750.* London: Routledge.

Israel, J.I. 1985: *European Jewry in the age of mercantilism, 1550–1750.* Oxford: Clarendon Press.

Konnert, M. 1989: Urban values versus religious passion: Chalons-sur-Marne during the wars of religion. *Sixteenth Century Journal* 20, 387–405.

Lehmann, H. 1984: The cultural importance of the pious middle classes in seventeenth-century Protestant society. In von Greyerz, K. (ed.), *Religion and society in early modern Europe, 1500–1800.* London: George Allen and Unwin, 33–41.

Martin, J. 1988: Salvation and society in 16th-century Venice: popular evangelism in Renaissance Italy. *Journal of Modern History* 60, 205–33.

Muir, E. 1989: The virgin on the street corner: the place of the sacred in Italian cities. In Ozment, S. (ed.), *Religion and culture in the Renaissance and the Reformation.* Kirksville, MO: Sixteenth-Century Journal Publishing, 25–40.

Parker, D. 1978: The Huguenots in seventeenth-century France. In Hepburn, A.C. (ed.), *Minorities in history.* London: Edward Arnold, 11–30.

Pettigree, A. 1986: *Foreign Protestant communities in sixteenth-century London.* Oxford: Clarendon Press.

Pullan, B. 1971: *Rich and poor in Renaissance Venice. The social institutions of a Catholic state, to 1620.* Oxford: Basil Blackwell.

Pullan, B. 1983: *The Jews of Europe and the Inquisition of Venice, 1550–1670.* Oxford: Basil Blackwell.

Rublack, H-C. 1987: Is there a new history of the urban Reformation? In Kouri, E. and Scott, T. (eds), *Politics and society in Reformation Europe.* London: Macmillan, 121–41.

Sacks, D.H. 1986: The demise of the martyrs; the feasts of St Clement and St Katharine in Bristol, 1400–1600. *Social History* 11, 141–69.

Scribner, R.W. 1989: *Popular culture and popular movements in Reformation Germany.* London: Hambledon.

Sheils, W.J. 1977: Religion in provincial towns: innovation and tradition. In Heal, F. and O'Day, R. (eds), *Church and society in England.* London: Macmillan, 159–67.

Terpstra, N. 1990: Women in the brotherhood: gender, class and politics in Renaissance Bolognese confraternities. *Renaissance and Reformation* **23**, 193–212.

Whaley, J. 1985: *Religious toleration and social change in Hamburg, 1529–1819.* Cambridge: Cambridge University Press.

White, A. 1987: The impact of the reformation on a burgh community: the case of Aberdeen. In Lynch, M. (ed.), *The early modern town in Scotland.* London: Croom Helm, 81–101.

Wykes, D.L. 1990: Religious dissent and the penal laws: an explanation of business success? *History* **75**, 39–62.

The urban fabric

Ackerman, J.J. 1989: Social stratification in Renaissance urban planning. In Zimmermann, S. and Weissmann, R.F.E. (eds), *Urban life in the Renaissance.* Cranbury, NJ: University of Delaware Press, 21–49.

Alldridge, N.J. 1983: House and household in restoration Chester. *Urban History Yearbook*, 39–52.

Argan, G. 1969: *The Renaissance city.* London: Studio Vista.

Aston, M. and Bond, J. 1976: *The landscape of towns.* London: Dent.

Boulton, J. 1987: *Neighbourhood and community. A London suburb in the seventeenth century.* Cambridge: Cambridge University Press.

Braunfels, W. 1988: *Urban design in western Europe. Regime and architecture, 900–1900.* Chicago: University of Chicago Press.

Calabi, D. 1993: Il mercato a la città. Piazze, strade, architettura d'Europe in età moderna. Venice: Marsilio.

Clark, P. 1983: Visions of the urban community: antiquarians and the English city before 1800. In Fraser, D. and Sutcliffe, A. (eds), *The pursuit of urban history.* London: Edward Arnold, 105–24.

Descimon, R. 1989: Paris on the eve of Saint Bartholomew: taxation, privilege and social geography. In Benedict, P. (ed.), *Cities and social change in early modern France.* London: Routledge, 69–104.

Konvitz, J.W. 1978: *Cities and the sea. Port city planning in early modern Europe.* Baltimore: Johns Hopkins University Press.

Laithwaite, M. 1973: The buildings of Burford: a Cotswold town in the fourteenth to nineteenth centuries. In Everitt, A. (ed.), *Perspectives in English urban history.* London: Macmillan, 60–90.

Laithwaite, M. 1984: Totnes houses, 1500–1700. In Clark, P. (ed.), *The transformation of English provincial towns.* London: Hutchinson, 62–98.

Mallett, M. and Hale, J. 1984: *The military organisation of a Renaissance state, Venice, c.1400 to 1617.* Cambridge: Cambridge University Press.

Palliser, D.M. 1982: Civic mentality and the environment in Tudor York. *Northern History* **18**, 78–115.

Power, M.J. 1972: East London housing in the 17th century. In Clark, P. and Slack, P. (eds), *Crisis and order in English towns 1500–1700*. London: Routledge, 237–62.

Power, M.J. 1978: The east and the west in early modern London. In Ives, E.W., Knecht, R.J. and Scarisbrick, J.J. (eds), *Wealth and power in Tudor England*. London: Athlone Press, 167–85.

Rosenau, H. 1982: *The ideal city in European history*. London: Methuen.

Stone, L. 1980: The residential development of the west end of London in the seventeenth century. In Malament, B.L. (ed.), *After the Reformation*. Manchester: Manchester University Press, 167–212.

Tittler, R. 1991: *Architecture and power. The town hall and the English urban community c. 1500–1640*. Oxford: Clarendon Press.

Poverty and poor relief

Black, C. 1989: *Italian confraternities in the sixteenth century*. Cambridge: Cambridge University Press.

Blockmans, W. 1981: Circumscribing the concept of poverty. In Riis, T. (ed.), *Aspects of poverty in early modern Europe*. Florence: Sijthoff, 39–45.

Clark, P. 1985: A crisis continued? The conditions of English towns in the 1590s. In Clark, P. (ed.), *The European crisis of the 1590s*. London: Allen and Unwin, 44–66.

Davis, N.Z. 1983: Poor relief, humanism and heresy: the case of Lyon. In Davis, N.Z. (ed.), *Society and culture in early modern France*. Cambridge: Polity Press, 17–64.

Flynn, M. 1985: Charitable ritual in later medieval and early modern Spain. *Sixteenth Century Journal* 16, 325–48.

Flynn, M. 1989: *Sacred charity: confraternities and social welfare in Spain, 1400–1800*. London: Macmillan.

Harvey, R. 1979: Recent research on poverty in Tudor and Stuart England: review and commentary. *International Review of Social History* 24, 237–82.

Herlan, R.W. 1976: Social articulation and the configuration of parochial poverty in London on the eve of the Restoration. *Guildhall Studies in London History* 2, 43–53.

Jütte, R. 1981: Poor relief and social discipline in sixteenth-century Europe. *European Studies Review*, 11, 25–52.

Jütte, R. 1994: *Poverty and deviance in early modern Europe*. Cambridge: Cambridge University Press.

Lis, H. and Soly, H. 1979: *Poverty and capitalism in pre-industrial Europe*. London: Croom Helm (revised edn 1982).

Martz, L. 1983: *Poverty and welfare in Habsburg Spain*. Cambridge: Cambridge University Press.

Mentzer, R.A., Jr. 1991: Organisational endeavour and charitable impulse in sixteenth-century France: the case of Protestant Nîmes. *French History* 5, 5–28.

Norberg, K. 1985: *Rich and poor in Grenoble 1600–1816*. Berkeley: California University Press.

Outhwaite, R.B. 1985: Dearth, the English crown and the 'crisis of the 1590s'. In Clark, P. (ed.), *The European crisis of the 1590s*. London: Allen and Unwin, 23–43.

Pearl, V. 1978: The London workhouse, 1649–1660. In Pennington, D. and Thomas, K. (eds), *Puritans and revolutionaries*. Oxford: Clarendon Press, 206–32.

Power, M. 1985: London and the control of the crisis of the 1590s. *History* 70, 371–85.

Pugh, W: 1974. Social welfare and the Edict of Nantes. *French Historical Studies* 8, 349–76.

Pullan, B. 1971: *Rich and poor in Renaissance Venice. The social institutions of a Catholic state, to 1620*. Oxford: Basil Blackwell.

Pullan, B. 1988. Support and redeem: charity and poor relief in Italian cities from the fourteenth to the seventeenth century. *Continuity and Change* 3, 177–208.

Pullan, B. 1992: Plague and perception of the poor in early modern Italy. In Ranger, T. and Slack, P. (eds), *Epidemics and ideas. Essays in the historical perception of pestilence*. Cambridge: Cambridge University Press, 101–17.

Riley, P.F. 1983. Hard times, police and the making of public policy in the Paris of Louis XIV. *Historical Reflections* 10, 313–34.

Slack, P. 1972: Poverty and politics in Salisbury 1597–1606. In Clark, P. and Slack, P. (eds), *Crisis and order in English towns 1500–1700*. London; Routledge, 164–203.

Slack, P. 1980. Books of orders: the making of English social policy 1577–1631. *Transactions of the Royal Historical Society* 30, 1–22.

Slack, P. 1984: Poverty and social regulation in Elizabethan England. In Haigh, C. (ed.), *The reign of Elizabeth I*. London: Macmillan, 221–41.

Slack, P. 1988: *Poverty and policy in Tudor and Stuart England*. London: Longman.

Wright, W.J. 1979. A closer look at house poor-relief through the common chest and indigence in sixteenth-century Hesse. *Archiv für Reformationsgeschichte* 70, 225–37.

Order and disorder

Archer, I. 1991: *The pursuit of stability. Social relations in Elizabethan London*. Cambridge: Cambridge University Press.

Ashton, R. 1983: Popular entertainment and social control in later Elizabethan and early Stuart London. *London Journal* 9, 3–19.

Beier, A.L. 1978: Social problems in Elizabethan London. *Journal of Interdisciplinary History* 9, 203–21.

Beier, A.L. 1986: The social problems of an Elizabethan country town: Warwick, 1580–90. In Clark, P. (ed.), *Country towns in pre-industrial England*. Leicester: Leicester University Press, 45–85.

Blickle, P. 1984: Social protest and reformation theology. In von Greyerz, K. (ed.), *Religion and society in early modern Europe, 1500–1800*. London: George Allen and Unwin, 1–23.

Bonney, R. 1978: *Political change in France under Richelieu and Mazarin 1624–1661*. Oxford: Oxford University Press.

Burke, P. 1983: The virgin of the carmine and the revolt of Masaniello. *Past and Present* 99, 3–21.

Cashman, J. 1991: The social uses of violence in ritual. Charivari or religious persecution? *European History Quarterly* 21, 291–326.

Chatellier, L. 1989: *The Europe of the devout: the Catholic Reformation and the formation of a new society*. Cambridge: Cambridge University Press.

Davis, N.Z. 1983a: The reasons of misrule. In Davis, N.Z. (ed.), *Society and culture in early modern France*. Cambridge: Polity Press, 7–123.

Davis, N.Z. 1983b: The rites of violence. In Davis, N.Z. (ed.), *Society and culture in early modern France*. Cambridge: Polity Press, 152–187.

Dewald, J. 1976: The 'perfect magistrate'. Parlementaires and crime in sixteenth-century Rouen. *Archiv für Reformationsgeschichte* 67, 284–300.

Ferraro, J. 1993: *Family and public life in Brescia, 1580–1650*. Cambridge: Cambridge University Press.

Fletcher, A. and Stevenson, J. (eds) 1985: *Order and disorder in early modern England*. Cambridge: Cambridge University Press.

Friedrichs, C.R. 1978: Citizens or subjects? Urban conflict in early modern Germany. In Chrisman, M.U. and Gründler, O. (eds), *Social groups and religious ideas in the sixteenth century*. Kalamazoo: Western Michigan University Press, 46–58.

Friedrichs, C.R. 1982: German town revolts and the seventeenth century crisis. *Renaissance and Modern Studies* 26, 27–51.

Friedrichs C.R. 1986: Politics or pogrom? The Fettmilch Uprising in German and Jewish history. *Central European History* 19, 186–228.

Hsia, R.P. 1989: *Social discipline in the Reformation: central Europe 1550–1750*. London: Routledge.

Kingdon, R.M. 1972: The control of morals in Calvin's Geneva. In Buck, L.P. and Zophy, J.W. (eds), *The social history of the Reformation*. Columbus, OH: Ohio State University Press, 3–16.

Koenigsberger, H.G. 1971: The revolt of Palermo in 1647. In Koenigsberger, H.G. *Estates and revolutions*. Ithaca, NY: Cornell University Press, 233–77.

Le Roy Ladurie, E. 1980: *Carnival: a popular uprising at Romans 1579–1500*. London: Scolar Press.

Lindley, K.J. 1983: Riot prevention and control in early Stuart London. *Transactions of the Royal Historical Society*, 33, 109–26.

Power, M. 1985: London and the control of the crisis of the 1590s. *History* 70, 371–85.

Riley, P.F. 1983: Hard times, police and the making of public policy in the Paris of Louis XIV. *Historical Reflections* 10, 313–34.

Schilling, H. 1987: 'History of crime' or 'history of sin'? Some reflections on the social history of early modern church discipline. In Kouri, E. and Scott, T. (eds), *Politics and society in Reformation Europe*. London: Macmillan, 289–310.

Schochet, G.J. 1969: Patriarchalism, politics and mass attitudes in Stuart England', *Historical Journal* 12, 413–41.

Slack, P. 1980: Social policy and the constraints of government, 1547–58. In Tittler, R. and Loach, J. (eds), *The mid-Tudor polity c. 1540–1560*. London: Macmillan, 94–115.

Villari, R. 1970: The insurrection in Naples of 1585. In Cochrane, E. (ed.), *The late Italian Renaissance 1525–1630*. London: Macmillan, 305–30.

Villari, R. 1985: Masaniello: contemporary and recent interpretations. *Past and Present* 108, 117–32.

Index of names

N.B. Names of modern scholars are given in italic.

Index of places

Subject index